Great Talk Outlines for Youth Ministry 2

40 more field-tested guides from experienced speakers

Great Talk Outlines *for* Youth Ministry 2

Includes CD-ROM with free trial version of MediaShout™ presentation software! *for Windows 98 or later*

Mark Oestreicher

with talks by **Dave Ambrose   Megan Hutchinson   Dan Jessup**

Kara Powell   Heather Flies   Will Penner *and others*

Youth Specialties

Great Talk Outlines for Youth Ministry 2: 40 more field-tested guides from experienced speakers

©2004 by Youth Specialties

Youth Specialties Book, 300 S. Pierce St., El Cajon, CA 92020, are published by Zondervan Publishing House, 5300 Patterson Ave. S.E., Grand Rapids, MI 49530.

Library of Congress Cataloging-in-Publication Data

Great talk outlines for youth ministry 2 : 40 more field-tested guides
from experienced speakers / [edited] by Mark Oestreicher.
   p. cm.
 Includes indexes.
 ISBN 0-310-25288-1 (pbk.)
 1. Youth sermons--Outlines, syllabi, etc. I. Oestreicher, Mark.
 BV4310.G64 2004
 251'.55--dc22

2004002250

Unless otherwise indicated, all Scripture quotations are taken from the *Holy Bible: New International Version* (North American Edition). Copyright © 1973, 1978, 1984 by International Bible Society. Used by permission of Zondervan Publishing House.

Web site addresses listed in this book are current at the time of publication. Please contact Youth Specialties by email (YS@YouthSpecialties.com) or by postal mail (Youth Specialties, Product Department, 300 South Pierce Street, El Cajon, CA 92020) to report URLs that are not operational and to suggest alternate URLs if available.

Editorial and art direction by Dave Urbanski
Proofreading by Kristi Robison
Editing by Laura Gross
Cover design by Left Coast Design
Interior design by Sarah Jongsma

Printed in the United States of America

04 05 06 07 08 09 / DC / 10 9 8 7 6 5 4 3 2 1

Dedication

o Michael Yaconelli, my friend and mentor

Acknowledgments

Many rich thanks to the amazing youth workers who contributed talk outlines to this book. Working on your outlines was devotional for me. Thank you for investing in other youth workers.

Thanks to the YS product team (Roni, Nicole, Rick, Urb, and Jay), especially for your patience with this absurdly late manuscript. Thanks to B, at B's Cajon Coffee Company, for the best writing spot in the world and for figuring out that a shot of espresso in my coffee makes me a happy writer! Thanks to Jeannie, Liesl, and Max—my pretty-darn-near-perfect family.

Contents

The Gift of God's Sucker Punch

The response to the first *Great Talk Outlines* surprised me! I'm so thrilled that tens of thousands of youth workers found these puppies as helpful as I'd hoped they would be. And this second volume is in direct response to the many requests we received for "more."

There's nothing quite like watching that glimmer of understanding flicker across a student's face while you're presenting God's truth to them. With that hope, here's a singular thought about making your talks better: *honesty*. If we, as youth workers, are honest about life—including our own messy lives—the kingdom of God, and God's great love for our students' messy lives, then we can do so much more than deliver snappy talks with decent content.

Preaching and Teaching are spiritual gifts. That not only has implications for the talk-giver—it has enormous implications for the talk-receivers! It means God will use our gifting to impact the spiritual lives of teenagers. This isn't a "maybe" or a "we hope so"—this is a God-given done deal.

We don't always know *how* God will use our youth talks in kids' lives—or *when!* In fact, many times the results of our efforts won't show up for years. And some of the *best* results we'll never see. But God *will* use you and your honest communication efforts to change the lives of teenagers.

A Few Technical User Tips

Pillage and tweak, please! These outlines shouldn't be used "as is." We trust that you know your students better than we do. Change the outlines, drop parts that won't work for you, add new stuff. Use these outlines as idea generators, suggestions, and examples.

Use the CD-ROM. There are a handful of way-helpful things on the enclosed CD. First, there are Word documents of all the talk outlines. Use these to customize an outline for your own use, then print it out for your presentation. Tweak and modify the questions at the end of each outline, and give them to small group leaders for discussion.

You'll also find that the main points from each outline have been turned into a set of "slides" for your presentation use. Using these will totally reinforce what you're talking about with kids. Project them using a VPU or hook up a laptop to a TV. We've included MediaShout scripts with each set of images because we believe MediaShout is the best media tool for youth ministry. But if you're still PowerPoint-shackled, you can easily pull the JPEG images into that format. Each set of images has one "blank" without any text, so you can even add new points of your own choosing.

MediaShout stuff. There are two special versions of MediaShout included on the CD-ROM. MediaShout EV is a fully functional evaluation version. You can use it to build and customize presentations—but it times out after 21 uses. ShoutPlayer is a limited edition player. You can't use it to build new presentations, but you can use it *forever* to play the MediaShout scripts included on the CD. If you want to consider buying MediaShout (a wise choice), you can find it in the online YS store (www.youthspecialties.com/store).

Movie start times. This is important, as it will save you a good deal of frustration. We've used the DVD versions of these films to determine the movie clip start and stop times, which are all timed from the start of the actual movie—when the distribution company logo appears on the screen (20th Century Fox and the like). Because VHS videos usually have forced-viewing previews, but *most* DVDs do not, we've chosen this standard.

We at Youth Specialties pray for you! We bless you as you connect teenagers with the great grace of God. Have fun!

Mark Oestreicher

Using the *Great Talk Outlines for Youth Ministry 2* CD-ROM

Minimum system requirements for Windows*

- Windows 98 or later
- Microsoft Word 6.0 or better
- 30 MB available hard disk space to load all graphics and outlines
- CD-ROM drive

Additional requirements for MediaShout™ EV presentation software

- 266 MHz Pentium II or equivalent
- 64 MB RAM
- 15 MB additional hard disk space
- *recommended:* two display cards (or a single card capable of independent dual-monitor display) to run in dual-monitor mode

Minimum system requirements for Macintosh

- Any PowerPC processor-based, Mac OS-compatible system (120 MHz minimum recommended)
- Apple System 7.5.5 or later
- Microsoft Word 6.0 or better
- 30 MB available hard disk space to load all graphics and outlines
- Color monitor or display supporting greater than 256 colors and 640x480 resolution
- CD-ROM drive

To install on a Windows PC

1. Close all open applications and insert the CD in your CD-ROM drive. Click the Start button, choose Run, then type *D*:\Setup.exe in the Open field, replacing the *D* with the actual letter of your CD-ROM drive.

2. Follow the setup instructions that appear on the screen.
   Note: You'll be given the option of installing MediaShout EV (evaluation version) on your computer. If MediaShout 1.5 or later is already installed on your computer, there's no need to install MediaShout EV. Just install the GTO Media component. Then presentations included on the disk will be ready to play from MediaShout.

To open a GTO outline in Microsoft Word

- Choose the File menu, click on Open, then browse to the C:\My Documents\GTO Outlines folder, then open the document you want.

A few tips when using the GTO outlines in Microsoft Word

- When you open a GTO outline in Word, you'll notice shaded boxes outlining sidebar material. To format this shaded area, click on the Format menu and scroll down to Borders and Shading, then choose the shading tab. Change or remove shading.
- If you would like to change or format bulleted items, click on the Format menu and scroll down to Bullets and Numbering. Make the desired changes.

To run a GTO presentation in MediaShout or MediaShout EV

1. Choose the File menu, click on Open, then browse to the GTO Media folder. If you chose the defaults during the installation, you'll find this folder in C:\My Shout.

2. Open the GTO Media folder. You'll find a folder there for each talk. Open the talk folder you want (e.g., GTO_01), then double-click the Script (MediaShout presentation) file in that folder. The Script will open in the MediaShout control screen.

3. To play the Script—
   - *In single-monitor mode:* Choose the Options menu, click on Overlay Display to bring up the display overlay, then hit the Space key to display the first screen. Hit Space again to play the next screen. To end the presentation, hit Escape. If the dis-played images don't fill the entire screen, you'll need to adjust the monitor's screen area. See Display & Sound: MediaShout on a Single Monitor in the Help file for details.

   - *In dual-monitor mode:* Double-click the first cue in the Script. Hit the Space key to play the next cue, and so on.

About MediaShout and ShoutPlayer

MediaShout EV is the evaluation version of MediaShout, a simple yet powerful presentation program optimized for ministry. EV allows you to open, create, edit, preview, and play a MediaShout Script (presentation file) for 30 days. After that it's automatically disabled, and you'll need to install either the full version of MediaShout or ShoutPlayer (free) to play the Scripts.

- *MediaShout*—the full version contains all the features found in MediaShout EV, plus dozens of backgrounds, video and sound clips, and extended Bible verses and song libraries. Choose Order Info in MediaShout EV to learn more.

- *ShoutPlayer* allows you to play Scripts even if you don't have MediaShout installed on your computer. Of course, its features are limited, but if all you want to do is play an existing Script, it does the job. A free copy of ShoutPlayer is included on the CD-ROM, but you must install it to use it.

*Microsoft Word files and jpeg images can be accessed by a Macintosh.

To install ShoutPlayer

1. Close all open applications and insert the CD in your CD-ROM drive. Double-click the My Computer icon on the Windows desktop, then browse to the CD-ROM drive and open the ShoutPlayer folder.

2. Double-click on *SPSETUP.EXE* and follow the instructions that appear on the screen.

Need more assistance?

*   For technical support for MediaShout™ software contact techsupport@mediashout.com or call (518) 423-4771.
*   For assistance with *Great Talk Outlines for Youth Ministry 2* Microsoft Word documents contact YS.Products@YouthSpecialties.com or call (619) 440-2333.

Index of Themes

Index of Bible Texts

When Good Desires Go Bad

Contributed by **Dave Ambrose**

Primary theme lust	
Themes accountability, desire, discernment, temptation, self-control, sin	
Scripture 1 Thessalonians 2:17; Luke 22:15; James 1:14-15; Romans 7:18; 1 Thessalonians 4:4-5; Galatians 6:2	
Approximate length through The Grand Finale 20-30 minutes	

You'll need

- ◄)) Copies of teen magazines
- ◄)) Videotape of TV commercials with sexual themes
- ◄)) TV and VCR
- ◄)) Mission: Impossible II (Paramount Pictures, 2000)
- ◄)) TV and DVD player
- ◄)) Hershey's Kisses, one for each person
- ◄)) Blank paper and pens for journaling

Most of the students we work with are bombarded with sexual images on a daily basis. For many of our kids, this can be an area of constant struggle and often a huge area of continual defeat. Youth workers may think of lust as a "guy issue," but that couldn't be further from the truth! The objective of this talk is to help your students discover where lust comes from and how to deal with the temptation to lust in such a way that brings them victory instead of defeat.

Use What You Have

Throughout this book, TV and DVD player are listed whenever a movie can be shown because we used the DVD versions of these films to determine the start and stop times for each movie clip. Of course, you can also use a VCR, video projection unit (VPU), computer, or whatever other technical resources fit your situation.

If an activity calls for a whiteboard to list ideas or responses, you can also use an overhead projector, a flip chart, or butcher paper taped to the wall.

It can get cumbersome if we list all the possible variations every time. So feel free to adapt to the technology you have available.

intro
The Opening Act

Begin with one or more of these options:

🔊 Activity: Magazine ads (see sidebar)

🔊 Videotape some television commercials that have sexual themes. Play the tape for your students and ask them to talk about what messages and values they see being displayed throughout the commercial.

🔊 Movie clip: *Mission: Impossible II* (see sidebar)

🔊 Transition to the body of the talk by explaining—No matter where we turn, it seems as though our society completely overwhelms us with sexual images and the idea that it's good to be physically desired by others. Many people go to great lengths to prove to themselves and others that they are physically desirable. But what does God have to say about this need that so many of us have to be desired or to desire someone else? In order to understand lust we first have to understand how desire works.

Activity

Magazine Ads

Lay out several popular magazines (not news mags, but ones that teenagers would actually read: *Seventeen*, *Rolling Stone*, *Teen People*, *YM*, and so on). Have a contest to see which group of two or three students can find the most advertisements with lustful themes in 60 seconds or less. Ask your students to explain why they think it was so easy to find sexual themes in these magazines. (Note: With young teens, you should first make sure everyone knows what "lust" is.)

Mission: Impossible II

Start 0:11:00 Ethan puts his empty glass on a tray.
Stop 0:12:17 Ethan scans the room looking for Nyah after she disappears.

Ethan (Tom Cruise) has been sent to find Nyah (Thandie Newton), the ex-girlfriend of Sean Ambrose (Dougray Scott), a former IMF agent who is planning to unleash a deadly synthetic disease, Chimera, on the world's population. Ethan's superiors hope he can convince Nyah to work with IMF to help them retrieve the vials of the deadly disease and stop Sean before he can carry out his plan for global bioterrorism.

In this clip, Ethan has tracked down Nyah at a party. As they circle around the dance floor, they can't take their eyes off each other. Ask your students to explain how necessary it is that real love start with some form of physical attraction.

heart of the talk

The Main Event

1. Our ability to desire is a gift from God.

- Scripture: 1 Thessalonians 2:17 ("But, brothers, when we were torn away from you for a short time (in person, not in thought), out of our intense longing we made every effort to see you.")

- Explanation (see sidebar)

- Personal illustration: Good Desires (see sidebar)

- Scripture: Luke 22:15 ("I have eagerly desired to eat this Passover with you before I suffer.")

- The ability to desire certain things in life is a gift from God and allows us to truly enjoy the world he has created for us.

- Object lesson: Hershey's Kiss Undressed (see sidebar)

1 Thessalonians 2:17

Paul is expressing his deep feelings of affection for the Thessalonians. He seems to be in agony over the fact that he had to leave them prematurely and wants them to know that he desires to be with them again. In this case, Paul is using the Greek word for lust in a positive sense, meaning an intense desire (not physical, of course!).

Personal illustration

Good Desires

Talk about some positive things that you desire (a good meal, close friendships, more time with your family, and so on). Then give your students a chance to share some of their positive desires. Ask—What are some of the good things you desire of life? After hearing a few responses, ask—Why do you think God gave you the ability to desire those things?

Desire alone is certainly not a bad thing! Even Jesus uses the word *desire*, showing that it's a good and normal thing.

Object lesson

Hershey's Kiss Undressed

Hand out enough Hershey's Kisses so that everyone in the room has one. With students holding their hands out flat in front of them, have each student hold his Kiss in the palm of his hand and just look at it. Talk about how incredible the Kiss looks and how desirable it is. Then have everyone follow you as you slowly peel back just a small corner of the foil wrapping and continue talking about how you just can't wait to eat this incredible piece of candy.

Next, have everyone pull out the little piece of paper sticking out of the Kiss as you continue talking about how wonderful this candy's going to taste. By this time everyone should be drooling, so just peel back all of the foil and have everyone look at his Kiss as it sits "naked" on top of the foil in the palm of his hand. Ask the students if anyone is lusting after the Kiss yet.

Talk about the differences between their desire for the chocolate Kiss and a desire for other things they may be tempted to lust after. Ask them if they think there's anything wrong with desiring a Hershey's Kiss. What makes one desire "good" and another desire "bad"? After the conversation, don't forget to eat!

2. Our ability to desire can bring us a lot of hurt and pain.

🔊 Because we may not always know what's best for us, we all have the opportunity to desire things that are not good for us. Many things that initially seem good may actually cause a tremendous amount of heartache in our lives.

🔊 Scripture: James 1:14-15 ("But each one is tempted when, by his own evil desire, he is dragged away and enticed. Then, after desire has conceived, it gives birth to sin; and sin, when it is full-grown, gives birth to death.")

- Even our God-given desires can lead us away from God if we allow them to. Uncontrolled desires have a way of turning into sin, which will always distance us from God.

- The ability to discern between good desires and bad desires can be difficult to do on our own. It's important to have people in our lives who can help us develop our discernment skills.

- Illustration: Hershey's Kiss Undressed Again (see sidebar)

Hershey's Kiss Undressed Again

This illustration will take a bit of advanced preparation. Before your talk, take another Hershey's Kiss and unwrap it very carefully so you're able to wrap it back up again. Do something to sabotage the Kiss, like soaking it in water or oil or hiding something inside of it, then wrap it up again.

Begin unwrapping the kiss in front of your students while you talk about how good it looks and how you can't wait to eat it. As the "problem" with this particular chocolate Kiss becomes clear, act shocked and disgusted while you explain to your students what's wrong with it. Then, as you hold the messed-up Kiss in your hand (as you did earlier), talk briefly about how you can't always tell what's good for you by the way it looks at first.

3. Our ability to desire also brings with it a responsibility to control our desires.

- Scripture: Romans 7:18 ("I know that nothing good lives in me, that is, in my sinful nature. For I have the desire to do what is good, but I cannot carry it out.")

- Explanation (see sidebar)

- Scripture: 1 Thessalonians 4:4-5 ("Each of you should learn to control his own body in a way that is holy and honorable, not in passionate lust like the heathen, who do not know God.")

- Activity: Keeping My Promise (see sidebar)

Romans 7:18

Even the apostle Paul, who wrote half of the New Testament, struggled with choosing to follow the good desires inside of him. He was constantly trying to figure out what it meant to conform his desires to God's desire for his life.

Activity

Keeping My Promise

Give each student a blank piece of paper and challenge them to "make a covenant" with a part of themselves that they have difficulty controlling—eyes, mouth, thought life, and so on. Ask students to write out the promise they're making between themselves, this particular part of their body, and God. Ask them to journal about some very specific steps they could take to make sure they're able to keep their promise.

closing

The Grand Finale

📣 Have students get into same-sex small groups and discuss some of the really good things they desire to do with their lives. Encourage them to dream a little bit!

📣 Invite students (who feel comfortable) to share what their "covenant" was all about. Ask the group to brainstorm ways they could help each other keep their promises to themselves. (Note: This would best be accomplished in small groups.)

📣 Ask the group to pray for each other and then encourage them to follow up with each other on a regular basis. Have them brainstorm some practical steps they could take as a group to enable one another to keep their promises.

discussion

Encore

Get It?	Middle School

📣 What's lust? Is lust always a sexual thing? What other things can you lust for?

📣 When is desire a good thing?

📣 If it seems almost impossible to resist some of our strongest desires, is it really possible to control them?

📣 When is it most difficult for you to control your desires?

📣 Talk about a time when God helped you control your desires.

Get It?   High School

🔊 When is desire good?

🔊 Why do you think God gave us the ability to desire since he knew we were going to struggle with giving in to evil desires that could hurt us?

🔊 Describe how you felt the last time you gave in to one of your bad desires.

🔊 Describe how you felt the last time you resisted a bad desire and gained victory in that area.

What If?   The Big Picture

🔊 What would it look like if our youth group modeled Galatians 6:2, which says, "Carry each other's burdens, and in this way you will fulfill the law of Christ"?

🔊 What does it mean to "carry each other's burdens"?

🔊 Why do you think one person can struggle with a certain desire continuously while another person never struggles in that area? What does this suggest about our need for one another?

🔊 In your opinion, how does desire conceive sin, which leads to death? What kind of death is James talking about?

So What?   It's Your Life

🔊 What are some positive steps you could take to enable yourself to understand how desire works in your life?

🔊 When are you most tempted? What causes you to give in? What type of strategy would it take to allow you to say no to harmful desires in your life?

🔊 How would your life look if you were able to get control of your harmful desires? Discuss.

🔊 Why do you think it's sometimes awkward to allow others to help us control our desires?

🔊 Is your youth group a place where you feel comfortable talking about this kind of stuff? Why or why not?

🔊 Against which area of lust do you especially need God's strength this week?

All By Myself

Contributed by **Dave Ambrose**

Primary theme loneliness	
Themes community, relationships, solitude, relying on God	
Scripture Psalm 25: 16-17; Psalm 22; Mark 1:45; Luke 5:16; Genesis 2:18; Psalm 68:6; Deuteronomy 31:6; John 16:32	
Approximate length through The Grand Finale 20-30 minutes	

You'll need

- *Rear Window* (Paramount Pictures, 1954)
- TV and DVD player
- Blank paper and pens
- A personal story about a time when you felt lonely
- A clip from a Cirque du Soleil performance (optional)

Think about the culture that surrounds most of your students on a daily basis. It seems they are in constant connection with someone. At school, teens are with their friends, teachers, coaches, and other people all the time. When they're at home, teens are not only surrounded by their families, but most of them also have instant access to an entire world of relationships through the Internet, instant messaging, chat rooms, and cell phones. So with all of those people available to them, how is it possible that there are more lonely and disconnected students than ever before? Our objective in this lesson is to see what God has to say about loneliness and how we can help your students experience real biblical community.

intro
The Opening Act

🔊 Activity: Separation (see sidebar)

🔊 Movie clip: *Rear Window* (see sidebar)

🔊 Ask a few of your students to describe a time when they remember being very lonely. Encourage them to give details and to talk about how that experience made them feel. Debrief these conversations with the entire group as you go along, asking others to jump in at anytime.

🔊 Transition to the body of the talk by explaining—
Most of you are around people all the time: your family, other kids at school, your teachers, and your friends. Many of you come home from school and immediately get on the telephone or the Internet and talk with more people, even though you were surrounded by friends all day long. In spite of all this interaction throughout the day, it seems there are more lonely people in our society today than ever before. So we're going to talk about loneliness and look at God's Word for some guidance in understanding what loneliness is really all about and how to help ourselves—or our friends—through the valley of loneliness.

Activity

Separation

Take your students outside (or into a large room with enough space for them to spread out). Choose two of your more confident students to participate in a little experiment. Ask them to move away from the group, in opposite directions from each other. They should move far enough away that they're unable to communicate, but still close enough to see and hear that something is going on back in the main group. Ask these two students not to say anything, but just sit there until you call them back.

Start a fun discussion about something your kids would enjoy talking and laughing about— the best movie they've seen recently or the worst song on the radio. After a while, call the two volunteers back to the group and ask them these questions:

• How did you feel while you were separated from the rest of the group?
• Did you have stuff you wanted to add to the conversation?
• How did not being allowed to participate make you feel?
• Is being alone easy or difficult for you? Why?

Then to the entire group ask—Do you think it's possible to be sitting with a group and still be lonely? (Ask them to explain their responses.)

Rear Window

Start 00:21:21 Jeff looks out his apartment window; the camera pans down the building and stops at Miss Lonelyheart's window.

Stop 00:23:28 Jeff says, "Miss Lonelyheart. Well, at least that's something you'll never have to worry about."

Jeff (Jimmy Stewart) watches as his neighbor, "Miss Lonelyheart," pretends she's having dinner in her apartment with a special someone. When she eventually realizes what she's doing and that it's all just a fantasy created out of desperate loneliness, she begins to cry.

Ask your students to describe the last time they felt completely alone. Then have them list some things people do to overcome their feelings of loneliness.

heart of the talk

The Main Event

1. Everyone experiences loneliness.

- Scripture: Psalm 25:16-17 ("Turn to me and be gracious to me, for I am lonely and afflicted. The troubles of my heart have multiplied; free me from my anguish.")

- Explanation (see sidebar)

- Meditation: Psalm 22 (see sidebar)

- Even though loneliness seems like a negative thing, there were times when Jesus purposefully searched for opportunities to be alone. (See Mark 1:45 and Luke 5:16.)

- Ask—
  In what ways do you see Jesus using loneliness positively? What could we learn from his example?

Psalm 25:16-17

Even the godly people who helped write Scripture struggled with feelings of loneliness at times. There are situations in life that can overwhelm even the most "spiritual" people and cause them to feel completely alone. You are not the only person who has struggled with feelings of loneliness and desperation.

Psalm 22

Explain to your students that you are going to read through a Psalm that describes one man's lonely journey. Ask them to bow their heads, close their eyes, and picture themselves as the writer of the Psalm.

Read through Psalm 22 slowly, at least twice. After you've finished, hand out paper and pens to your students and ask them to write down how they felt as you read through the Psalm. (You may want to read it through one more time once they have their journaling tools.)

Have a few of your kids read their journal entries and explain to them that Psalm 22 is a prophecy depicting the crucifixion of Jesus. Ask them to discuss the feelings of loneliness Jesus must have experienced on the cross.

2. God cares for the lonely, and so should we!

- Scripture: Genesis 2:18 ("The Lord God said, 'It is not good for the man to be alone.'") Immediately after God created Adam and placed him into the Garden of Eden, God stated that it wasn't good for Adam to be alone and he created someone (Eve) to share a relationship with Adam.

- Scripture: Psalm 68:6, NASB ("God makes a home for the lonely.") God promises to take care of the lonely by placing them in families. A family is a group of people who come together to care for one another. Youth group should be a safe place where students have the opportunity to experience genuine community in Christ.

- Ask—
  How could our group be a place where students experience the type of "family" that Psalm 68 talks about?

- Scripture: John 16:32 ("But a time is coming, and has come, when you will be scattered, each to his own home. You will leave me all alone. Yet I am not alone, for my Father is with me.") Jesus could have wallowed around in self-pity, for he knew that his disciples would abandon him during his final hours of life on earth. But Jesus also knew that his father would never leave him, and he took great comfort in that fact. We can, too.

- Scripture: Deuteronomy 31:6 ("Be strong and courageous. Do not be afraid or terrified because of them, for the Lord your God goes with you; he will never leave you nor forsake you.") What an incredible promise from God! No matter how lonely we may feel at times, we're promised that God is always with us. Situations change, people may forget about us at times, but God never does! God promises to go with us no matter where we go.

- Personal illustration: When God Met Me (see sidebar)

- Activity: The Great Balancing Act (see sidebar)

When God Met Me

From your own life, share an illustration of a time when you felt very lonely, but God met you in that place. Talk about your feelings, what happened, and the end result.

The Great Balancing Act

Have students stand up and try to see how long they can balance on one foot while holding their other leg out behind them (not touching the floor) and stretching out their arms like airplane wings. After a while it should become difficult for most students to maintain their balance. Ask—What are a couple ways we could learn to control our bodies to allow us to balance for a longer period of time?

There are two primary ways:

• Practice. Consider showing a clip from a Cirque du Soleil video (available through Amazon.com). This amazing group of performers includes balancing artists who are able to hold an uncomfortable pose for a long time because they've practiced it over and over. Similarly, as we experience what it means to rely on God over and over again, we also get better at it!

• Partnership. Suggest that the students try their balancing act again, only this time they should grab hands with the students on either side of them and help each other remain standing. Afterward, ask your students to explain the point of this illustration as it relates to combating loneliness.

closing

The Grand Finale

🔊 Exercise: We Are Family (see sidebar)

🔊 Activity: Letter Writing (see sidebar)

Exercise

We Are Family

Have students sit in a circle (use small groups of up to a dozen in each). Give each student as many pieces of paper as there are people in the circle, and a pen or pencil. Using one sheet of paper for each person in their small group, ask your students to write the person's name on the piece of paper and one sentence about one unique thing that person adds to your youth group family.

After they've had some time to think and write, go around the circle and ask the students to take turns sharing what they've written about the other students in the circle. Discuss how your group would be different if these qualities were not represented.

If you think it will encourage your students to do so, ask them to collect the statements that the other students wrote about them. They can take these home as reminders of how the kids in their youth group value their positive qualities.

(Note: This exercise will have to be dropped or modified if your group doesn't know each other very well.)

Activity

Letter Writing

Have students write letters of encouragement to someone they know who has been going through a very lonely time in their life. Or if any of your students have been feeling lonely lately, encourage those kids to write letters to themselves using the themes of this talk as encouragement.

If they totally can't think of anyone to write a letter to, have them write to an imaginary lonely friend (just to get them thinking through the application of this talk).

Consider ending your time with a bit of solitude. Ask students to go off by themselves for about 10 minutes. During this period of forced loneliness, they can either listen to God, draw, or journal.

discussion
Encore

Get It? | Middle School

- Describe how you felt the last time you were "left out" of something.

- What's the most difficult part of being alone?

- Where is God when we're lonely? How does that work? How can we be more aware of his presence?

- Have you ever met someone who came across as if she didn't need anyone in her life? How do you respond to people like her?

- What are some ways Jesus may have responded to her?

Get It? | High School

- What are some ways you could use a period of loneliness in your life in a positive way during this upcoming week?

- Describe a time when you felt abandoned by your friends or family.

- What's it feel like to be separated from someone you love?

- How do you think Jesus felt while he was on the cross and separated from his heavenly Father?

- Why do you think God created us to be dependent on one another? Wouldn't it have been easier to make us independent?

- Why do you think our culture values independence so highly?

What If? | The Big Picture

- Do you think it's possible for our youth group to genuinely care for each person in our group so that no one ever feels left out or lonely? Why or why not?

- What's keeping our group from being that kind of community?

- How could knowing that Jesus went through some incredible moments of loneliness on the cross help you when you're struggling with feelings of loneliness?

- Identify some lonely groups of people in your community. What are some ways our youth group could genuinely care for some of these people?

- Ask someone in your group who has recently moved to the area to describe some of the feelings of loneliness he faced during this transition. What are some things the group could have done to help make it easier for him?

So What?	It's Your Life

◄» Why do you think some people tend to isolate themselves from others?

◄» What are some ways your group could help them overcome their fears and become part of your youth group community?

◄» What can we do—really—to move our group toward genuine community?

◄» Are there other students who attend your church but never come to youth group? Why do you think they don't attend? What could your group do to get them involved?

◄» How do you think consciously spending time with others helps us get over our own feelings of loneliness?

◄» What will you do the next time you feel lonely?

What Time Is It?

Primary theme false and true prophets
Themes discerning God's voice, truth, judgment, disillusionment, the church, revival, trust
Scripture Jeremiah 28: 1-17
Approximate length through The Grand Finale 20-30 minutes

You'll need

- 🔊 *Batman* (Warner Bros., 1989)
- 🔊 TV and DVD player
- 🔊 Jars filled with various liquids
- 🔊 Some pH paper strips (available at most pharmacies)

This talk simply recounts a story about a moment in the history of Israel. Although the story is from a long time ago, it still seems very relevant to our current situation in the church in the Western world. (Note: This talk is best suited for older students.)

Contributed by **Jonny Baker**

intro

The Opening Act

🔊 Ask students to pair off and come up with a definition of *prophet*. Have some or all the pairs read their definitions to the group.

🔊 Quote: Walter Brueggemann (see sidebar)

🔊 Activity: True/False (see sidebar)

🔊 Discussion: What's the Illusion? (see sidebar)

🔊 Transition by saying something like—Today we are going to look at a story from the Old Testament about a prophet named Jeremiah. It is a story about true and false prophets, where God's people have to try and work out which prophet knows what time it is, so to speak. It's also a story that shows how some people are only too ready to believe an illusion and end up very disillusioned.

Quote

"A prophet is someone who knows what time it is."
—Walter Brueggemann

Activity

True/False

Read aloud each of the 10 items below. Ask for a vote of true or false after each one is read. Allow students to work in pairs to come up with their answers.

• The largest bats have a wingspan up to 6 feet. (True—the flying fox in Indochina)
• People with diabetes should inspect their feet daily. (True—people with diabetes can unknowingly develop numbness in their feet. When the feet are numb, the patient can have injuries that go undetected which could develop into serious problems unless daily foot inspections are performed.)
• Water always drains clockwise. (False—it depends on whether you're in the northern or southern hemisphere.)
• There are seven continents. (True—can any of your students name all seven of them?)
• Isaac Newton was a priest. (True—he was an ordained minister of the Church of England.)
• Greece is to the northeast of Egypt. (False)
• If your nose runs and your feet smell, you are built upside down. (False)
• Mat, pot, and squidger are terms used in wrestling. (False—they're terms used in tiddlywinks.)
• Chinese checkers did not originate in China. (True)
• Coffee is the only beverage to receive the papal seal of approval. (True)

After working through the list, ask the pairs how they decided whether to vote true or false. What could have helped them as they made their guesses?

What's the Illusion?

Ask the group if any of them has ever been disillusioned. Get one or two students to share about a situation when this happened to them. And come prepared to share one or two of your own personal experiences with disillusionment as well.

Tell your students—When you are disillusioned it is good to look back and ask, What was the illusion that I wanted to believe? See if this question can be used with any of the stories that were recounted in order to illustrate the concept.

If it is going well, you could press this a bit further by asking whether anyone has ever felt disillusioned by God or by the church. In the same way, get them to recount their stories and then ask them to identify the illusions they believed.

heart of the talk

The Main Event

1. Sometimes the truth isn't pretty.

🔊 Scripture: Jeremiah 28:1-9 (The conflicting prophesies of Hananiah and Jeremiah.)

🔊 Explanation: Israel in Crisis (see sidebar)

🔊 Movie clip: *Batman* (see sidebar)

🔊 Explanation: The Church in the West (see sidebar)

Israel in Crisis

At the time of this Scripture story, Israel was in crisis. The unthinkable had happened. Captives had already been taken from the northern kingdom, but now the first captives had also been seized from Jerusalem. Babylon took treasures from the temple, along with the king. How could God have let this happen? And what is he going to do about it?

Two voices are heard at this time, each one proclaiming a very different message. Hananiah the prophet delivers the popular message of triumph, victory, and a swift resolution to the problem at hand: God will bring back the exiles and the treasures of the temple. Surely this is a message of faith in the midst of adversity—faith in God who won't let his people down.

The other message is Jeremiah's. He has been threatened with death for uttering it. It is not very cheery: God is judging his people for not obeying the law. They will live in exile for 70 years! It is easy to imagine Jeremiah being labeled a pessimist and a doubter who lacks faith. And it is not too difficult to see why his message wasn't very popular either.

Ask the students—Which one would you have believed? Why?

Batman

Start 01:38:26 The Joker is riding on a parade float as it makes its way through the streets of Gotham.

Stop 01:42:35 Batman uses the Bat Plane to pull the balloons away from the crowd.

This scene needs very little explanation. The evil Joker (Jack Nicholson) wants to destroy the people of Gotham City. But he deceives them by throwing free money into the crowd during a parade. The Joker crows, "Hubba, hubba, hubba. Money, money, money. Who do you trust? Me? I'm giving away free money!" and his henchmen throw bags full of bills into the crowd.

All seems to be well with world, but unknown to the onlookers, the large clown balloon that's tethered to the Joker's float is filled with poisonous gas. Those who have believed the illusion that the Joker is trustworthy (and really giving away free money) are about to be disillusioned! Fortunately, Batman knows the truth. He rescues the people in the nick of time by flying down in his Bat Plane and dragging the deadly balloons up into the sky and away from the crowds.

The Church in the West

We find ourselves in a similar situation today. There are two voices in the church that are very different from each other. In lots of places people have said that great spiritual revival is coming. God has promised it, and we must get ready.

A very different message is that the church in the West (in other words, the United States and Europe) is dying. And if she doesn't reform her ways, she will not exist in 50 years time. Statistics on church attendance in most Western countries show a decline. While there is openness to spirituality, people are not looking to the church to find it. She is becoming increasingly irrelevant. She once held unspeakable riches, but these treasures have been carried away. This second message is less popular. To believe it is to be labeled a cynic and a doubter, whereas believers of the first message are considered to be full of faith.

2. God's Word is the ultimate test.

◁)) Object lesson: The Acid Test (see sidebar)

◁)) Scripture: Jeremiah 28:10-17 (Jeremiah's response to Hananiah)

- Jeremiah turns out to be the prophet who knows what time it is. The people are exiled for 70 years and the treasures are not brought back to the temple within two years. Hananiah is judged and dies for his false prophecy. Those who believed Hananiah end up disillusioned.

- Ask the students what the acid test for prophecy is. (If they struggle to respond, point them to verse 9—the acid test is whether or not a prophet's words come true!)

- In our own situation, the two messages of revival or decline in the relevance of the church will face the acid test. But whichever one is true, Jeremiah's reaction to Hananiah is one we can learn from: "Amen! Let it be so! But you still need to reform your ways." The church must address and reform her irrelevance.

Object lesson

The Acid Test

Before your meeting, fill a few small jars with a variety of liquids, one liquid per jar. And make sure the liquids you choose have a range of acidity levels. For instance, cola, orange juice, and coffee all have higher levels of acidity than apple juice or water. You could also make some mixtures of water and baking soda, or water and laundry detergent.

In addition to the jars of liquids, you'll also need some pH or litmus paper. (If you can't find any at your local pharmacy, ask a science teacher at your local junior high or high school where to purchase some.) These paper strips will turn a whole range of colors depending on the levels of acid or base in the liquid. (Pinks and reds on the paper indicate an acid; blues and greens indicate a base; and purple indicates a neutral substance like water, which is neither an acid nor a base.)

Ask students to name some things that they believe are acidic (lemon juice, vinegar). Then ask them to name some things that are alkaline or bases (baking soda, soap). Briefly explain how the pH paper works, then test all the liquids and let your group see the results.

Now ask your students if they've ever heard the phrase "the acid test" used outside of a science classroom and, if so, what it means. Then explain that people sometimes use that term when they're talking about finding out the real truth in a situation.

closing

The Grand Finale

- Ask the group memebers what things they have learned from the story of Jeremiah.

- Reread Walter Brueggemann's definition of a prophet as someone who "knows what time it is."

- Pray for your own church and the church nationwide to know what time it is and to reform her ways.

discussion

Encore

Get It? — Middle School

- How do you know when to trust someone?
- Should you trust someone just because she is a leader?
- Should you trust someone because he says, "God says…" before he shares something?
- How can you learn to hear God's voice for yourself?
- What part does the Bible have in that?
- What part do friends have in that?
- What part does the church have in that?

Get It? — High School

- Who do you think are today's false prophets?
- Who do you think are today's true prophets?
- How do we tell the difference?
- Should we believe something someone says just because she says, "God says…"?
- Read some other parts of the story of Jeremiah. He had a tough job. What do you think kept him going?
- What do you think God is calling you to do for him?

What If? — The Big Picture

- Moving from believing and doing what others say without even thinking about it, to thinking and weighing things for yourself is an important part of maturing in your faith. How can you develop this skill?
- What things help you discern the truth and what God might be saying to you?
- Rank the following in terms of importance for discerning God's voice: feelings, the Bible, friends, parents, prayer, church leaders, gut instinct.
- When do you think it's okay to say to someone, "God says…"? Be prepared for the acid test.

So What?	It's Your Life

◀)) Make a list of dreams for your church and for your youth group. Pray that God will make some of these dreams happen.

◀)) Make a list of times when you remember being disillusioned—either by a friend, a situation, a family member, the church, or a leader. Try and work out what the illusion was that you believed. Offer them to God and then write down what the real situation was. Even if the illusion is more pleasant, throw it away and hold on to the real situation. Ask God to help you hold on to what is real.

Cross-Cultural Mission

Contributed by **Jonny Baker**

Primary theme missions	
Themes outreach, evangelism, culture, prejudice, change, diversity	
Scripture Acts 10; Acts 15:1-35	
Approximate length through The Grand Finale 30 minutes	

You'll need

- *Shrek* (DreamWorks SKG, 2001)
- TV and DVD player

MThe period in the church's history as recorded in Acts 10-15, is a very exciting and significant moment where the gospel moves from the Jews to the Gentiles. Peter and Cornelius are caught up in a move of the Spirit of God that changes the course of history. Peter is called to let go of some of his assumptions of how the gospel is culturally clothed in Jewish culture and to follow the call of God into the future.

The church had to wrestle with the complex challenge of working out what was essential to the gospel and what was essential to keeping relations good between Jewish believers and the emerging Gentile churches. This may seem a tricky passage to consider with young people, but it is worth taking on for two reasons.

One is the obvious importance and challenge of relating the gospel across different cultures. But the second is that insights from cross-cultural missions have a lot to offer us. Our own culture has experienced huge changes over the last 30 years, so much so that we find ourselves in a situation where the inherited ways of being part of a church seem to be very alien to people in the culture of the teen world.

The question of how we share the gospel in the emerging culture is essential for the future of the church, but how the inherited church maintains relationships with the emerging church is crucial. (Note: This talk is best suited to older students.)

intro

The Opening Act

🔊 Ask the group members if they have ever traveled to another country or culture. What did they notice that was different? What did they notice about their own culture when they returned?

🔊 Illustration: Soccer Skills (see sidebar)

🔊 Ask if anyone in the group has had a cross-cultural embarrassing moment they'd like to share with the group.

🔊 Reading: They Speak with Other Tongues (see sidebar). You could either read this story aloud to your students or ask a few of your leaders to act it out in typical "Who's on First?" fashion, with people playing the parts of the narrator, Ed, and Denise.

Illustration

Soccer Skills

A youth minister traveled to Morocco and wanted to build friendships with the local young people. They were all into soccer, and he was a pretty good player. So it was a natural way for him to build relationships. The teens soon wanted the youth worker to teach them some new skills.

He had noticed they weren't very good at heading the ball. However, he had to use hand signals to communicate with them because the teenagers didn't speak English. So he tried to show them how to do it by pointing to his forehead. At first the young people looked shocked, then they burst out laughing. And this happened every time he made the gesture. Eventually he figured out that the sign he was using was actually a very rude insult along the lines of "Your mother is a—"!

heart of the talk

The Main Event

1. God wants to reach all cultures.

🔊 Scripture: Acts 10 (The story of Peter going to Cornelius's house)

• This is a long passage. Depending on your group and your preferred method of storytelling, you could do one of three things:

a) Read the passage and then do the explanations;

b) Read the passage while pausing along the way to interject the explanations as you go; or

c) Retell the passage in your own words and read aloud a few significant verses.

- But the story speaks for itself. All you need to do is make a few connections.

🔊 Explanation: Peter and Cornelius (see sidebar)

🔊 Discussion: Unpacking the Story (see sidebar)

🔊 Movie clip: *Shrek* (see sidebar)

Explanation

Peter and Cornelius

Here are a few points you can use as you read the story:

- After verse 8: God is at work in his world. He speaks to Cornelius without the intervention of any of the apostles.

- After verse 23: Peter's dream confuses him because in it God seems to be telling him to do something that God has forbidden! In Jewish law, as seen in Leviticus, it is forbidden to eat "unclean" food. But this dream seems to nudge Peter into thinking he should go with the Gentiles and enter their house, even though that is also "against the law."

- After verse 48: When Peter takes the risk of crossing a previously forbidden border between the Jews and the Gentiles, he finds that God is ahead of him beckoning him to join in with what the Lord is already doing among the Gentiles. And much to the amazement of the circumcised believers, the Holy Spirit came upon the Gentiles—just as he had come upon the Jews earlier.

Discussion

Unpacking the Story

Imagine if Peter hadn't taken the risk of going into the Gentile's house. Where would we be now? Why do you think the Jewish believers are so surprised when the Holy Spirit comes upon the Gentiles? Are there groups of people today who you would be surprised to see the Holy Spirit coming upon? What borders is God calling us to cross?

Movie clip

Shrek

Start 00:26:17 Shrek and Donkey are walking through a field of sunflowers.

Stop 00:28:03 Shrek says, "End of story. Bye-bye. See ya later!"

In this clip Donkey (voice of Eddie Murphy) is trying to understand why Shrek (voice of Mike Myers) agreed to go on a dangerous quest to slay a dragon and free Princess Fiona just so the evil Lord Farquaad can marry her. While making his argument, Donkey lists a number of typical ogre behaviors that Shrek should have used to get his way instead: throttling Lord Farquaad, laying siege to his fortress, or grinding his bones to make bread—the "whole ogre trip." So Shrek attempts to explain to Donkey that there is more to an ogre than those scary stereotypes.

2. Separating our stuff from God's stuff.

🔊 Illustration: Hymn Singing and Falling Asleep in Africa (see sidebar)

🔊 Quote: Charles Kraft (see sidebar)

🔊 Scripture: Acts 15:1-35 (circumcision for the new Gentile believers?)

🔊 Explanation: I Have to Cut What? (see sidebar)

Illustration

Hymn Singing and Falling Asleep in Africa

This story highlights an age-old issue in the history of cross-cultural mission. Where missionaries share the gospel, it is often wrapped up in their own cultural forms. So when people are being persuaded to accept Christ, they are also being persuaded to accept the cultural baggage of the missionaries. The challenge is how to share the gospel in ways and forms that grow out of the culture of the people you are living among and ultimately how to get them to develop and lead their own expressions of church and worship.

Roberta King tells the story of missionaries who were trying to reach the Senufo peoples on the Ivory Coast in West Africa (now called Côte d'Ivoire), when they experienced a problem during their worship times:

The Senufo peoples always slept during hymn singing. Hymns like "Come Thou Fount of Every Blessing" worked like sleeping pills. The church leaders had no idea what to do. The missionary had recently discovered that the "Hallelujah Chorus" sounded like crying music to these people. Yet he knew that the Senufo people love their own music. Finally, in desperation at the end of one service, he challenged the people: "Don't you have something to sing to God?" An old woman stood up and began singing a call-and-response-style song. The atmosphere turned—electric people were captivated and became totally involved in the song.

Quote

"I have nothing against those who as part of their devotion to Christ choose to follow Christ according to the patterns of Europeanized African culture. These are truly God's people. But my heart yearns for the 300 million who will not Westernize in order to become Christian."
— Charles Kraft (at a Pan-African assembly in 1976)

Explanation

I Have to Cut What?

As with the previous passage, choose your own method of telling the story. Introduce it by saying that the same issue they're facing in Africa today was faced by the early church. Did people have to act Jewish in order to become Christian?

• After verse 1: The Gentiles' explosive response to the gospel was incredibly exciting. But some Jewish believers were getting upset because the Gentiles were doing things differently. The big issue seemed to be circumcision. Certain believers were saying that people weren't saved unless they had been circumcised!

• After verse 21: This all came to a head at a big church council meeting that was called to decide what should be done. Peter, who had earlier seen the Spirit at work among the Gentiles, persuades them not to impose their own cultural baggage on the Gentile believers.

• After verse 35: They write a letter to the Gentiles with some stipulations. The Message concludes the letter with these words, "These guidelines are sufficient to keep relations congenial between us" (verse 29). In other words, the important thing is that the Gentile believers were given freedom to develop the church in ways that were true to their own culture, but at the same time it was essential that they kept good relations with the Jewish Christians.

closing

The Grand Finale

🔊 The early church had the courage to recognize that the gospel required different expressions and developments of the church in different cultures. Now we can thank God that there is incredible diversity between churches around the world.

🔊 It is tempting for us to think that our ways of doing things are the right way, but that isn't necessarily so.

🔊 Lessons from cross-cultural missions need to be applied in our own situations. Inherited ways and emerging ways of being a church are often very different. Those people with the inherited ways need to have the courage to free up the people with the emerging ways rather than imposing their cultural baggage on the new expressions—all while keeping good relations between the two.

🔊 Discussion: What about Us? (see sidebar)

Discussion

What about Us?

Spend some time talking about the implications for your own city or town:
- In what ways is the culture of this decade different than the culture of 30 or 40 years ago? (Your adult leaders may need to help the kids answer this question.)
- What about the way your church practices Christianity doesn't make sense to people in this current culture?
- Which parts of the church service, programs, or constitution are essential to hold on to?
- Which parts might we consider moving away from if we want to reach people in this culture with the Good News of Jesus Christ?

discussion

Encore

Get It?	Middle School

- If culture is "the way we do things around here," describe the culture of your church.
- Describe the culture of your friends outside the church.
- Is there a gap between the two cultures you've just described? If so, according to this story, what should you do about the gap?
- Find out if there are any people your church keeps in touch with who have gone as mission partners to another culture. Get their newsletters and pray for them.

Get It?	High School

- If God was at work in Cornelius, who was outside the Christian community, where do you think he might be at work in your town or city? How can you join in with what God is doing?
- Peter took the risk of following God's beckoning to cross a border. Are there any borders God might be calling you to cross?
- Jews and Gentiles were insiders and outsiders—the assumption was that God favored one group more than the other. Who are the insiders and outsiders in our church today?

What If?   The Big Picture

🔊 Circumcision was a big issue for the Jews and Gentiles. What are the big issues for your church? What can you learn from the early church by studying how they dealt with their particular issue?

🔊 Write a drama reenacting the church council in Jerusalem, but rewrite it so it concerns contemporary issues rather than circumcision and food sacrificed to idols.

So What?   It's Your Life

🔊 Does your church have links with any churches in other countries? Find out if there are any young people (who are close in age to your group) in one of those churches. Make contact with them either by letter or e-mail. Ask the link to pray for your youth group, and your group should do likewise. Eventually have some members from your group travel to visit them and vice versa.

🔊 The passage in Acts 15 records how the church dealt with their differences in how to go about doing things in order to keep relations good between the inherited church and the emerging church, all while remaining faithful to the gospel. Split your group into two. Ask one half to imagine they are your church leaders and to write a letter to your youth group that outlines what is important for keeping relations good with the inherited church and for remaining faithful to the gospel. Ask the other half to do the same thing, but they should write their letter from the youth group to the church leaders. Discuss what the students have written.

Reading

"They Speak With Other Tongues" by Bob Cohen

This reading opens the issue of culture closer to home. Our churches have cultures. Culture is "the way we do things around here" that is often invisible to us when we are inside it. But as soon as someone from outside comes in or we go somewhere else, we can see that our ways of doing things are just one way, not the only way.

"Have you ever been saved?" A rather wide-eyed young fellow startled me with his question as we waited for the bus. He handed me a booklet with a picture of hell on the front.

"Sure," I responded. "Once when I was nine years old, I was swimming at Jones Beach on Long Island, and a strong undertow began to drag me out to sea. My uncle heard my call for help and..."

"No, no," he interrupted, "redeemed! Have you ever been redeemed? You know, reborn...washed in the blood?"

"What," I inquired, "in the world are you talking about?"

"Convicted. Have you ever felt convicted?"

"No, of course not!" I replied. "I've never been in trouble with the law."

He looked at me square in the eye. "I think you need to be delivered."

"Delivered? I was just waiting for the bus home. I think I'll stick with that, but thank you very much." He looked at me as if I were speaking another language.

"Can we have lunch together sometime?" he asked. "I work just down the street."

"Sure, that would be fine." He looked harmless enough, but I must admit he was an unusual fellow and quite difficult to understand.

That Wednesday I had lunch with Ed. He was a little late but explained that he was having some quiet time.

"Quiet time?" I asked. "What do you mean?"

"Each day just before lunch I have some time in my prayer closet," he responded.

I was puzzled. "Do you pray in a closet at work?"

"No," he answered. "It's in my car."

"A closet in your car?!" He changed the subject. Like the first day I met him, again he left me confused. This Ed is quite a unique fellow, I thought.

As we parted that day, Ed gave me a little booklet that explained how someone could come into a relationship with God through Jesus Christ. I read it and understood it and knew that was exactly what I needed. That night I submitted my life to Jesus, and I was "born again" as it stated in the booklet. Two days later I told Ed. He was overjoyed.

The following week we got together again, and Ed strongly urged me to find a good body. I was surprised at his suggestion, but it sounded good to me. I took his advice and proceeded to comb the local health clubs for an attractive woman. When I met Denise, I knew she was the one. We began to date and soon she became a believer, too. Ed rejoiced and told us that it was crucial that we get planted so that we could grow together.

"Sometimes it's hard to understand this guy," I confided to Denise. I told Ed that I wasn't quite sure what he meant by planted.

He responded, "Committed! You both need to be committed now that you know Jesus."

"Now wait a minute," I protested. "Just because I don't understand what planted means doesn't mean I'm nuts. Anyway, I think that trusting Jesus is the most sane thing that I've ever done in my life."

It was obvious that Ed's patience was growing thin. He explained, "Bob and Denise, you have to get plugged in. Don't you understand?" No we didn't! But I did wonder if getting plugged in had any connection with "going out under the power," something that I had heard Ed mention but hoped it would never happen to me.

Regretfully, I had to miss worship the next Sunday. But Ed and I had breakfast together Monday morning, and he filled me in on what happened.

"God moved!" he said with excitement. "God really moved yesterday!"

"Where is he now?" I pleaded. "I was just getting to know him, and now he's gone?"

"No, no, Bob, God hasn't gone anywhere." I was relieved. "It's just that so many people were stepping out and moving in the gifts."

"You mean people were leaving during the meeting?" I asked. "And what's this about presents?"

"No, it's the gifts. The gifts were really flowing," he said.

"That's beautiful," I answered. "People were giving gifts to each other. I wish I was there." Now Ed seemed confused.

"Anyway," he said, changing the subject, "Denise was there, and boy, was she on fire."

"Fire? Denise got burned? What happened? Is she okay?"

"No, Bob, you don't understand." (That sure is an understatement, I thought.) "Denise is just fine. It's just that I believe she is really called, and that God wants to use her." Things were not getting clearer. "Did Denise mention that she's getting too many phone calls or something? And what's this about God wanting to take advantage of her?" I asked.

Ed sighed, "Can I walk in the light with you?"

"Where do you want to go?" I answered. "Of course we can walk in the light. It's daytime, Ed." He just shook his head. I don't know what it is, but sometimes it seems that Ed and I have a hard time communicating.

It's been two years since I was saved and delivered. Now I'm plugged in, planted, and committed to a good body. God has been moving, and I've been stepping out in the gifts. I can hardly believe how God has been using me! I have developed one new problem, though. It seems that all my old friends just don't understand me anymore. When I share about my redemption, that I've been washed as white as snow and that I desire to follow the Lamb, they seem to tune me right out. I guess they're just convicted when they see that I'm on fire.

The Adventures of Mr. Potato Head®

The Adventures of Mr. Potato Head®

Contributed by **Heather Flies**

Primary theme the body of Christ	
Themes spiritual gifts, celebrating others, serving others	
Scripture 1 Corinthians 12:4-7,11; 1 Corinthians 12:15-19,26; 1 Peter 4:10; 1 Timothy 4:12	
Approximate length through The Grand Finale 20-30 minutes	

You'll need

- Copies of the Yellow Pages (enough for each team of three to have a copy)
- *Sister Act* (Touchstone Pictures, 1992)
- TV and DVD player
- A Mr. Potato Head® doll (buy or borrow!)
- A whiteboard
- Dry erase marker
- Half sheets of paper or 3" x 5" cards, one per student
- Pens or pencils for each student

Imagine this: You drive up to the church building and are greeted by a smiling eighth-grade boy who points you in the direction of the nearest parking spot. As you make your way up the sidewalk, the door swings open as a sophomore girl hands you a program and shows you where the coat rack is located. But it doesn't stop there! You see a student collecting the offering while another one sings the special music and yet a third adjusts the volume levels behind the soundboard. Are you dreaming? Some would say yes, but this could be an incredible reality if we empower our students to discover and use the gifts they've been given to bless the church and the kingdom!

intro

The Opening Act

🔊 Game: Yellow Pages Teams (see sidebar)

🔊 Movie clip: *Sister Act* (see sidebar)

🔊 Transition by saying something like—Ever wonder why some activities and assignments come really easily for you and others seem impossible? Ever wish you had the same ability your friend has? Ever done a school project with a group that just seemed to click? As much as we would all love to do everything with ease and perfection, that's not the way life is. We were created to have different abilities and gifts. Wouldn't it be boring if we all had exactly the same abilities? The apostle Paul lays it out perfectly for us in his description of the body of Christ.

Game

Yellow Pages Teams

Before your meeting collect multiple copies of the Yellow Pages. Divide your group into teams of at least three. One is blindfolded and holds the book in her lap. A second student is the only one of the three allowed to speak. The third serves as the runner.

From the front you say, "Find me a place where I could—" (buy a wig, rent a karaoke machine, get my toilet fixed, and so on). Only the blindfolded student can turn the pages as the speaking student instructs her to do. When a team finds the correct business, the runners run up to whisper their answers to you, and the team with the first correct answer receives a point. Repeat the process, using a new service request each time, until one of the teams scores five points or you run out of ideas!

Movie clip

Sister Act

Start 00:46:56 Sister Mary Clarence asks, "Is this the choir rehearsal?"
Stop 00:52:28 Sister Mary Patrick squeals, "Oh, we did it! We actually sang a chord!"
This clip is a great example of a "team" coming together. Deloris, also known as Sister Mary Clarence (Whoopi Goldberg), thought she was just going to sing in the choir. But once the other nuns learn that she has some singing experience, they talk her into taking over as choir director.

The choir knows they're awful. So Mary Clarence briefly works with them and then asks them to try singing a three-note chord together. When they finally get it, Sister Mary Patrick (Kathy Najimy) and the other nuns are elated to hear how good they sound together.

(Note: If you have time to show a longer clip, let the movie keep running until 00:57:42. This will take you through the end of the choir's first performance under Sister Mary Clarence's direction, where they amaze everyone with how well they can sing.)

heart of the talk
The Main Event

1. The Holy Spirit gives all believers unique gifts to build up the body of Christ.

🔊 Scripture: 1 Corinthians 12:4-7,11 ("There are different kinds of gifts, but the same Spirit.")

🔊 In order to identify what gift or gifts you might have, think about your answers to the following questions:

- What do I love to do?
- What abilities or characteristics have people noticed in my life?
- What are the themes that run through the activities I spend a lot of time doing?
- When do I feel most energized?
- Where do I feel most comfortable?

🔊 Scripture: 1 Timothy 4:12 ("Don't let anyone look down on you because you are young.") You don't have to wait until you're old to use the gifts God has given you! He wants to use you right now to glorify him and build up the church!

🔊 Object lesson: Mr. Potato Head® (see sidebar)

Object lesson

Mr. Potato Head®

Ahead of time, purchase or borrow a Mr. or Mrs. Potato Head®. (Many families with young kids will have one you can borrow.) As you pull the naked spud out in front of the kids, remind them that we're never too old to play. Ask the students to help you accessorize the spud as they wish— they'll choose some crazy combos.

Now put the parts where they actually belong. Talk about how each of those pieces fit and give definition and personality to Mr. or Mrs. Potato Head®. It's the same with how we make up the body of Christ. And we're all necessary! Pull off an ear and comment on how incomplete Mr. Potato Head® is with even one part missing.

2. As Christians we should celebrate all the gifts and parts of the body.

🔊 To celebrate all gifts means we don't try to take over a part of the body (ministry) we were not designed to fill. Instead we should allow those who were crafted for that part to use their gifts.

🔊 Object Lesson: Mr. Potato Head® Revisited (see sidebar)

🔊 Scripture: 1 Corinthians 12:15-19,26 ("But in fact God has arranged the parts in the body, every one of them, just as he wanted them to be.")

🔊 There are lots of things that could keep the body of Christ from working as it was intended to work, such as:

- We compare our gifts to others' gifts, resulting in jealousy and feelings of inadequacy.

- We try to force ourselves into other parts of the body, which causes great frustration.

🔊 Scripture: 1 Corinthians 12:4-6 ("There are different kinds of gifts...but the same God works all of them in all men.")

- Will all the parts of the body always work together in harmony? Unlikely. But when we disagree with other Christians, we need to remember the one thing we share that unites us—our relationship with Christ.

🔊 Illustration: The Pyramid Problem (see sidebar)

🔊 Illustration: Our Body (see sidebar)

Object lesson

Mr. Potato Head® Revisited

Come back your Potato Head creation. Comment on what a "hot potato" they've created and say: What do you think would happen if I did this? (Take the nose and feet off and switch them around. Then try to make Mr. or Mrs. Potato Head stand up—impossible.) Ask your students why that doesn't work. After fielding their answers, talk about how each of us was specifically created to fit into a certain part of the body of Christ.

The Pyramid Problem

Ask for volunteers and call six students of varying sizes up to the front of the room. Explain that their job is to form a pyramid. As they move toward their natural spots (big guy on the bottom, small girl on the top), assign them the opposite spots. On your watch, time how long they can stay in formation (without killing the small girl!). After they pick themselves up from the heap, ask them to try again. This time let them to do it as they see fit. Have the students talk about why one formation was more difficult to sustain than the other.

Our Body

Think about the individual giftedness of the students and leaders in your group. Make this Scripture come alive by drawing (on a whiteboard or someplace where all the students can see) what the body of Christ looks like in your group. For instance, draw the head and put the name of an intelligent student there. Draw the ears and next to them write the names of any student leaders with whom your students always share their problems. Allow the students to make additions, too!

closing

The Grand Finale

🔊 Invite students to identify a possible gift or function in the body of Christ that they see in other students. Beforehand ask your leaders to be prepared to point out gifts they've witnessed in the students, especially those gifts that other students might miss—hospitality, good listening, the ability to bring people together—in other words, not just the "up front" leadership gifts.

🔊 Scripture: 1 Peter 4:10 ("Each one should use whatever gift he has received to serve others, faithfully administering God's grace in its various forms.")

🔊 Pass out half sheets of paper or 3" x 5" cards and something to write with. Ask your students to write down at least three characteristics or abilities they have that could be used to build up the body of Christ.

🔊 Have sign-up sheets available for students to sign up for service opportunities in the church according to their gifts—sound technicians, nursery workers, peer counselors, working at a homeless shelter, the welcoming team, and so on.

discussion
Encore

Get It? Middle School

- What if you don't know what your gifts are yet? How can you discover them?
- Do you feel like our church gives you opportunities to use your gifts? How about our youth group? (Discuss.)
- Give an example of a time when you and another person combined your gifts?

Get It? High School

- What makes it hard to celebrate the gifts of others in the body of Christ?
- In what ways do you tend to compare yourself with others?
- How do those comparisons affect your unity in Christ? How about your ministry for Christ?
- When is the last time someone affirmed you for your gifts? How did you feel? How did you respond?

What If? The Big Picture

- Do you tend to spend time being grateful for the gifts you do have or being envious of those you don't have? Talk about how that could affect you. How could it affect your group?
- What kinds of things could people with the gift of helping do in our ministry? What about the gift of encouragement? The gift of wisdom? The gift of mercy? (You may need to describe a few of these gifts to your students first.)
- What could you learn about the body of Christ by watching the adults in our church?
- Is it possible to be united with another believer, even if you don't like that person? Talk about your answer.
- What do you think you should do if another believer is jealous of one of your gifts?
- Do the things we've talked about also relate to people who don't know Jesus yet? Why or why not?

So What?   It's Your Life

🔊 How would our youth group be different if we really combined our gifts to be the body of Christ, even though we are different? What do you think others would think when they came to our gatherings?

🔊 What keeps you from working with others in the body of Christ to reach out to others?

🔊 What is one way you could work with other Christians to reach out to students at school?

Contributed by **Heather Flies**

Contentment or Splinters?

Primary theme contentment	
Themes God's faithfulness, patience, trust, God's provision, desire	
Scripture Psalm 23:1-4; Psalm 37:3-4; Proverbs 3:5-6	
Approximate length through The Grand Finale 20-30 minutes	

You'll need

- ◄» Videotape you've recorded of preschoolers answering the question, "What do you want to be when you grow up?"

- ◄» TV and VCR

- ◄» A personal story about a time when you wanted to be older

- ◄» A board, five feet long and a couple inches thick (any width under a foot will do)

- ◄» A blindfold

So many students spend the majority of their teenage years longing to be a different age. The junior high girl longs to be 16 so she can finally date the guy of her dreams. The junior high guy longs to be old enough to drive his grandpa's car and pick up that girl for a night out on the town. When they finally reach that age, though, it's not enough. Now, that girl wants to be in college with unlimited freedom, and that guy can't wait to get a real job so he can sell his grandpa's car and buy a truck. Although some of this is normal and to be expected in your students' developmental stage, they end up missing so much of what God wants for their lives at this moment.

intro
The Opening Act

🔊 Video: When I Grow Up (see sidebar)

🔊 Ask—If you could be any age right now, what age would you be and why?

🔊 Personal illustration: What I Wanted (see sidebar)

🔊 Transition to the body of the talk by explaining—Imagine I was holding a magic wand and said to you, "If you could magically change any three things about your life with a simple wave of this wand, what would you change?" Most of us could rattle off three things in 10 seconds flat! We'd want to be taller, skinnier, older, more popular, in a different family, whatever. Why is it so hard to be content with who we are and what we have? Will we ever truly reach a point in life when we're content? King David gives us an incredible picture of this truth in Psalm 37.

Video

When I Grow Up

Before your session, videotape a group of preschoolers answering the question, "What do you want to be when you grow up?" Most answers will be either cute or humorous and will get your students laughing. You'll make the connection to the lesson later on.

Personal illustration

What I Wanted

Share about a time in your life when you wanted to be older or at a different place than you were. (For example, you wanted to be on the varsity team instead of the junior-varsity squad. Or you wished you were done with high school.)

heart of the talk
The Main Event

1. God can be trusted with our lives.

🔊 Scripture Psalm 37:3 ("Trust in the Lord and do good; dwell in the land and enjoy safe pasture.")

🔊 Scripture Psalm 23:1-4 ("The Lord is my shepherd, I shall not be in want.")

🔊 Explanation: Living in Pastures? (see sidebar)

🔊 Scripture: Proverbs 3:5-6 ("Trust in the LORD with all your heart and lean not on your own understanding; in all your ways acknowledge him, and he will make your paths straight.") When we let God do his job, life is always better.

🔊 Object lesson: The Trust Plank (see sidebar)

Living in Pastures?

Does the Lord put us in protected pastures to steal the fun and excitement from our lives? During the time of David, shepherding was a common occupation—and it was David's job before he became king of Israel, so he knows what he's talking about in Psalm 23! Shepherds would spend days in the hills feeding, watering, and protecting their flocks. During the night, the shepherd would make a pen out of rocks and brush and then lie down across the opening of the pen in order to prevent intruders (lions and tigers and bears, oh my!) from entering and harming the flock. The boundaries of the pen were not meant to steal all the fun from the flock, but to keep them safe and in the care of the shepherd.

The same thing holds true today: God encourages us to trust him with our lives—trust that he'll protect us, take care of us, restore us, and give us the desires of our hearts. So why is it so hard to trust God with our lives?

The Trust Plank

Bring out a five-foot-long and two-inch-thick board. Call four kids up front—two burly guys, a taller kid, and a kid who won't mind getting a tiny bit embarrassed. (Ahead of time you should brief all but the last "volunteer" so they know their roles—but call them up now as if they were just volunteers.) Blindfold the last volunteer. Have the two strong guys lift the board just two inches off the ground and have the blindfolded volunteer step onto the board. Have the tall kid stand next to her and allow the blindfolded volunteer to put her hand on his shoulder for balance.

Tell the blindfolded volunteer: I want you to trust me. Ask the guys to lift the board two feet higher—they shake with power but really only lift the blindfolded girl another inch off the ground. The student acting as the balance should crouch down about two feet as the board-holders are shaking the board, to simulate the board being raised.

Say again, "I want you to trust me." Have them lift "two feet higher" again, while the balance student crouches lower again. Repeat the process one last time. Make sure you're not standing next to the blindfolded volunteer, or she'll realize from the direction of your voice that she's not actually being raised.

Now tell her to jump off the board while she's still blindfolded. She'll hesitate, but encourage her. When she jumps, she'll hit the ground after five inches of air, but think she's falling 10 feet!

Follow up the object lesson by explaining that as we go through life, we're blinded by our humanness and sin—oftentimes we can't see our situation clearly, but God can. Even when what we think or feel seems uncertain or scary, we need to trust God, knowing that he is our great Shepherd and wants what's best for us.

2. God wants to give us the best.

🔊 The only time we get second best in life is when we jump for it instead of waiting for the ultimate best.

🔊 Review Psalm 37:3-4 ("Trust in the Lord and do good; dwell in the land and enjoy safe pasture. Delight yourself in the Lord and he will give you the desires of your heart.")

🔊 Explanation: This Sounds Confining! (see sidebar)

🔊 Illustration: Danger Zone (see sidebar)

Explanation

This Sounds Confining!

There are lots of things that keep us from dwelling in the pasture where God has placed us. We might plaster ourselves against the fences around our pastures, desiring what others are experiencing in their pastures. Or we feel like we've already learned enough in our pastures and we try to bust through the gate into the next pasture.

If we're honest, some of us have a hard time dwelling, period. Being still. Staying. Not moving. Frankly, it's scary! But when we allow our Shepherd to protect us and provide for us—when we truly delight in him—we find relationships, experiences, gifts, and joys that could only be found within the safe boundaries of our pastures.

You may wonder, "What if the desires of my heart aren't the same as God's desires?" No need to worry! Because when we truly get to know God through worship, prayer, Christian friends, reading the Word, and meditation, his desires will become our desires!

Illustration

Danger Zone

Tell students to think about something they've gotten in the last year—a mountain bike, curling iron, video camera, contacts, weight set, and so on. It's likely that they would have enjoyed getting the same thing when they were four years old, but the same item could have been extremely dangerous for them at that age! Imagine riding that mountain bike as a four-year-old! Can you imagine a four-year-old trying to put in contacts before watching Barney or curling her hair before running out the door to preschool? When we receive things at the proper time, they enhance our lives. When we push to get them too soon, we put ourselves in the danger zone.

closing
The Grand Finale

- Invite students to think about a time in their lives when they wanted to be somewhere else, have something more, or have life be different somehow. Allow them a quiet moment to ask God to forgive them for their discontentment.

- Invite students to turn to the student sitting next to them and share their response to this question: What are three things about my pasture that I am thankful for right now?

- Encourage students to go find someone in the room whose pasture they have longed to be in—someone whom they have been jealous of—and encourage them to turn it into an affirmation by saying something like, "I really admire how athletic you are!" or, "I think you're really funny!"

discussion
Encore

Get It?	Middle School

- If we're supposed to be content with where we are, how can I grow as a Christian?

- What are some of the things that you tend to be jealous of in others?

- Who are the most content people in your life? How can you tell?

- Can you think of a time when God worked in a way that wouldn't have been possible had you not been dwelling in the pasture where he placed you? (For example, a friend you wouldn't have met if you hadn't switched schools, an award you wouldn't have gotten if you had a talent other than the one you have.)

Get It?	High School

- In what ways has God shown that he's trustworthy in your life so far?

- What is something he has protected you from?

- Is there a chance you can become too content in your pasture? What would that look like? How would you correct that?

- What would you say are the desires of your heart today?

What If? — The Big Picture

- How can you see feelings of discontentment in the world around you?

- At what time of your life have you felt the most discontented? What about most content?

- How does the phrase "Delight yourself in the Lord" play out in your everyday life?

- What pasture do you think the Lord will lead you into next? What does he want you to experience before that happens?

- Have you developed the art of "being still"? How can you try to impart stillness into your life?

- If you chose to be content where you are, what would change in your life during the next month?

So What? — It's Your Life

- What is it about other peoples' pastures that causes you to plaster yourself up against your fence?

- What specific thing do you need to give up to God in order to relax and stop trying to jump too soon?

- What could you do to encourage your friends to dwell in the pastures where God has placed them?

- Is being content primarily a choice or an emotion? How can you tell the difference?

Do You Know the Mind of God?

Do You Know the Mind of God?

Contributed by **Curt Gibson**

Primary theme God's will	
Themes leadership, humility, listening to God, discerning God's voice, false and true prophets	
Scripture Mark 14:3-9; 1 Kings 18:19-39; 1 Kings 19:3-13	
Approximate length through The Grand Finale 20-30 minutes	

his talk exposes how the disciples were trying to act on Jesus' behalf, but they were dead wrong when they rebuked the woman who anointed Jesus with perfume. The disciples seemed to have all of Jesus' interests in mind—the poor, good cash flow—but they completely missed the point. You'll show students how Christians have missed the point and done things that were completely wrong—supposedly in the name of God. Then you'll turn the corner and talk about what the voice of God sounds like.

You'll need

- Sheets of paper and markers for each game contestant (optional)
- Whiteboard or large sheet of paper (optional)
- A marker (optional)
- A personal story about a time when you thought you knew God's will—but were completely wrong
- Copies of Who Said This? handout, page 76 (optional)
- Blank paper and pens for journaling (optional)

This outline is saved as GT02_07 on the CD-ROM.

intro

The Opening Act

🔊 Activity: My Buddy and Me (optional, see sidebar)

🔊 After the game has ended, transition by saying—An exercise like this helps us to see that we may not always know someone as well as we thought we did.

🔊 Activity: The Good Disciple (optional, see sidebar)

🔊 Transition by saying something like—Let's take a look at the disciples as they discover they are dead wrong in determining Jesus' will.

🔊 Scripture: Mark 14:3-9 (The woman anoints Jesus' head with expensive perfume.)

Activity

My Buddy and Me

Set up something similar to *The Newlywed Game*, where pairs of friends are tested on their knowledge of each other. Send one person from each pair out of the room. Now ask the remaining contestants the following questions—

• What is your favorite color?

• If given the chance to date a famous person, would you date Elvis or Kurt Cobain?

• You have a choice of two careers—butcher or foot masseuse. Which would you choose?

• Would you rather skateboard or bicycle down a really steep hill, knowing you were going to lose control and crash?

• If you had to choose one body piercing, would you choose your tongue or your eyebrow?

Have the contestants write their answers on sheets of paper—one answer per sheet, which they will hold up during the next portion of the game when their partners try to guess how they answered the questions.

Now bring in the other half of the pairs and see how well they know their partners. Ask them to answer the same questions for their friend and see how their answers compare. After each answer is given, ask the students who stayed in the room to hold up the sheet of paper containing the correct answer.

When all the pairs have shared and compared answers, split them up again, this time sending the other half of the pairs out of the room. Give the remaining students new sheets of paper and markers. Then ask them to record their answers to these questions:

• Would you rather chug a gallon of warm milk or drink a quart of used hot dog water?

• If you could be on one television show, would you choose MTV's *Punk'd* or CBS's *Survivor*?

• If abducted by aliens who can neither taste nor smell, which would you choose to give up—your tongue or your nose? (They have promised to return the body part after you undergo some painful experimentation.)

Have the second group return to the room and repeat the answer and reveal portion of the game.

The Good Disciple

Ask your students to help you create a list of the characteristics of a good disciple. Write their ideas on a whiteboard or someplace where the whole group can see it. Here are a few ideas to prime the pump: they should imitate Jesus; they should be able to understand Jesus' teaching; they should know God's will; they should have courage; and so on. Once you have a list together, conclude by saying—Certainly someone who has spent three years eating, sleeping, and living with Jesus would know him well enough to speak for him or on his behalf. Right?

heart of the talk
The Main Event

1. Missing the point

◀ᴺ Ask—
Can I 100-percent believe I am doing the will of God and be dead wrong?

◀ᴺ Personal illustration: When I Was Wrong (see sidebar)

◀ᴺ Illustration: They Were Wrong (see sidebar)

◀ᴺ Return to the Scripture story. Point out that many of us would have missed the point—we would have rebuked the woman just like the disciples did (or at the very least we would have thought she was wrong, even if we didn't say anything). In doing so, we would have insisted that we knew what Jesus wanted.

◀ᴺ Quote: Hitler's Spiritual Conviction (see sidebar)

When I Was Wrong

Share a personal example of a time when you were convinced you knew God's will and were, in fact, completely wrong. If you can't think of a time like this, use the following They Were Wrong illustration instead.

Illustration

They Were Wrong

A church located in an affluent, upper-middle-class neighborhood in the heart of Los Angeles was a vital presence in its community for years. Over time the community transitioned, and the neighborhood became more integrated as poor people moved in. The all-white pastoral staff soon found themselves leading an urban, poor, multiethnic congregation.

Eventually they believed it was God's will for them to sell the facility and move to a suburban area, rather than give their building to the new church that had developed or choose to stay and make some changes in the leadership staff to reflect the new congregants. The building was sold, and it is no longer used as a church. Those who still live in the neighborhood, many of whom do not own a car, no longer have a church within walking distance of their homes.

Quote

Hitler's Spiritual Conviction

If you have an opportunity to use MediaShout or PowerPoint®, project the following quote on a screen (without the speaker's name, of course) and ask—What famous person said this?

> In boundless love as a Christian and as a man I read through the passage which tells us how the Lord at last rose in his might and seized the scourge to drive out of the temple the brood of vipers and of adders. How terrific was his fight for the world against the Jewish poison. Today, after two thousand years, with deepest emotion I recognize more profoundly than ever before—the fact that it was for this that he had to shed his blood upon the cross. As a Christian I have no duty to allow myself to be cheated, but I have the duty to be a fighter for truth and justice.
>
> — Adolf Hitler

(Part of a speech given in Munich, Germany, on April 12, 1922)

On the next slide, show a picture of Hitler and the following statement: 56 MILLION PEOPLE DIED IN WORLD WAR II WHILE ADOLF HITLER BELIEVED HE WAS DOING THE WILL OF GOD. If you don't have access to these software tools, make copies of the handout at the end of this lesson (see page 76). Hitler's name has been left off the page so you can still ask students to guess who said it.

While the students are trying to guess, consider giving them the following clues (with pauses in between to allow for more guessing):

- An historical figure
- Male
- Politician
- Leader during World War II

After you reveal the speaker's identity, ask your students if they were surprised that Hitler said that. And if so, why were they surprised?

2. Listening for God's voice

🔊 Ask—What does the voice of God sound like?

🔊 Scripture story: Elijah and the Prophets of Baal (see sidebar)

🔊 Scripture: 1 Kings 19:3-13 (Elijah hears the still small voice of God.)

🔊 God spoke in—

- "A still small voice" (verse 12, KJV)

- "A gentle whisper" (verse 12, NIV)

- "A gentle and quiet whisper" (verse 12, The Message)

🔊 Ask—Is this how we'd expect to hear God's voice?

🔊 Ask—What are some of the implications of God choosing to communicate this way? (He wants us to listen; if we don't slow down and really listen, we'll miss what he has to say.)

Scripture story

Elijah and the Prophets of Baal

Telling this story is just a precursor; you'll look at the back story to the Scripture passage in a minute. But it's important for your group to get the context.

Read or retell the amazing story of Elijah and the prophets of Baal from 1 Kings 18:19-39. Whether you tell it or read it, make sure you build a sense of excitement and energy as the drama of the story unfolds. Elijah heckles the prophets! Then there's the tense moment when he makes it seem as though it'll be impossible for his offering to light—then BAM! God torches the whole thing!

After telling the story, talk about how Elijah must have felt after this event—massively pumped up and spiritually stoked! Nope, just the opposite. Elijah fell into depression! And he really needed to hear from God.

closing

The Grand Finale

🔊 Reading: Dangerous Wonder (see sidebar)

🔊 Say something like—If Elijah could learn to hear God's whisper, then let's spend some time listening together.

🔊 Send your students off for a time of silence and listening. This would be best accomplished if they can spread out and get comfortable (as opposed to sitting in rows of metal folding chairs!). Ideally you could give them about a half-hour. But try to give them at least 10 minutes. Consider passing out paper and pens for them to use for journaling.

Dangerous Wonder

In the book *Dangerous Wonder* (NavPress, 1998) Mike Yaconelli shares the story of a one-day adult retreat and a teenager who showed she was able to hear God's voice. Give your students the necessary background information and then read aloud the teen's dialogue portion of the quote.

We spent the day reading different Scriptures, meditating on Scripture and then journaling an assigned task. All participants were asked to journal, individually, what they thought Jesus might say to them if he wrote them a letter. When we gathered as a group to read our journal entries, the adults found it difficult to read theirs. Many were so concerned about interpreting Scripture correctly that they were afraid to be embarrassed by their lack of understanding. Janie, a 17-year-old high school girl, volunteered to read hers first.

"First of all," she said hesitantly, "I think I messed up. You wanted us to write about what Jesus would say to us, and instead I wrote a dialogue between Jesus and me." (Interesting, isn't it? Her first concern was that she messed up, which is why children lose their ability to listen to God.) We assured her that whatever she had written was fine. Here is her dialogue:

i feel awkward
because it's been so long
since I've been near you.
        i've missed you too;
        i think about you every day.
But i've messed up;
i've done a lot of things
that i regret.
        it's okay, child.
        i forgive you.
i don't understand
i turn away,
i ignore you…
        i'm still here
        right beside you.
i try to live without you
even though i know deep inside
that you're still a part of me.
        you don't have to make yourself lovable;
        i love you how you are.
even after everything i've done,
and everything that has happened,
would it offend you if i called you bizarre?
        i am bizarre;
        more so than you'll ever know.
this may seem strange,
but could i please ask you
to hold me for a little while?
        my child, i've been waiting for
        you with outstretched arms.

After Janie read her dialogue, there wasn't a dry eye in the place…and all the adults said, "I'm not reading mine." Janie was still able to hear the "thin silence" of God.

discussion

Encore

Get It?	Middle School

🔊 Describe a time in your life when you thought you knew for sure what your parents or a teacher wanted you to do—and you were wrong.

🔊 How do you tell the difference between what you want and what God wants for you?

🔊 If God were trying to communicate a message to you right now, would you be able to hear him? What time of the day would God best find you?

🔊 If God were to give you a message today, what do you think it would be?

Get It?	High School

🔊 If you had spent three years with Jesus, walking and ministering next to him, do you think you would know his will better than the disciples in this story? Why or why not?

🔊 Have you ever seen your church or Christian leaders make decisions based on what they thought God wanted, but you felt they were wrong? What happened?

🔊 Does your daily routine include time to be silent enough to hear the voice of God?

🔊 If God were to whisper in your ear right now, what would he say?

What If?	The Big Picture

🔊 If God called you to anoint Jesus by purchasing perfume that was so expensive you had to sell everything you owned in order to buy it, how would you respond? How would you feel as Jesus' closest friends and co-workers rebuked you for doing what God told you to do?

🔊 Do you think it is unusual for God to ask us to do something that is weird or unaccepted in our culture? (Discuss.) What might those requests of God's look like today?

So What?	It's Your Life

🔊 Where will you go to hear the still small voice of God?

🔊 What will you have to do to reach a point where you can tell the difference between what you think God wants you to do and what God is actually telling you to do?

75

Who Said This?

In boundless love as a Christian and as a man I read through the passage which tells us how the Lord at last rose in his might and seized the scourge to drive out of the temple the brood of vipers and of adders. How terrific was his fight for the world against the Jewish poison. Today, after two thousand years, with deepest emotion I recognize more profoundly than ever before—the fact that it was for this that he had to shed his blood upon the cross. As a Christian I have no duty to allow myself to be cheated, but I have the duty to be a fighter for truth and justice.

Insiders and Outsiders

Contributed by Curt Gibson

Insiders and Outsiders

Primary theme becoming others centered	
Themes accepting others, evangelism, the church, exclusivity	
Scripture John 2:13-16	
Approximate length through The Grand Finale 25-35 minutes	

You'll need

- A personal story about a church rule regarding the handling of money
- Copies of the The Temple in the City handout, page 84, or project this image using MediaShout or PowerPoint (see sidebar)
- *Big* (20th Century Fox, 1988)
- TV and DVD player
- $420 cash (42 $10 bills)—the real stuff gets the point across VERY well!
- Monopoly money
- Three stuffed animals
- Whiteboard
- Marker

Students who have been raised in your church will often pick up an insider's knowledge of how things work. Whether we mean to or not, church can easily become an exclusive social club with a "members only" feel. On the other hand, a visitor to your church or youth group brings an outsider's eye; they often see the church quite differently than we intend it to be seen. There are only a few times in the gospels where we read about Jesus being angry—one is when he is dealing with religious leaders, and another is when people are misusing the center of worship. Back in Jesus' day, there was a grand system in place in the temples. Unfortunately, it changed the focus of these holy places from worshiping the almighty to making a profit. Real people with real needs were not the focus, as they should have been, and it slowly became a "members only" system that took advantage of outsiders. This talk will help your students examine their own place of worship and determine if it exists for the insiders or for the outsiders.

intro
The Opening Act

🔊 Scripture: John 2:13-16 (Jesus clears out the temple courtyard.)

🔊 Personal illustration: Soda on Sundays (see sidebar)

🔊 Transition by saying something like—Here's the problem: Some churches take a story like that and just apply it today without thinking a bit about the culture in which it took place. The first question we have to answer is: Why was Jesus so ticked off?

Personal illustration

Soda on Sundays

If you have a personal story about a church rule (maybe the church you grew up in) that involves the handling of money on Sundays, tell it. If you can't think of a story, use this one: First Church had soda machines that were owned by the youth department. They were allowed to use them all week long but not on Sundays (when they were expected to unplug the machines). When the youth worker asked for an explanation, a church leader told him, "If Jesus were in our church today and the soda machines were on, he would tip them over and throw you out."

heart of the talk
The Main Event

1. God's House is not about turning a profit.

🔊 Say something like—The temple was designed so that each person (regardless of their ancestry, race, or gender) would have a place to seek God and the forgiveness of their sins. But the Court of Gentiles had become a busy passageway for greedy merchants, moneychangers, and bankers to take advantage of outsiders.

🔊 Explanation: The Temple in the City (see sidebar)

🔊 Melodrama: The Temple Run by the Sopranos (see script on page 85)
(Note: if the HBO mafia series *The Sopranos* has no cultural presence by the time you use this—or if your kids haven't heard of it—change the name to "The Temple Run by the Mafia.")

🔊 Explanation: A Day's Wage (see sidebar) Ask your students to point out the obvious problems with this system.

🔊 Ask—What was Jesus so upset about?

The Temple in the City

Make copies of the temple drawing on page 84 or go to http://www.youthspecialties.com/store/downloads (password: gto2) for a downloadable image to project using MediaShout or PowerPoint.

While students look at the image, explain what each of the courts was for:

• The Court of Gentiles—anyone, Jew or Gentile, could come and pray here; this was the largest of all the courts, and it provided room for anyone in the city to come in and seek God.

• The Court of Women—any Jewish man or woman was welcome here to pray and seek God.

• The Inner Court—the court where Jewish men would go.

A Day's Wage

Based on a day's wage for a skilled laborer, a half shekel was worth approximately $160 in today's currency.

Temple tax: a half shekel, which was equivalent to two days' pay for a common laborer.

Today, a construction laborer makes $80 per day. Cost of temple tax: $160 per year.

Price of a sacrifice (without blemish):

Dove—inside the temple courtyard, $50-70

Dove—outside the temple courtyard, $3

Sheep—inside the temple courtyard, $400-$700

Sheep—outside the temple courtyard, $80

2. God's House is not an exclusive, "members only" club.

Ask—What do "outsiders" look like in our churches today? Have your group brainstorm a bit on this. The list would obviously include visitors but could also include people like those who don't know how to behave during a worship service, people who don't understand our beliefs or those who have different beliefs, people who don't have the "right" clothes, those who don't know how to speak our language, and so on.

Ask—How are we doing at caring for the outsiders in our church?

Ask—How are we doing at caring for the outsiders in our youth group?

Movie clip: *Big* (see sidebar)

Movie clip

Big

Start 00:49:14 The elevator doors open, and Josh enters the office Christmas party.
Stop 00:53:05 Josh and Susan leave the party.

Set up the movie clip by explaining that Josh, a 13-year-old boy, wished to be big and woke up the next morning to find he now lives inside a man's body (Tom Hanks). In this scene he's managed to get a job at a toy company, and he's now attending the formal office Christmas party, only he doesn't know how to behave because he's never been to one before. Watch how he is treated by his officemates. (Note: You may want to edit the clip due to some swearing by one of the other characters.)

closing

The Grand Finale

📢 Start by examining your neighborhood and identifying the outsiders. Write on a whiteboard all of the ways that we knowingly and unknowingly create obstacles for people to come and seek God.

📢 If you want to get more personal, ask students to think of ways they may have been obstacles to someone who was seeking God.

📢 Also mention that some of the students in your group have probably felt like outsiders at times. Remind them of the Bible story and suggest that they recognize Jesus as their advocate in knocking down those obstacles and doing whatever it takes to clear a path to God.

📢 Close in prayer, asking God for forgiveness for all the ways we create obstacles for people in their pursuit of God. Pray that your group would be just the opposite—a place where everyone is welcome and accepted.

discussion

Encore

Get It?	Middle School

📢 How does Jesus feel about cola machines being left on at church on Sundays?

📢 What was the problem with how things were done in the temple courtyard?

📢 What makes Jesus angry?

📢 Which part do you play in the story—an Insider or an outsider?

Get It? | High School

- Summarize the problem that existed in the temple.

- Why did this make Jesus so upset?

- What have you done that could be an obstacle to people seeking God?

- If Jesus were to visit your church, would he tip anything over?

- Do the demographics of your church look any different than the demographics of your community? If so, why? What's standing in the way of neighborhood people becoming involved in your church or youth group? Is there a system at play that makes them feel like outsiders?

- How would your church respond to a real outsider? If you don't think there is one, think about how your church members would respond if a homeless person entered the sanctuary. Or a gangbanger. Or a couple that is clearly gay. Or a biker guy with tattoos all over his body.

What If? | The Big Picture

- What if anyone could walk into your church or youth room to seek forgiveness and worship God? What would have to happen for that to be the case? How would your group be different if this were really true?

- What does the church have to gain by allowing anyone to come?

- How will you ever know if someone feels like an outsider?

So What? | It's Your Life

- As you look around and see outsiders who are seeking God, what are you doing to remove the obstacles that stand in their way?

- What are the consequences of the church existing as an elite social club?

- Do you ever feel resentment toward someone new trying to break into your group of friends from church? What can you do about that?

- Does the church deserve its reputation for being judgmental, exclusive, racist, and condemning?

- What should the church be known for? How can you help make that a reality in your group?

Herod's Temple

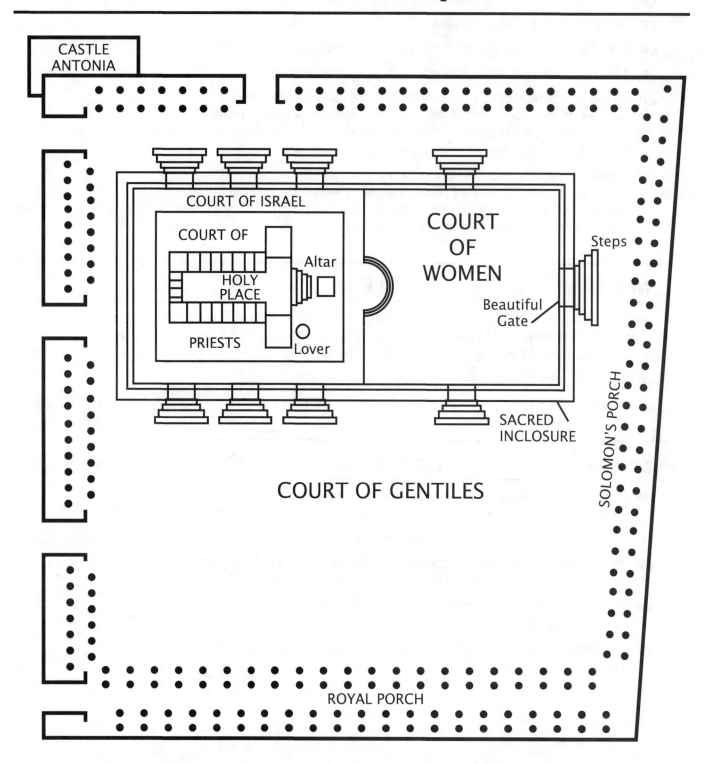

CASTLE ANTONIA

COURT OF ISRAEL

COURT OF

HOLY PLACE

PRIESTS

Altar

Lover

COURT OF WOMEN

Steps

Beautiful Gate

SOLOMON'S PORCH

SACRED INCLOSURE

COURT OF GENTILES

ROYAL PORCH

The Temple Run by the Sopranos

You play the part of the narrator and choose volunteers for the following cast members. Have them play their parts—with gusto!—as you read them. Any spoken parts should just be repeated in character.

Cast

Tony Soprano, also known as "The Priest"

Cousin Vinnie, a Temple Guard

Cousin Louie, a Temple Guard

Cousin Alfredo, a Temple Guard

Giovanni (Gino) the Accountant, also known as "The Money Changer"

Pasquali (Patsy), also known as "The Dove Salesman"

Mickie, local Italian who is young and connected, also known as "The Insider"

Herman the German, also known as "The Outsider"

Props for Skit

- $420 cash for Herman to hold (Yeah, you can fake it if you need to!)
- Monopoly money (also known as shekels) for Mickie to hold
- Three stuffed animals for animal sacrifices (one for Mickie, one for Herman, one for Patsy)

Mickie and Herman approach the temple with their animal sacrifices. The only way Mickie and Herman can be purged of their sins is to sacrifice a temple-approved animal in the temple courts.

The first layer of protection to the inner court is the temple army (that's the three temple guards—Vinnie, Louie, and Alfredo). At this time the temple had its own military under the direction of the priests.

Mickie approaches the temple guards and is greeted with hugs and a very Italian-sounding, "How you doin'?"

Vinnie asks, "How's your mother, family, cousins?"

Mickie says that they're doin' fine.

Alfredo asks, "Mickie, how you been doin' in school? Nobody's been hasslin' you, right?"

Mickie says that he's doin' fine.

Mickie hands a shekel to Louie and is escorted straight through with a big hug and pat on the back. Mickie is like family!

The three guards say in unison, "That's a fine boy!"

Next Herman approaches the guards. They ask if he's paid his temple tax. He answers no while pulling out $200, or two day's wages.

Louie says, "Your foreign money's no good here—you gotta go see cousin Gino, the money changer. Next time show some respect by bringin' the right kinda money!"

Herman the German is roughly escorted to see Gino. Gino asks how much money he needs.

Herman explains that he must pay his temple tax.

Gino is preparing to take Herman's money in exchange for a half shekel when he asks, "Your name is Herman? Wait a minute—you're not from around here, are you? You are disrespecting generations of tradition here. Sorry, but the rate for outta-towners is $300."

Herman hands Gino $300, and Gino happily turns over the half shekel.

Herman returns to the temple, pays the guards, and is finally allowed inside where he shows his sacrifice to Tony, the priest. Tony inspects the animal quietly, pauses, and stares at him for a long moment.

He says, "When someone comes as a guest to my house to make a sacrifice to my God, I expect them to bring their very best. When I see what you have brought here, it's obvious that you have brought less than your best. Don't come back and see me with less than your best."

Tony looks to the temple guards and says, "Boys, show this gentleman the door." The three guards escort Herman to meet Pasquali.

Alfredo says to Herman, "Hey Meatball, I'm sure your mother raised you better than this."

Meanwhile, back to Mickie. Mickie brings his sacrifice to Tony, who greets him like family with open arms. In fact, Tony hugs Mickie and lifts him off the ground. Tony takes Mickie's animal for a sacrifice and sends Mickie into the inner court so he can worship and make things right with his Maker.

Meanwhile, Pasquali, also known as Patsy, explains to Herman that he can take his sacrifice in on trade and offers him a new sacrifice that will be acceptable to Tony for a mere quarter shekel.

Frustrated, Herman says, "I can buy a perfect sacrifice a mile down the road for only $3!"

Patsy says, "Yeah, but Tony and I are family, and he respects my product."

Herman reluctantly hands him $80 cash, but Patsy says, "Sorry, I don't take money with that face on it; you'll have to go back to see cousin Gino. Tell him I sent you, and he'll take good care of you."

Herman sees Gino, pays him another $120 to get the quarter shekel, and returns to Patsy to purchase the animal.

Patsy sends Herman on his way, saying, "Make sure you tell Tony that Patsy took care of you."

Herman returns to the inner court to see Tony, who inspects the animal closely. Once the priest finds out where Herman got the animal, he lets him right through to worship.

Tony then announces that he is having a family dinner. All the family (Tony, Gino, Louie, Vinnie, Alfredo, and Patsy) come together. They hug and kiss each other's cheeks. Each family member pulls out the cash they've received, slipping Tony's "take" into his pocket while telling him how good it is to be a part of the family.

You're God, I'm Not

Contributed by **Curt Gibsom**

Primary theme lordship	
Themes obedience, discerning God's voice, following God, God's sovereignty, self-reliance	
Scripture Psalm 139, 1 Samuel 15	
Approximate length through The Grand Finale 25-30 minutes	

You'll need

- State maps from your state (one map per every group of five students)
- Paper (one sheet per group)
- Pens or pencils (one per group)
- A personal story about a time when your parents caught you in a lie

This talk looks at Saul's unwillingness to follow God's instructions. The premise is that Saul's actions reveal that he thought he knew what was best, not God. Oftentimes our actions reveal the same misguided thinking. We turn following God into a giant game of control. We're always trying to take control, rather than giving control to God. When you think about it, that's a pretty stupid thing for us to do because God has a perspective based on knowing the future. Our perspective is limited to things that have already happened. So our control grabbing is about as crazy as driving backward down the freeway.

intro
The Opening Act

🔊 Illustration: Aerial Perspective (see sidebar)

🔊 Scripture: Psalm 139 (see sidebar) Read this passage aloud to your kids. This Psalm works as a great preamble for the talk, recognizing that God knows us and knows the days of our lives before we have lived them. It doesn't need to be explained.

Illustration

Aerial Perspective

Divide your group into smaller groups of five students each. Hand out a state map, a sheet of paper, and a pen or pencil to each group. First have them find their present location on the map. Then name some out-of-the-way place for them to find. Once the destination point is located, have the students plan a route and write out an itinerary of how they will go about getting to the destination. It will work best if you've actually been to this place and can describe some of the pitfalls they may encounter along the way.

They'll need to figure out where to stop for gas (tell them their car will go 200 miles on one tank) and how long it will take them to get there. The story will work even better if you have a story to share about traveling to this destination without a map, knowing it would have been much easier to get there if you had perceived an overall picture of where you were going.

Scripture

Psalm 139 (The Message)

GOD, investigate my life; get all the facts firsthand.
I'm an open book to you;
even from a distance, you know what I'm thinking.
You know when I leave and when I get back;
I'm never out of your sight.
You know everything I'm going to say
before I start the first sentence.
I look behind me and you're there,
then up ahead and you're there, too—
your reassuring presence, coming and going.
This is too much, too wonderful—
I can't take it all in!

YOU'RE GOD, I'M NOT

Is there anyplace I can go to avoid your Spirit?
to be out of your sight?
If I climb to the sky, you're there!
If I go underground, you're there!
If I flew on morning's wings
to the far western horizon,
You'd find me in a minute—
you're already there waiting!
Then I said to myself, "Oh, he even sees me in the dark!
At night I'm immersed in the light!"
It's a fact: darkness isn't dark to you;
night and day, darkness and light, they're all the same to you.
Oh yes, you shaped me first inside, then out;
you formed me in my mother's womb.
I thank you, High God—you're breathtaking!
Body and soul, I am marvelously made!
I worship in adoration—what a creation!
You know me inside and out,
you know every bone in my body;
You know exactly how I was made, bit by bit,
how I was sculpted from nothing into something.
Like an open book, you watched me grow from conception to birth;
all the stages of my life were spread out before you,
The days of my life all prepared
before I'd even lived one day.
Your thoughts—how rare, how beautiful!
God, I'll never comprehend them!
I couldn't even begin to count them—
any more than I could count the sand of the sea.
Oh, let me rise in the morning and live always with you!
And please, God, do away with wickedness for good!
And you murderers—out of here!—
all the men and women who belittle you, God,
infatuated with cheap god-imitations.
See how I hate those who hate you, GOD,
see how I loathe all this godless arrogance;
I hate it with pure, unadulterated hatred.
Your enemies are my enemies!
Investigate my life, O God,
find out everything about me;
Cross-examine and test me,
get a clear picture of what I'm about;
See for yourself whether I've done anything wrong—
then guide me on the road to eternal life.
(From *The Message* by Eugene M. Peterson. NavPress, 2002).

heart of the talk

The Main Event

1. Saul thinks he knows best.

🔊 Explain—This is a story about a man who was called by God to be king of his people.

🔊 Explanation: Saul's Bio (see sidebar)

🔊 Scripture: 1 Samuel 15 (The Lord rejects Saul as king.) Prior to reading the passage, you may need to briefly mention that Samuel was a guy who spoke for God—a prophet. Also highlight the problem: Saul is given clear instructions and only partially follows them. Point out how Saul tried to lie to cover up his disobedience.

Explanation

Saul's Bio

Saul had everything a person could want: He was tall, handsome, the first king in Israel's history, and anointed by God's Spirit. A close encounter with God himself affected his personality from that day forward. He led repeated successful military campaigns, was publicly crowned as king, and never had to run for office. But he had one fatal flaw: He wasn't good at following instructions.

2. We think we know best.

🔊 Ask if students can see parallels to their own lives. After getting a few responses, mention that we are all great at doing the same thing—modifying God's instructions so they better suit us.

🔊 Personal illustration: Caught in My Own Lie (see sidebar)

🔊 Explanation: Rationalization (see sidebar)

🔊 Case study: To Tell the Truth (see sidebar)

Caught in My Own Lie

Tell a personal story of a time in your childhood or teenage years when your mother or father caught you lying. If you can't think of one offhand, feel free to use this one. Just say, "There's a guy who tells this story…"

As a boy I remember my mother specifically telling me not to have any more candy from the box she kept out of my reach on top of the refrigerator. Instead I created a makeshift ladder by opening all the drawers of the cabinet next to it, climbed onto the counter, grabbed the candy, and left a trail of wrappers that led to my bedroom.

My mother came into my room and asked, "Did you take the candy?"

With chocolate all over my face and holding the box with both hands behind my back, I answered, "No. Now leave me alone."

Rationalization

There's something interesting about this story that teenagers are famous for—rationalization. When Samuel confronts Saul about the sheep and goats (with a comedian's sarcasm, say: "Baa! Maa!"), Saul not only lies, but he also does so in a way that reveals he's convinced himself he really did do the right thing. Explain to your group that we refine this skill and use it all the time. You might consider sharing a story of a time when you did this or asking students to share their own stories.

To Tell the Truth

Read this case study and ask your students to decide if Charlene is telling the truth.

Charlene is grounded from hanging out with her best buddy Marquita because Marquita has been in trouble with the law, and Charlene's mom doesn't think Marquita is a good influence. Charlene is invited to a party with her church friends. Her mom says she can go to the party and hang out, telling her, "I'll pick you up at 11." Charlene goes to the party, having made secret arrangements to meet Marquita there to hang out later in the neighborhood. Charlene comes back to the party by 10, and her mom picks her up at 11, as planned. The next morning at breakfast Charlene's father asks, "Did you go to that church party last night?" Charlene answers, "Yes, I did."

Ask—Did Charlene lie? Do you think she thought she was lying?

3. God does know best.

🔊 Use the "driving down the freeway backward" example from the introductory paragraph to this outline, which illustrates that our perspective is based only on the past. So deciding that we know what's best (rather than obeying God, who knows the future) is like driving down the freeway backward!

🔊 Ask—Why does God know what's best for us? (He knows us better than we know ourselves. He has a future perspective and knows the consequences of our choices.)

closing
The Grand Finale

🔊 Close your talk with prayer, asking for forgiveness for all the times we ignore or modify God's instructions and for courage to follow him, even when we don't feel like it.

discussion
Encore

Get It?	Middle School

🔊 Describe a time when you lied to cover your own tracks just like Saul.

🔊 Why do you think Saul thought he was smarter than God?

🔊 What was the difference between how Samuel responds to God's instruction and how Saul responds?

🔊 What does rationalization mean, and how did Saul do this?

Get It?	High School

🔊 We live in a different day when God rarely speaks to us through the voice of a prophet. How do we recognize God's instructions to us?

🔊 Why is it often difficult to act decisively on what we believe God is asking us to do?

🔊 Describe a current situation in your life where you are struggling to know what God wants you to do.

🔊 Talk about rationalization. What is, it and where do you see it in your own life?

What If?   The Big Picture

- What if you were number one in command of Saul's army and knew he wasn't carrying out the Lord's instruction—what would you have done?

- What difference will it make in your life if you never obey God's instructions?

- What if you made a commitment to stop rationalizing and to stop making excuses for your modification of God's instructions? What would the impact be in your life?

So What?   It's Your Life

- Saul lost his kingship because of his disobedience. What opportunities will God take away from you if you choose not to carry out his instructions?

- How can you know God's instructions to you?

- How can you get a "Samuel" in your life, someone who will help you see where you're modifying God's instructions?

- In what area(s) of your life are you currently disobeying God? How can you change that?

Contributed by **Megan Hutchinson**

Talk to Me: How to Communicate So Your Family Will Listen

Primary theme communication	
Themes family, parents, honesty, reconciliation, anger, forgiveness	
Scripture 1 Peter 2:17; Ephesians 6:1-3; Matthew 5:23-25; Ephesians 4:29 Ephesians 4:26-31	
Approximate length through The Grand Finale 25-30 minutes	

You'll need

- A student who is ready to share a personal story about how their family communicates
- *Meet the Parents* (DreamWorks SKG, 2000)
- TV and DVD player
- Copies of the Rate Myself quiz, cut into half-sheets, page 102, one half sheet per student
- Pens or pencils

There are millions of teens in America. It is estimated that over a third of them have a problem that's so serious—like an eating disorder or a chemical dependency—that if it's not dealt with, it could easily destroy their lives. One of the major issues leading to these problems is a lack of communication with their parents. But even in the homes of healthy teenagers communication with parents is a challenge! As students move toward independence, it's natural that evolving communication will, at times, be strained. This talk presents three helpful suggestions for improving family communication.

intro

The Opening Act

🔊 Before your meeting ask a student (or two) to come prepared to share a personal story that illustrates how their family communicates with one another (positively or negatively). (If you can't think of a student who could do this effectively, move on to the role-play.)

🔊 Role-play: The Camping Trip (see sidebar)

🔊 Transition by saying something like—We all want to be heard and understood, yet it seems like getting parents and teens to communicate effectively can be like pulling teeth. What are some things that can help with this?

Role-play

The Camping Trip

Ask for volunteers to come up and play parts in a role-play. You'll assign them their roles, give them a setting, and then allow them to create the dialogue. (Note: High school students and older teens tend to be quite good at this impromptu drama. Younger teens are capable of it but often not in the context of a large group. If you're speaking to junior highers, consider using small groups for the role-play instead.)

Recruit someone to play Mom, Dad, the 16-year-old sister, and the 10-year-old brother. Have Mom and Dad sit on chairs while the two siblings stand on either side of them. (All of them should be facing your group so everyone can hear the dialogue.)

Describe the setup:
- This is a very conservative home.
- The parents are very nervous about the daughter dating.
- The daughter is a great girl, a solid follower of Jesus; she makes good decisions and never gets in trouble.
- The daughter wants permission to go on a camping trip with a bunch of friends. The only chaperone will be the older sister of one of the kids who's going.
- Little Brother wants to see his sister fry! He'll do anything, including lie, to see that she doesn't get to go.

Tell the actors to start by having the girl ask her parents if she can go on the trip. Give them about five minutes (or until it spins out) to play the roles and create a live case study for you.
- After you cut them off (with applause), ask your students: How was this like your family? How was this NOT like your family?

heart of the talk
The Main Event

1. Communicate with respect.

🔊 Scripture: 1 Peter 2:17, NLT ("Show respect for everyone. Love your Christian brothers and sisters.")

🔊 Scripture: Ephesians 6:1-3 ("Children [teens], obey your parents in the Lord, for this is right. 'Honor [respect] your father and mother'—which is the first commandment with a promise—'that it may go well with you and that you may enjoy long life on the earth.'")

🔊 Respect = acknowledging another person's position of authority (parent, law enforcement, judge) or their dignity (everyone!).

🔊 Ask—What does it look like to communicate with respect?

2. Communicate with appreciation and understanding.

🔊 Scripture: Ephesians 4:29, NLT ("Let everything you say be good and helpful, so that your words will be an encouragement to those who hear them.")

🔊 Let others know you appreciate them—express your love for them.

🔊 Illustration: One More Time… (see sidebar)

🔊 Reread Ephesians 4:29 (see above) When we express ourselves with appreciation and understanding, we win the right to be heard.

Illustration

One More Time…

An article in the paper told about an old husband whose wife had just died. He said he longed to talk to his wife just one more time because he didn't say all that he needed to say to her. One youth worker was so struck by this comment that she's since made a conscious effort to treat people like it's the last time she will see them. An interesting thought worth trying. She says the payoff has been immeasurable.

3. Communicate in the spirit of reconciliation.

📢 Warning: This takes time!

📢 Define reconciliation (resolve, settle, patch up, make right)

📢 Scripture: Matthew 5:23-24 ("Therefore, if you are offering your gift at the altar and there remember that your brother [or sister] has something against you, leave your gift your gift there in front of the altar. First go and be reconciled to [them]; then come and offer your gift.") In other words, when you've wronged someone or someone has wronged you, go and talk to them honestly and make things right.

📢 Scripture: Ephesians 4:26-31, NLT ("Don't let the sun go down while you are still angry, for anger gives a mighty foothold to the Devil.")

📢 Movie clip: *Meet the Parents* (see sidebar)

📢 Acknowledge that some students in your group may have been deeply hurt by their parents or family. But it's important that in those worst-case situations we don't let our families teach us how to hate, to be unfair, to be unethical, or to be mean.

📢 Illustration: Becoming a Slave (see sidebar)

Movie clip

Meet the Parents

Start 01:32:06 A flight attendant says to a boarding passenger, "Enjoy your flight, sir."
Stop 01:35:01 Greg says, "…and tried to pry it from my dead, lifeless fingers."
Before you show this scene, explain that Greg Focker (Ben Stiller) has had a fight with his future father-in-law and feels as though his fiancée's entire family hates him. He is really hurt and angry, and that anger is carrying over into other parts of his life. In this scene Greg blows up at the flight attendant (Kali Rocha) when she tells him that his luggage is too big for the overhead compartment. (Note: Make sure you stop the movie quickly because Greg swears at the flight attendant in his next line.)

Illustration

Becoming a Slave

A student was in so much trouble that he was headed for jail. The police said he needed counseling, so he asked to see a pastor from the church he grew up in.

The boy told the pastor, "Do you know why I steal, drink, curse, and party? Because I'm getting back at my father for all the hurt he has caused me."

The pastor responded, "Well, here's what you're really doing: In the process of trying to get back at your father, you've filled yourself with hate. You have become a slave to your father—he has become your master. In other words, your dad's pain still has power over you."

closing

The Grand Finale

🔊 Exercise: Rate Myself (see sidebar)

🔊 Prayer: Forgiveness (see sidebar)

🔊 Final thought—God loves families. He created our families and his dream for us is that our families can be places of healthy communication.

Exercise

Rate Myself

Pass out copies of the Rate Myself quiz on page 102 and pens or pencils. Give your students a few minutes to complete it. When time's up, acknowledge that you don't know the family backgrounds of all your students or what goes on in all their homes, but you do know that this communication thing is a big issue in every home with teenagers.

Prayer

Forgiveness

Say something like—I have a hunch that some of you need to forgive and restore some relationships with family members. Some of you might need extra help or counseling for the really big stuff. But all of us need to seek forgiveness from God for our part in poor communication. Think of one person in your family with whom you'd like to improve your communication. Then lead your students in this prayer:

> God, forgive my bitterness toward this person. Forgive me for the role I've played in breaking down communication. Help me to look to you for strength in repairing communication and do so with respect, appreciation, understanding, and a spirit of reconciliation.
>
> God, go before me and lead me;
> God, go beside me to encourage me;
> Go behind me and push me;
> Go under me to sustain me;
> And go over me to protect me.
> Amen.

(Note: You may want to consider projecting this prayer onto a TV or screen using MediaShout or PowerPoint.)

discussion

Encore

Get It?	Middle School

- What is communication?
- What does good communication look like in families?
- What does it mean to communicate with respect? How can you do that when you struggle with respecting your parents?
- What does it mean to communicate with appreciation and understanding?
- What does that look like when we're dealing with our parents?
- What is reconciliation? What does it mean to communicate with a "spirit of reconciliation"?

Get It?	High School

- Why do you think God cares about how we communicate with our families?
- What part are we supposed to play in creating healthy communication in our families?
- How does that work if a family is really messed up?
- What does each of these phrases mean?
    - Communicate with respect.
    - Communicate with appreciation and understanding.
    - Communicate with a spirit of reconciliation.

What If?	The Big Picture

- How would your parents react if you suddenly started treating them with more respect? What might that look like? How could you do it?
- What about your parents do you need to appreciate or understand that would help your communication with them?
- What would happen if you really made an attempt to reconcile with a parent or sibling with whom you have strained communication? How do you think they would react, assuming you do this with humility and love?

So What?	It's Your Life

- What one action will you attempt this week to improve communication with your parents? What's your starting point?

- What one action will you attempt this week to improve communication with a sibling?

- What advice would you give to a student who wants to improve communication with her parents but has been treated poorly by them?

- What's the worst thing that could happen if you attempt to improve communication? How could it backfire?

- What role does God play in this? How can you draw on God's strength?

Rate Myself

Rate yourself on each of these scales, with 1 = Really Bad and 5 = Amazing.

Communication with my parents

1 • • • • • • • • 2 • • • • • • • • 3 • • • • • • • • 4 • • • • • • • • 5

Communicating with respect

1 • • • • • • • • 2 • • • • • • • • 3 • • • • • • • • 4 • • • • • • • • 5

Communicating with appreciation and understanding

1 • • • • • • • • 2 • • • • • • • • 3 • • • • • • • • 4 • • • • • • • • 5

Communicating in the spirit of reconciliation

1 • • • • • • • • 2 • • • • • • • • 3 • • • • • • • • 4 • • • • • • • • 5

Rate Myself

Rate yourself on each of these scales, with 1 = Really Bad and 5 = Amazing.

Communication with my parents

1 • • • • • • • • 2 • • • • • • • • 3 • • • • • • • • 4 • • • • • • • • 5

Communicating with respect

1 • • • • • • • • 2 • • • • • • • • 3 • • • • • • • • 4 • • • • • • • • 5

Communicating with appreciation and understanding

1 • • • • • • • • 2 • • • • • • • • 3 • • • • • • • • 4 • • • • • • • • 5

Communicating in the spirit of reconciliation

1 • • • • • • • • 2 • • • • • • • • 3 • • • • • • • • 4 • • • • • • • • 5

The All-Access Pass

Contributed by **Megan Hutchinson**

Primary theme the future	
Themes choices, myths and truths about God, heaven, perseverance, discipleship, submission, obedience	
Scripture Revelation 1-3	
Approximate length through The Grand Finale 30-40 minutes	

You'll need

- *Night of the Living Dead* (Columbia Pictures, 1990) or some similar movie about zombies

- TV and DVD player

- MediaShout or PowerPoint to project the closing prayer or copies of the prayer at the end of this outline (see page 113), one per student

W e always joke that if you poll your students, the two topics they want to hear about the most are the end times and sex. In fact, a talk on "sex during the end times" may just be the ultimate youth talk! Well, this outline talks about one of those topics—and from the Revelation reference, you can probably guess which one! It's really a look at five of the seven churches mentioned in Revelation and the lessons we can learn from them. The real point of the talk is that the choices we make today will impact us for eternity. (Note: This outline is fairly long. You'll have to move along at a brisk clip to finish in the approximate time listed above. It would also be a great outline to split into a multipart series.)

intro
The Opening Act

📣 Discuss questions about the end times, such as—

- Why do you think there is so much interest in the "end times" in our world these days?

- Do any of you ever think about this subject? (Discuss.)

- What's exciting about the future?

- What makes you nervous about the future?

📣 Explanation: Myths about God (see sidebar)

📣 Scripture: Revelation 1:1-2, NLT ("This is a revelation from Jesus Christ, which God gave him concerning the events that will happen soon. An angel was sent to God's servant John so that John could share the revelation with God's other servants. John faithfully reported the word of God and the testimony of Jesus Christ—everything he saw.") The word *revelation* in the original Greek literally means "apocalypse" or "unveiling." So God starts the first chapter of Revelation by telling us what this entire book is about.

📣 Scripture: Revelation 1:11 ("[The angel] said: 'Write on a scroll what you see and send it to the seven churches: to Ephesus, Smyrna, Pergamum, Thyatira, Sardis, Philadelphia and Laodicea.'")

📣 We talk about these letters today because what was true for the churches 2,000 years ago is true today—we need to GET READY! Jesus is coming. It's not a question of "if" but "when."

📣 Explanation: Letter Structure (see sidebar)

📣 Transition by saying something like—So today we look at these letters to the churches and see what we can learn. Each letter starts out by saying, "To the angel of the church" in Ephesus, in Smyrna, in Pergamum, and so on. It could just as easily say, "To the students of our church."

Explanation

Myths about God

MYTHS about God	TRUTHS about God
He wants to zap some to hell ASAP.	He wants ALL to come to him; he is patient.
He wants us to be afraid.	He wants us to trust in him.
He wants us to be clueless and in the dark.	He wants us to know what will happen; he has a plan (he's not out of control).

Letter Structure

All of the letters to the churches include three things:
- An affirmation: the areas where you're doing great!
- A challenge: what you're still lacking (or areas where you need to "get ready")
- A reward: the consequences of obedience

What you'll be revealing to students is similar to the law of inertia: To every action there is a reaction. In the following letters, the churches are being challenged to change something; if they do, a reward is promised. Similarly, as we live in obedience to Jesus, we will have an eternal reward.

heart of the talk

The Main Event

1. Ephesus—the church of weak lovers

🔊 Affirmation: You have persevered!

🔊 Scripture: Revelation 2:2-3, NLT ("I know all the things you do. I have seen your hard work and your patient endurance. I know you don't tolerate evil people. You have examined the claims of those who say they are apostles but are not. You have discovered they are liars. You have patiently suffered for me without quitting.")

🔊 Challenge: Be true to your first love.

🔊 Scripture: Revelation 2:4-5, NLT ("But I have this complaint against you. You don't love me or each other as you did at first! Look how far you have fallen from your first love!") The Lord desires a loving relationship with us. We so often try to substitute our work, our efforts, and our abilities because we think that will get us closer to God. Not true!

🔊 Reward: Heaven!

🔊 Scripture: Revelation 2:7, NLT ("Everyone who is victorious will eat from the tree of life in the paradise of God.")

2. Smyrna—the persecuted church

🔊 Explanation: The Persecuted Church of Smyrna (see sidebar)

🔊 Jesus starts by recognizing their pain and suffering.

🔊 Affirmation: Jesus sees our hurts—and hurts with us!

🔊 Scripture: Revelation 2:9, NLT ("I know about your suffering and your poverty.")

🔊 Challenge: Be faithful.

🔊 Scripture: Revelation 2:10 ("Do not be afraid of what you are about to suffer. I tell you, the devil will put some of you in prison to test you, and you will suffer persecution for ten days. Be faithful, even to the point of death, and I will give you the crown of life.") In the Roman world, prison was usually not punitive but a prelude to trial and execution; hence the words: "Be faithful, even to the point of death."

🔊 Reward: the crown of life!

🔊 Scripture: Revelation 2:10 ("I will give you the crown of life.")

🔊 Explanation: The Crown of Life (see sidebar)

Explanation

The Persecuted Church of Smyrna

The church of Smyrna went through a tremendous amount of suffering. It is estimated that six million Christians were martyred during this time. Some of them were fed to lions (there's a fairly brutal, but not graphic, scene portraying this in the "Deleted Scenes" section of the *Gladiator* DVD), some were stretched on the racks, and some crucified because the Romans wanted to stamp out Christianity.

Many people want to stamp out Christianity today: God is very popular these days, but talk about Jesus and you'll make people angry or uncomfortable. In many countries people are still being tortured and killed because of their faith. (For more information on the persecuted church today go to www.opendoorsusa.org, the Web site of Open Doors, or to www.persecutedchurch.org, the Web site for the National Day of Prayer for the Persecuted Church.)

The Crown of Life

For those who would face martyrdom out of loyalty to Christ, there was to be a "crown of life" given by Christ himself. People at Smyrna were familiar with the term "the crown of Smyrna," which no doubt alluded to the beautiful skyline formed around the city by the hill Pagos and the public buildings on its sloping sides. The "crown" usually referred to a garland of flowers worn chiefly in the worship of the pagan gods. Faithful servants of the city appeared on coins with laurel wreaths on their heads. As the patriots of Smyrna were faithful to Rome and to their crown city, so Christ's people are to be faithful unto death to him who will give them the imperishable crown of life.

(From the Zondervan *NIV Bible Commentary*, 1994)

3. Thyatira—the church of the easily misled

🔊 Explanation: Thya-what? (see sidebar)

🔊 Ask—What are some of the idols we worship in our culture? Like the people of Thyatira, do different groups of people in our culture worship different things? (Discuss.)

🔊 Affirmation: You are growing!

🔊 Scripture: Revelation 2:19, NLT ("I know all the things you do—your love, your faith, your service, and your patient endurance. And I can see your constant improvement in all these things.")

🔊 Challenge: Be smart! (Don't be deceived.)

🔊 Scripture: Revelation 2:20, NLT ("But I have this complaint against you. You are permitting that woman—that Jezebel who calls herself a prophet—to lead my servants astray. She is encouraging them to worship idols, eat food offered to idols, and commit sexual sin.") People will try to deceive you. Watch out for false teachers and pretenders.

🔊 Reward: authority with God!

🔊 Scripture: Revelation 2:26, 28 ("To him who overcomes and does my will to the end, I will give authority over the nations...I will also give him the morning star.")

🔊 Explanation: The Morning Star? (see sidebar)

Explanation

Thya-what?

Background about Thyatira: It wasn't a huge city or all that important, but it was known for its wool, linen, apparel, dyed stuffs, leather work, tanning, and excellent bronze work. Each of these industries had a membership organization (almost like a labor union or a club). These groups all worshiped different gods and had pagan worship rituals that were a normal part of their everyday lives. In other words: lots of idol worship!

Explanation

The Morning Star?

The promise to the church at Thyatira is two-fold. First, they're promised authority with God. To a church in constant persecution, this would have been an enormous encouragement.

Second, the overcomers in Thyatira are promised "the morning star." Some link this expression to Christ himself as in 22:16; believers receive Christ as their very life. Or it may refer to the resurrection in the sense that the morning star rises over the darkness of this world's persecution and offers victory over it. Perhaps a combination of the two thoughts is intended. The promise of Christ's return is like the "morning star."

(From the Zondervan *NIV Bible Commentary*)

4. Sardis—the church of the living dead

- Background: Sardis was a much wealthier city than one that hadn't experienced much war.

- Scripture: Revelation 3:1, NLT ("I know all the things you do, and that you have a reputation for being alive—but you are dead.")

- Affirmation: You had a good reputation of being alive! (You had life!)

- The church in Sardis was attractive! They were alive and full of excitement. That is what God wants our church and youth group to be like—something that outsiders want to come to.

- Challenge: Be prepared! Be ready for anything!

- Scripture: Revelation 3:2-3 ("Wake up! Strengthen what remains and is about to die, for I have not found your deeds complete in the sight of my God. Remember, therefore, what you have received and heard; obey it, and repent. But if you do not wake up, I will come like a thief, and you will not know at what time I will come to you.")

- Movie clip: *Night of the Living Dead* (see sidebar)

- What a cool challenge—wake up! Snap out of your zombie-like life and experience the real life I have for you!

- 🔊 Reward: acknowledgment before God!

- 🔊 Scripture: Revelation 3:5, NLT ("I will announce before my Father and his angels that they are mine.") Jesus will put his arm around us and say, "Welcome!"

- 🔊 Activity (optional): Ask the students to think about the last time they felt really welcome somewhere. Where were they? What happened? How did they feel?

Movie clip

Night of the Living Dead

Show a short scene from the classic horror film *Night of the Living Dead*, or any other movie with zombie-like "living dead." Show a little discretion, please, and don't show some disgusting people-munching scene. Just pick any of a dozen scenes with the zombies walking around moaning.

Then talk about what it means to be "the living dead" as a group of Christians. What would that mean? Why do so many churches fit this description today?

5. Laodicea—the room-temperature church

- 🔊 This is the final letter, and it ends with a bang!

- 🔊 Affirmation: none!

- 🔊 The church of Laodicea isn't affirmed at all. This is significant! It shows that Jesus isn't just "finding something nice to say" about the other churches. And it shows how bad the situation was in the Laodicean church.

- 🔊 Ask—Why do you think there is no affirmation of this church? (There was nothing to affirm.)

- 🔊 Explanation: Laodicea (see sidebar)

- 🔊 Challenge: Be committed.

- 🔊 Scripture: Revelation 3:15-16 ("I know your deeds, that you are neither cold nor hot. I wish you were either one or the other! So, because you are lukewarm—neither hot nor cold—I am about to spit you out of my mouth.")

- 🔊 Explanation: Lukewarm (see sidebar)

- 🔊 Reward: dinner with Jesus!

- 🔊 Scripture: Revelation 3:19-21 ("Those whom I love I rebuke and discipline. So be earnest, and repent. Here I am! I stand at the door and knock. If anyone hears my voice and opens the door, I will come in and eat with him, and he with me. To him who overcomes, I will give the right to sit with me on my throne, just as I overcame and sat down with my Father on his throne.")

- 🔊 Jesus is only disciplining them because he loves them! But this lazy group of people still has hope: Jesus wants to hang with them!

Explanation

Laodicea

Laodicea was a very wealthy city—wealthier than even Sardis. The whole city had a reputation very much like the church. In other words, the church was merely a reflection of the culture of the city: wealthy, arrogant, lazy, compromising.

Explanation

Lukewarm

It's important to understand both the context for the example and what is meant here. First, some context: While the city of Laodicea had a lot going for it, their one significant natural weakness was water. They got water two ways: nearby hot springs (from which the water would be cooled), and an aqueduct from another city that had a source of cold water. During the trip down the aqueduct, the cold water would become lukewarm. The people of Laodicea were familiar with lukewarm!

Second, what was meant: We often use these words of Jesus to imply spiritual hotness or coldness. The people of this time would not have understood that concept. Instead the important idea here is "usefulness." Cold water has great uses, as does hot water. But lukewarm water is distasteful and useless. Jesus is slamming them because they are not "useful" to God! They thought they had it all together, but the reality is just the opposite.

closing

The Grand Finale

🔊 Ask—How do we give God our all? (Open the door of your heart.)

🔊 Scripture: Revelation 3:20, NASB ("Behold, I stand at the door and knock; if anyone hears My voice and opens the door, I will come in to him and will dine with him, and he with Me.") This verse was written to the people of the church at Laodicea, but it applies to all of us.

🔊 Many people make the mistake of assuming this verse was written to non-Christians ("Let Jesus into your life"), but that is taking it out of context. The true context is to the seven churches. Jesus is saying to them (and to us), "Let me into your lives!"

🔊 Illustration: All-Access Pass (see sidebar)

🔊 Prayer: The All-Access Pass Prayer (see sidebar)

Illustration

All-Access Pass

Ask—What is an "all-access pass"? (for concerts or other large events). Then ask what the difference is between a "backstage pass" and an "all-access pass." (Backstage passes allow the holder to get backstage, but only into the common areas. All-access is just that—it gives the holder unlimited access to every area of the venue.)

When Jesus asks us to "open the doors of our hearts," he's asking for an all-access pass into our lives. Brainstorm with your group what this would look like in real life.

Prayer

The All-Access Pass Prayer

Lead your students in unison as they recite this closing prayer. (You can either use the MediaShout or PowerPoint screen provided on the CD-ROM in this book or copy it from page 113 and give the copies to your students.)

God, I don't really know where to start, but I do know that I want to be ready when you return. In fact, I want to be ready now. So I open the door of my heart and give you an all-access pass to every area of my life. I give you permission to change me and make me more like you. Do what you must—but get me ready. Thank you for second chances! Amen.

discussion

Encore

Get It?	Middle School

🔊 What were some of the issues these churches were dealing with?

🔊 In what ways were they blowing it?

🔊 Why do you think these messages were sent to them?

🔊 What does it mean to give Jesus an "all-access pass" to your life?

Get It?   High School

🔊 Why do you think all five of these letters had each of the following components—
  - Affirmation
  - Challenge
  - Reward

🔊 Do you think challenges are a good thing? Why?

🔊 Why do you think the original audience (the churches) needed to hear about a "reward"?

🔊 Which of the five churches do you feel you can most relate to in your—
  - Family life
  - Social life
  - Youth group

🔊 What does it mean to give Jesus an "all-access pass" to your life?

What If?   The Big Picture

🔊 If someone told you, "Get ready—you only have 30 days to live!" what would you do?

🔊 Who would you want to see?

🔊 Would you change anything about the way you behave now? What?

🔊 What do you think God would say about your answers above? Would he add anything? Take away anything?

🔊 Describe your understanding of that "hot, cold, and lukewarm" comment Jesus made to the church at Laodicea (Revelation 3:15-16: "I know all the things you do, that you are neither hot nor cold. I wish you were one or the other! But since you are like lukewarm water, I will spit you out of my mouth!" NLT)

🔊 Who do you know who seems to have really given Jesus an all-access pass into his life? How can you tell? What does that look like?

So What?   It's Your Life

🔊 If God were to give your life an affirmation, a challenge, and a reward, what area(s) would he target?

🔊 What is one way you can begin thinking more about eternity? Who will help you do this consistently?

🔊 In what way(s) have you only given Jesus a "backstage pass" to your life, rather than an "all-access pass"?

🔊 What areas of your life would you rather he stay out of? What can you do about that? What are you willing to do about that?

🔊 God wants to be your first love. What is one way you can invite him into your life this week?

The All-Access Pass Prayer

God, I don't really know where to start, but I do know that I want to be ready when you return. In fact, I want to be ready now. So I open the door of my heart and give you an all-access pass to every area of my life. I give you permission to change me and make me more like you. Do what you must—but get me ready. Thank you for second chances! Amen.

The All-Access Pass Prayer

God, I don't really know where to start, but I do know that I want to be ready when you return. In fact, I want to be ready now. So I open the door of my heart and give you an all-access pass to every area of my life. I give you permission to change me and make me more like you. Do what you must—but get me ready. Thank you for second chances! Amen.

The All-Access Pass Prayer

God, I don't really know where to start, but I do know that I want to be ready when you return. In fact, I want to be ready now. So I open the door of my heart and give you an all-access pass to every area of my life. I give you permission to change me and make me more like you. Do what you must—but get me ready. Thank you for second chances! Amen.

The All-Access Pass Prayer

God, I don't really know where to start, but I do know that I want to be ready when you return. In fact, I want to be ready now. So I open the door of my heart and give you an all-access pass to every area of my life. I give you permission to change me and make me more like you. Do what you must—but get me ready. Thank you for second chances! Amen.

Choosing Life over Death

Contributed by **Dan Jessup**

Primary theme living for Jesus	
Themes life, death, choices, heaven, discipleship, the kingdom of God	
Scripture Matthew 13:44; Hosea 2:21; Daniel 7:13; Genesis 1:14-16; 2 Corinthians 12:1-4; John 14:1-3; Hebrews 12:22-24, 28-29; Luke 17:21; Deuteronomy 30:19-20	
Approximate length through The Grand Finale 20-30 minutes	

You'll need

- Videotape of a dating game segment from TV
- Clippings from the obituary section of your local newspaper (optional)
- *Braveheart* (20th Century Fox, 1995)
- TV and DVD player
- A personal story about a time when you felt great anticipation about something in the future
- Paper and pencil for each student

It wasn't very long ago that dying was the last thing on most kids' minds. Visions of going to the movies, playing sports, and hanging out with friends consumed their free time. But times have changed. In the post 9/11 years, war, terrorism, bombings, and school violence are added to the already chaotic world of car accidents and cancer, filling the students' world with the reality of death more than it was just a few short years ago. This reality changes the way kids read and hear Scripture, and we, as youth workers must change the way we present God's Word to our young friends. Oddly enough, in a world full of unpredictability and global chaos, our kids still live in a day-to-day, consumer-driven, get-as-much-as-you-can culture. Perhaps focusing on what kids choose to live for will be more productive than focusing on what they must live without.

intro
The Opening Act

🔊 Video: Dating Game Choice (see sidebar)

🔊 Discussion: Funerals (see sidebar)

🔊 Movie clip: *Braveheart* (see sidebar)

🔊 Transition by saying something like—Most teens tend to think that the Christian life is dominated by living "without." You know, without sex (until you are married), without drinking (until you are 21), without having fun like the rest of the world. This isn't totally wrong; but we often miss the excitement of the life God wants for us now! We need to spend more time thinking about living, not living without.

Video

Dating Game Choice

Ahead of time, record a clip or two from one of the many dating games that are now shown on television. Find a section without massive sexual innuendo (good luck!). You'll need to show a scene where someone is choosing between two potential dating partners and they are talking about why they made that particular decision. Use it to begin a discussion on how your students think before making decisions.

Discussion

Funerals

Ask for a show of hands of those who've been to a funeral in the last year or two. Have them talk about what they remember people saying about the person who died. Hopefully, one or two students will be able to talk about what the person's life was all about and what they lived for. (Note: This wouldn't be the most productive idea to use if your community recently experienced a significant death that greatly affected your students.)

If this is too risky for your group, or if you know that a family member of one of your students just passed away, you could choose this alternative instead. Cut out a few obituaries from the newspaper and read them aloud to the group. Ask your students to talk about what this person may have lived for and what he may have valued in life.

Movie clip

Braveheart

Start 02:31:08 Prison guard says, "Your highness."
Stop 02:33:58 Princess Isabelle leaves the prison cell.
William Wallace (Mel Gibson) has been charged with committing treason against England, and he is sentenced to undergo purification the next day (a slow, torturous, public death). Princess Isabelle (Sophie Marceau) visits William in his prison cell and begs him to confess to the charge of treason so he might receive mercy—in other words a quick death—instead. She says she can't bear the thought of him dying by purification. However, he declines, saying, "Every man dies, not every man really lives."

Why is this statement so memorable and why does it connect with us on such a deep level? Maybe it's because there's so much freedom in the thought that we can actually choose some things in life. Much of life is dealt to us—who our parents are, how tall we'll be, what we'll look like, where we're born. And people spend a lot of time fretting over the unchangeable things of life. But not Jesus. He didn't seem to be too worried about where people were born (in occupied Roman Israel in a time of great hardship and persecution).

Jesus came to set people free, but not in the external things. Rather he spent most of his life encouraging people to choose something that was 100-percent available to all—life!

heart of the talk
The Main Event

1. Jesus invites us into the kingdom of heaven!

🔊 Ask—What do you think heaven is like?

🔊 Scripture: Matthew 13:44–45 ("The kingdom of heaven is like treasure hidden in a field...like a merchant looking for fine pearls.")

🔊 Explanation: Heaven in the Bible (see sidebar)

🔊 One thing we know about heaven: We'll be there for eternity!

🔊 Personal illustration: It Seemed Like Forever (see sidebar)

🔊 We have such a hard time understanding the concept of "forever" because we don't have any examples of it now in our lives. Everything we know ends.

Explanation

Heaven in the Bible

(Note: This sidebar isn't really for you to read to your group. It's more like background information for you as you lead this discussion—though you may want to use some of these pieces to explain how unclear the Bible is about heaven.)

There are lots of images that appear in Scripture about heaven, but none of them are conclusive—most are more poetic or metaphorical. We are told of a first Heaven, a second Heaven, and a Third Heaven. Nobody is quite sure exactly what these are, but we have a guess that the first heaven might be the sky (Hosea 2:21; Daniel 7:13), the second heaven might be the stellar places (stars and planets) mentioned in Genesis 1:14-16, and the third heaven may be where God the Father, the Son, and the Holy Spirit dwell (2 Corinthians 12:1-4; John 14:1-3; Hebrews 12:22-24, 28-29).

We also see that heaven is described as a lush city: "The foundations of the walls of the city are described as garnished with all manner of precious stones…The twelve gates are set each one so that they consist of one huge pearl. The seer's city is said to be pure gold. No temple is there because the Triune God is unveiled in all of his glory. No light is needed because the unobscured glory of God is revealed in the city." From *The New Unger's Bible Dictionary* (Moody Press, 1988)

The truth is, we don't know exactly what the kingdom will be like. But we do know that it will be more exciting than we could ever dare to imagine!

Personal illustration

It Seemed Like Forever

Tell a story about a time when you were a child or teenager and you knew something great was coming your way, but you had to wait for it. Maybe this was a family vacation or a special gift you knew you were going to receive at Christmas. Maybe you saved your own money for a long time to buy something. Maybe it was getting your driver's license. Whatever the item, stress how that reasonably short period of time seemed to take forever to come! And if you're a parent, you could use the example of waiting for one of your children to be born or share a time when one of your kids was waiting (impatiently) for something.

2. We can start living in the kingdom now!

🔊 We don't have to wait until we die to experience the kingdom. Jesus said that the kingdom of God is within you—right now!

🔊 Scripture: Luke 17:21 ("Nor will people say, 'Here it is,' or 'There it is,' because the kingdom of God is within you.") This is the unbelievable news of life in Christ! It is NOT like Christmas where we have to wait for it; it is here now. God's kingdom isn't "out there" and "someday"—it's here and now.

🔊 Scripture: Deuteronomy 30:19-20 ("Now choose life, so that you and your children may live and that you may love the Lord your God, listen to his voice, and hold fast to him. For the Lord is your life...") Every day—every moment—you can choose life or death, living in God's kingdom or not.

🔊 Ask—Think about what it means to choose life: Where do you struggle with choosing life? What makes that so hard? What would it be like, in the midst of that occasion, to choose life? How would that change your day?

🔊 Apparently it is possible to "choose death." How crazy is that? You can be alive, but choose to be living in death!

🔊 Activity: Influences (see sidebar)

🔊 When you live for Jesus, you choose to be influenced by what he cares about—you choose to desire the things he desires. This is choosing life, choosing to live in God's eternal kingdom now.

Activity

Influences

Say something like—Think about how many decisions you make in a day, an hour, or a minute for that matter! We are making decisions all day long, for all kinds of reasons. Think about how many different reasons there were for people in this group to be here today. There are thousands of things that go into most of our decisions: feelings, knowledge, desires, parents, friends, opportunities—you name it. And they all influence what and why we choose what we do!

Give each student a piece of paper and a pencil. Ask them to think about their day yesterday as they make two columns on their paper. In one column, students should list five decisions they made yesterday. In the second column, ask them to list the influences that went into making each of those five decisions. Then ask one or two students to share about some of the choices they made.

closing
The Grand Finale

🔊 Exercise: When I Chose Life (see sidebar)

🔊 Have students turn over the piece of paper they used in the Influences activity. On the back they should each make a list of some choices they know they will need to make during the next month. Ask them to keep a journal of these choices and report back on them each week.

◀ᴕ Have each student take a moment to reflect on the most recent choices they've made, especially the poor ones—or their "death" choices! For most of us, just as there are positive reasons to choose life, there are usually a bunch of reasons that influence us not to choose life. Now ask them to make a list of the reasons and influences that play a part in their negative decision making. Why are these influences important to them? Are there some proactive things they can do to begin to minimize the impact that these have in their lives this next week?

◀ᴕ Say something like—Those who choose life are wonderful to be around. Think about the people you like to spend time with. Are they choosing life? Or are you choosing friends who are clearly choosing death?

◀ᴕ Close in prayer, thanking God for life and for the opportunity to experience his kingdom here and now. Ask for courage and insight to allow Jesus to influence our choices and to help us choose life.

Exercise

When I Chose Life

Tell students to think about a recent time when they made a choice and allowed Jesus to influence their decision. Ask—What was going on in your life? What gave you the strength to make that decision? How did you feel? Was that an experience that you could draw on to help you choose life next time?

discussion

Encore

Get It?	Middle School

◀ᴕ Talk about heaven—what will it be like?

◀ᴕ What does it mean that heaven isn't just "out there" and "someday"?

◀ᴕ What does it mean to "choose life"?

◀ᴕ What does it mean to "choose death"?

◀ᴕ Why is it easier to choose death than it is to choose life?

◀ᴕ Think about the kids you hang you with; do they tend to choose life or death? Why do you think this is?

Get It? — High School

- What about heaven sounds great?

- What concerns do you have about heaven? (Be honest!)

- What does it mean that heaven isn't just "out there" and "someday"?

- What does it mean to "choose life"?

- What does it mean to "choose death"?

- What are the most important things you need in order to make decisions about your high school life?

- What are you doing to help you make good life decisions?

- Name two people you know who are choosing life. What do you like about them? In what ways would you like to be like them? In what ways would you not like to be like them?

What If? — The Big Picture

- What major decision in your life might have been different if you had allowed Jesus to influence that decision? How would the outcome have been different?

- How can you know what Jesus' desires for you are?

- How would your relationships be affected if you constantly chose life? How would that impact your relationship with your parents? With your friends?

So What? — It's Your Life

- What if you made a decision to begin choosing life today? What difference would it make in your life? What would you need to deny?

- What would you need to do to have the strength to choose life?

- What part does Scripture play in your choosing life? Would you like it to have more of an influence? How might you help make this happen?

- What major decisions do you see on the horizon of your life? How can you choose life in those situations?

Relationship, Not Religion

Contributed by **Dan Jessup**

Primary theme realtionship with Jesus	
Themes freedom, religion, discipleship, behavior, rules	
Scripture Galatians 5:1; 1 Corinthians 10:29; 2 Corinthians 3:17; Galatians 2:4; Galatians 5:13; Ephesians 3:12; 1 Peter 2:16; Exodus 20:1-17; Matthew 5:1-12; John 15:16-17; 1 John 5:3	
Approximate length through The Grand Finale 30-45 minutes	

You'll need

- 📢 Whiteboard
- 📢 Marker
- 📢 Bibles
- 📢 A marionette, ventriloquist's dummy, or hand puppet
- 📢 Blank paper and pens for journaling

t's far easier to live out a religion than it is to live out a relationship. Religions have rules, lists of do's and don'ts, rights and wrongs. When you look at the religions of the world, you can vividly see how people who are fanatically religious will die for what their religion tells them is holy. Rules—we hate them, but we seem to gravitate toward them all the same. And this isn't just about "other" religions. We Christians are big into rules too! We tend to teach proper behavior and Christian etiquette, how not to offend older people, and how "good Christians" should vote. This is, however, precisely what Jesus did NOT come to teach. Jesus came to set us free from an oppressive religious structure. Free from lists of behavioral practices, free from the law, and free from feeling like we can never measure up to a worldly or religiously imposed standard of behavior. So let's explore how we might begin to understand and live out this freedom of a relationship with Jesus Christ.

intro

The Opening Act

🔊 Ad-lib drama The Rules of Dating (see sidebar)

🔊 Brainstorming: Two Columns (see sidebar)

🔊 Transition to the body of the talk by explaining—Isn't it funny? We hate to be told what to do; but when it comes to religion, we look for the list of "do's" and "don'ts". We want to know what we're allowed to do and what we're not allowed to do so we can get on with our lives while still being good Christians. Yet Jesus came to give us freedom from those religious behavior lists. Instead he wants his followers to walk with him, live with him, desire to know him, love him, and imitate him.

Drama

The Rules of Dating

Ahead of time, ask an outgoing guy and girl to ad-lib a short drama. It's kind of like a role-play, but you'll give them more direction. (Note: This will be really tough to pull off with middle school students. If you're using this talk with young teens, consider having some adult volunteers perform the drama instead.)

Tell the group that this couple has just started dating. The guy should ask the girl a long series of very specific questions regarding how she wants to be treated, what she wants him to do, and how she wants him to act. Allow this line of questioning to go on until it becomes ridiculous. Eventually, the girl should get exasperated and say something like, "I don't want you to perform a list of actions! I want you to fall in love with me, like me, and want to be with me!"

Brainstorming

Two Columns

Using a whiteboard or flip chart, make two columns, but do not put headings on them. In one column, you'll record specific actions or behaviors. In the other column write down core desires or longings. Ask the kids to shout out a list of things that most people think a Christian should be like and begin to fill in the columns. (Most, if not all, input will be placed in the specific action or behavior column.) When the responses stop coming, write the headings above the two columns and then explain how this shows that we tend to think of "being a Christian" in terms of behavior.

heart of the talk

The Main Event

1. Jesus came to give us freedom!

📢 Scripture: Galatians 5:1 ("It is for freedom that Christ has set us free. Stand firm, then, and do not let yourselves be burdened again by a yoke of slavery.")

📢 Scripture: Freedom Passages (see sidebar)

📢 Ask—How can we have freedom without total chaos? (Freedom must come with responsibility.)

📢 In order for a relationship to flourish in freedom, the following must be present:

- Limits—a relationship cannot happen without self-imposed limits on behavior, thoughts, and desires.

- Choice—love involves freedom, and love involves choice. More than anything Jesus wants our love.

- Responsibility—we can't be a follower of Jesus on Sunday and a wild sinner Monday through Saturday! Our real desires are shown most of the time by our actions.

- Sacrifice—ultimately, either you live for yourself or you live for Jesus.

📢 Point out the difference in tone between the Ten Commandments (Old Testament laws; Exodus 20:1-17) and the Beatitudes (Jesus' New Testament teaching; Matthew 5:1-12).

- The Ten Commandments—clear and concise commands. People chose either to follow them or disobey them.

- Beatitudes—the tone is completely different from the commandments. They are not requirements. Rather they bring blessing with them. You can choose how to respond to the various circumstances of life.

📢 Illustration: The Gift of Boundaries (see sidebar)

Freedom Passages

The Bible talks about freedom a lot! Have individual students find and read these passages out loud to the group:

- 1 Corinthians 10:29 ("For why should my freedom be judged by another's conscience?")
- 2 Corinthians 3:17 ("Now the Lord is the Spirit, and where the Spirit of the Lord is, there is freedom.")
- Galatians 2:4 ("This matter arose because some false brothers had infiltrated our ranks to spy on the freedom we have in Christ Jesus and to make us slaves.")
- Galatians 5:13 ("You, my brothers, were called to be free. But do not use your freedom to indulge the sinful nature; rather, serve one another in love.")
- Ephesians 3:12 ("In him and through faith in him we may approach God with freedom and confidence.")
- 1 Peter 2:16 ("Live as free men, but do not use your freedom as a cover-up for evil; live as servants of God.")

The Gift of Boundaries

There was a study done on children playing in fields. When there was a fence surrounding the field, the kids explored every nook and cranny of the field. They would play right up to the fence. When the fence was taken away, the kids tended to huddle together in a small section in the middle of the field, afraid to wander too far from each other.

When Jesus gave us our freedom, he did so with boundaries. These invisible, behavioral boundaries were not given to detract from life, freedom, or pleasure. They were given to enhance our lives. The boundaries Jesus gives are nothing short of a huge gift to us!

2. Jesus wants relationship, not religion.

🔊 Object lesson: Marionettes and Dummies (see sidebar)

🔊 Scripture: John 15:16-17 ("You did not choose me, but I chose you and appointed you to go and bear fruit—fruit that will last. Then the Father will give you whatever you ask in my name. This is my command: Love each other.") Jesus' goal for us is that we love. Love can't exist without the freedom to choose it.

🔊 Explanation: Rules Are Easy (see sidebar)

Marionettes and Dummies

Ideally, you should borrow both a marionette (a puppet controlled by strings attached to its arms, legs, and head) and a ventriloquist's dummy (although one or the other will be sufficient). And if you have no way to get ahold of one of these, a simple hand puppet will work just as well.

Give a quick demonstration of how the puppet works. It doesn't matter if you're not good at it—just establish the concept. Then ask—Now what would you say if I told you that my doll here is the best relationship I have in my life? You'd say I'm a freak, right? God could have made us with no freedom at all—we would do exactly what he wants us to do at all times. (Demonstrate by showing again how you make the puppet move and talk.) Life would be easier for us—and for God! But it would also be so boring! God is much more interested in having a relationship with us than he is in having us performing a list of religious do's and don'ts.

Rules Are Easy

What makes living in relationships harder than living with rules? You have to think! When you're a part of a relationship, you have to actually think about the other person involved—what she wants, feels, hopes, fears, likes, and dislikes. This is hard. We have to put ourselves aside and discover what she desires.

By comparison, rules are so easy—we either follow them or we don't. You don't have to give too much of yourself when you're following the rules. And your behavior is the only measure of success. This makes things really simple—and really boring!

closing

The Grand Finale

🔊 Ask the students to take a moment and think about what they prefer—rules or relationships?

🔊 Then ask them to consider why what we want and what we ask for are often opposites.

🔊 Wrap up by saying something like—This is a tricky concept. We can't really love God without obedience; but we could be obedient to God without ever loving him. Jesus wants our love—a genuine relationship with us. But this relationship is only possible if we choose to follow him. We know that we love him if we obey his commandments.

◀)) Scripture: 1 John 5:3 ("This is love for God: to obey his commands. And his commands are not burdensome.")

◀)) Ask students to spend some time journaling about what they love about Jesus' desire to have a relationship with them instead of just giving them a list of rules.

discussion

Encore

Get It?   Middle School

◀)) Does this mean we have no rules? Is it all about our freedom? Why or why not?

◀)) Why do most people think attending church is all about doing the right thing?

◀)) Does the whole idea of freedom with boundaries or "freedom with limits" sound kind of like a rip-off to you? Does it sound like something your parents might say? Does it sound like real freedom? (Discuss.)

◀)) Explain the point about the puppet again. What was the point of that example?

Get It?   High School

◀)) Is freedom with boundaries really freedom? (Discuss.)

◀)) Why is a relationship plan a riskier, gutsier move for God?

◀)) Do you think most people think Christianity is just another religion?

◀)) How do you see it as being different from other religions?

◀)) What does a "relationship with God" look like? How can you have a relationship with a being you never see?

What If?   The Big Picture

◀)) How would life be easier if it was all about rules? How would you like to live in that system? What would be good about it? What would you have to give up?

◀)) What do you think are some areas of life where God gives us freedom, but Christians turn that freedom into a set of rules?

◀)) Think about someone you know who has an active relationship with Jesus. How does this relationship show up in his life?

So What?   It's Your Life

🔊 What might you want to consider changing in your life after thinking about these things?

🔊 If Jesus came to preach freedom, why do we feel guilty so often? What do you think Jesus would like to say to us about this feeling?

🔊 How would you change our youth group meetings to help other students enjoy more freedom in Christ?

🔊 What will you do tomorrow or this week to grow in your relationship with Jesus?

Why Should I Suffer?

Contributed by Jeff Mattesich

Primary theme suffering	
Themes salvation, following Jesus, sacrifice	
Scripture Luke 9:18-26	
Approximate length through The Grand Finale 20-25 minutes	

You'll need

- A personal story about the greatest gift you ever received
- The actual gift mentioned in your personal story (or a picture of it that you can show using MediaShout or PowerPoint)
- A personal story about a time when you felt lonely
- *Braveheart* (20th Century Fox, 1995)
- TV and DVD player
- Short, personal stories about suffering, rejection, death, and resurrection (the last two are metaphorical)
- 3"x 5" cards for each student
- Pencils or pens for each student
- Whiteboard
- Marker

If you just accept Jesus into your life, then your life will be great, right? Isn't that what some modern preachers tell us? Whether you know it or not, we've all been influenced by this type of thinking. It creeps in when we forget to focus on the actual words of Jesus. So it can be refreshing and healthy when we communicate to hurting students that Jesus is right there with them, that he has emotionally experienced the same feelings they're dealing with now. This talk invites students into a conversation with Jesus about the "real life" he tells us about—a life that is full of suffering, rejection, death, and resurrection. It will invite students to evaluate their own ideas about what life with Christ is like.

intro
The Opening Act

🔊 Personal illustration and activity: Greatest Gift (see sidebar)

🔊 Transition by saying something like—Although we have all just shared stories about great gifts we've received, we're going to learn about a gift that Jesus gives us that puts all other gifts to shame. It's a gift that gives us insight into our lives and Jesus' life.

🔊 Personal illustration: My Life (see sidebar)

🔊 Transition by saying something like—Life is a tough thing to navigate. So many times we all experience some form of rejection, suffering, or loneliness. We're going to spend some time listening to Jesus, as he has some words for us that might give us a better perspective on life during those difficult times.

Personal illustration and activity

Greatest Gift

Ask students to think about the best gift they've ever received for Christmas, their birthday, or another special occasion. Let them talk about this gift with another student sitting nearby, then ask a few students to share about their best gifts with the whole group.

Now it's your turn. Create a detailed story about the greatest gift you've ever received. Talk about how old you were when you received it, how much you wanted it and for how long, and anything else that will show your students how wonderful it was when you finally received the item. Spend some time talking about who gave it to you and how much they knew you and loved you. (See where this is going?) But don't tell them what the actual gift was until the very end. When you do reveal the item to your students, you may either show the actual gift or a picture of it.

Personal illustration

My Life

Share about some time in your life when you experienced rejection, loneliness, and suffering (whether it was that time you didn't get picked for a kickball team or something more serious like the death of a friend or relative). Share about those experiences and discuss what it felt like to be lonely.

heart of the talk
The Main Event

1. The wrong Christ

🔊 Set up the Scripture passage you're about to read: Jesus just fed 5,000 or more people and is now resting with his disciples a short distance away from the crowds. He asks the 12 disciples a few very simple questions.

🔊 Scripture: Luke 9:18-20 ("But what about you?" he asked. "Who do you say I am?") The crowd thought Jesus was a great religious figure (like John the Baptist, Elijah, or an old prophet). Peter said he was the Christ of God.

🔊 Explain by saying something like—When Peter says "the Christ," his definition is a little bit off. People had been waiting for Jesus to come for so long that they were envisioning a military Messiah who would take over the world by force and power while still eliminating all sin and suffering. So when Peter says "the Christ," he's only half right.

🔊 Movie clip: *Braveheart* (see sidebar)

🔊 Jesus had to redefine who he is, who the Messiah is, and what he's all about: freedom from false expectations about life!

Movie clip

Braveheart

Start 01:15:50 A Scotsman says, "It's William Wallace."
Stop 01:18:52 The Scottish army shouts, "Freedom!"
William Wallace (Mel Gibson) and his men join other Scottish clans on the battlefield as they prepare to fight the English army. As a few of the clansmen begin to discuss the identity of the mysterious, blue-faced man on a horse, William says, "Sons of Scotland, I am William Wallace." A few don't believe him, saying he's not tall enough to be the legendary Scottish fighter. William has also heard the legends told about him, and he sets the men straight, declaring that he's come to fight the English for freedom—his and that of his country. In the same way that the Scottish people had the wrong image of William Wallace, in Jesus' day people had the wrong idea about the Messiah.

2. Jesus' job description

🔊 Scripture: Luke 9:22 ("And he said, 'The Son of Man must suffer many things and be rejected by the elders, chief priests and teachers of the law, and he must be killed and on the third day be raised to life.'") This verse contains the redefined job description for the Christ as Jesus predicts his own future:

- Suffering
- Rejection
- Death
- Resurrection

🔊 Illustration: Jesus' Last Days (see sidebar)

Explanation

Jesus' Last Days

When Jesus redefines the role of the "Christ," he chooses four very powerful words. In each one we can hear a prophetic statement of what will come.

Suffering

When Jesus says he "must suffer many things," we know that to be true! In the last couple days of his life on earth, Jesus experienced extreme physical suffering:

- He was given 39 lashes with a "cat o' nine tails." This is a long leather whip that has nine pieces of knotted cord or line attached to one end. To each of these mini-whips were tied pieces of bone, rock, or glass. As Jesus was being whipped, these jagged fragments would stick into his back, thus tearing off his flesh every time they were pulled out.
- A robe was placed on his raw, bleeding back, then pulled off again.
- He had a crown of thorns shoved onto his head. These thorns were strong and long, piercing the skin of his scalp.
- He had to carry a heavy wooden cross on his back (which was now covered with long, painful cuts) while being paraded through a jeering crowd.
- Then he was nailed to the cross through each wrist and through his feet. He hung for hours until he could no longer pull himself up to draw breath and suffocated.

Jesus knows suffering.

Rejection

Jesus also knew rejection. He was turned in by one of his followers and rejected by most of the people who had the power to save him. When he carried the cross through the crowd, people were yelling and spitting at him. "Loser" and "liar" were very familiar names to Jesus. Jesus knows rejection.

Death

Even though he was perfect and sinless, he died a painful and humiliating death on the cross. Jesus knows death.

Resurrection

On top of all that, Jesus was raised from the dead! Rather than show his divine power against those people who abandoned him and falsely accused him during the last hours of his life on earth, Jesus chose to show his power over death instead. Jesus knows resurrection.

3. Our job description

🔊 Transition by saying something like—Jesus doesn't just give a job description for himself; he also uses this time with the disciples to give them a charge in their own personal job descriptions.

🔊 Scripture: Luke 9:23-26 ("For whoever wants to save his life will lose it, but whoever loses his life for me will save it.")

🔊 Say something like—When Jesus tells us to pick up our cross and follow him, he's telling us to expect a life like his. So our job description should look like his.

- Suffering—share a short personal illustration of suffering (or, with permission, talk about the suffering of one of your group members).

- Rejection—share a short personal illustration of rejection.

- Death—share a short personal illustration of death. (Think of death more abstractly—a time when you experienced death to someone or something, such as a relationship or a very low point in your life.)

- Resurrection—say something like—This is all not negative. While Jesus is with us in our times of suffering and rejection, he also promises that we'll be "resurrected" from those things. Now share a short personal illustration of a time when you were "brought back to life" (obviously, this would also be metaphorical!).

🔊 (Note: As you go over the job description for your life again, spend some time making it personal and share about some times in your life when you have experienced each of the four things. Make sure to include a statement like—It is in these times of rejection, suffering, death, and resurrection that we are very much like Jesus and can feel closer to him.)

closing

The Grand Finale

🔊 There are a couple different ways to end this talk—

Evangelistic invitation: The Eternal Question (see sidebar)

Reflection: My Current Place (see sidebar)

Evangelistic invitation

The Eternal Question

You've just talked about our Messiah and his work on the cross. This is an opportunity for you to offer a time of response and ask students if they want to join in God's story. Yup, it's one of pain and suffering, but we all have that! Jesus offers to walk with us through those difficult times and bring about "resurrection"—real life!

Reflection

My Current Place

Pass out 3" x 5" cards and pencils to everyone. Ask them to evaluate where they are in the "job description" that Jesus reveals. (It would be helpful if you had the four words—SUFFERING, REJECTION, DEATH, and RESURRECTION—projected on a screen or written on a whiteboard for all the kids to see.) After they reflect for a few minutes, ask the students to write down their thoughts.

Then ask them to turn over their cards and write a short letter to Jesus, asking him to help them through whatever difficulties they are currently experiencing. Have them start their notes to him by writing something like:

Dear Jesus,

Right now I'm in the _____ part

of the job description you gave us. I know that you

understand because _____.

But I need you to _____

_____.

discussion

Encore

Get It?	Middle School

- 🔊 Have you ever thought a Christ follower's life should be easier? Why isn't it?

- 🔊 Is it normal to face rejection? Don't only losers experience rejection? (Discuss.)

- 🔊 Do you think God makes people go through difficult experiences? Why or why not?

- 🔊 What does it mean to "take up your cross and follow Jesus"?

- 🔊 To someone who doesn't know much about Jesus, how would you describe what Jesus promises us in Luke 9? ("For whoever wants to save his life will lose it, but whoever loses his life for me will save it.")

Get It?	High School

- 🔊 What are the ramifications for life if we'll always be facing some sort of rejection and suffering?

- 🔊 What makes Jesus' speech so revolutionary in regards to suffering, rejection, death, and resurrection?

- 🔊 In light of this talk, what does it mean to follow Jesus?

What If?	The Big Picture

- 🔊 Why do so many people try to avoid pain and suffering instead of embracing them?

- 🔊 What if life is just one big process of suffering, rejection, death, and resurrection? What would that mean for the way you view life?

- 🔊 What would you say to someone who thinks that Christianity is for people who have no real problems? Or to someone who thinks following Jesus should make life easy?

- 🔊 How would you share the story of Jesus with your friends who are in the middle of hard times?

So What?	It's Your Life

🔊 How can you cope with suffering and rejection, knowing what you've just learned?

🔊 In what ways do you try to avoid pain and suffering?

🔊 What difference will it make in your life this week to know that Jesus has experienced pain and suffering like you do?

🔊 What hope does resurrection offer?

Don't Be a Sucker!

Contributed by **Mark Oestreicher**

This outline is saved as GT02_15 on the CD-ROM.

Primary theme leaving Christianity	
Themes discipleship, choices, peer pressure, priorities	
Scripture Philemon 23-24; Colossians 4:14; 2 Timothy 4:9-10; Jonah 1:1-3; Judges 16:4-21; 2 Samuel 11:2-17	
Approximate length through The Grand Finale 30-40 minutes	

You'll need

- 🔊 Whiteboard
- 🔊 Marker
- 🔊 A personal story about a time when a friend (or you) walked away from her faith because it was just too hard
- 🔊 A personal story about a time when a friend of yours walked away from his faith because he loved worldly things more
- 🔊 A personal story about a time when a friend slowly turned away from God

This is a talk about fading away from Christ. So many of the teenagers in our youth groups will not be walking with Christ in any meaningful way in 10 years. This talk addresses that issue by looking at the rarely noticed New Testament example of Demas, one of Paul's disciples. After spending a considerable amount of time traveling with Paul and being discipled by Paul, we're told that Demas left Paul because of his love for the world. There are no clear answers given as to Demas' reasons for fading away (other than his love for the world). So this talk considers three ways people tend to fall away from Christ and looks at a biblical case study for each possibility.

intro
The Opening Act

🔊 Approximately 50 percent of churchgoing teenagers fade away from their faith within 10 years.

🔊 Brainstorming: Faith Chuckers (see sidebar)

🔊 Ask—What would it be like to have traveled around with the apostle Paul for five years? What impact would that have on your life?

🔊 Explanation: Paul's Disciples (see sidebar)

🔊 Scripture: Philemon 23-24 ("Epaphras, my fellow prisoner in Christ Jesus, sends you greetings. And so do Mark, Aristarchus, Demas and Luke, my fellow workers.") When Paul wrote to Philemon, he was in prison. It seems that Demas wasn't in prison with him but was somewhere in town nearby.

🔊 Scripture: Colossians 4:14 ("Our dear friend Luke, the doctor, and Demas send greetings.")

🔊 Scripture: 2 Timothy 4:9-10 ("Do your best to come to me quickly, for Demas, because he loved this world, has deserted me and has gone to Thessalonica.") Those first two passages were written at about the same time, but this last one was written about five years later.

🔊 Ask—What happened to Demas? Why did he toss his faith and desert Paul? And why do so many young adults desert their faith in the same way?

🔊 Transition by saying something like—One of the best ways to prevent this from happening in our own lives is to look at ways others have gone wrong. We're going to look at three common ways people fade away from their faith in God.

Brainstorming

Faith Chuckers

Using a whiteboard or overhead, work with your group to brainstorm a list of reasons why teenagers and young adults might walk away from their faith or settle for a watered-down, wimpy faith. This might include things like unanswered questions, busyness, or just a desire to walk on the wild side for a while. Don't respond one way or another to their ideas, just affirm them and write them on the list. (In other words, don't try to counter them or comment on them at this point.)

Paul's Disciples

Explain that just as Jesus traveled with a group of disciples, so did Paul. One of Paul's disciples was a guy named Demas. We know Demas was with Paul for a while because he's mentioned at the close of three of Paul's letters. (The first two were likely written around AD 62, and the last was written during his Roman imprisonment in AD 67.)

Explain that many of the pastoral books of the New Testament (books that were originally written as letters of encouragement and instruction to churches or individual people) close with some personal comments. Paul often sends greetings to certain people and mentions who is with him or what his needs are. This is the simple context in which Demas is mentioned.

heart of the talk

The Main Event

1. Wimping under the heat

- There is a strong possibility that this is what happened to Demas, as Paul was under constant persecution for his ministry. (He was in prison when he wrote all of these letters!)

- If you really live your life for Jesus, you're very likely going to take some heat for it.

- Personal illustration: My Wimpy Friend (see sidebar)

- Biblical illustration: Jonah (see sidebar)

My Wimpy Friend

Ideally, you will share an illustration of someone you knew who walked away from the faith for this reason. It could even be a part of your own story at some point in your past. For me, this is a story of a friend named John who got involved in a destructive and highly physical relationship. When several of his friends tried to lovingly suggest he reconsider the choices he was making and the effect these were having on his life, he responded by walking away from our friendship and his faith.

Jonah

Read Jonah 1:1–3. Explain that God was calling Jonah to a very specific, but challenging, task: Go confront the people of the city of Nineveh about their sin. Jonah freaked out and then wimped out. Instead of obeying God, he tried to run away! (As if we can really run away from God!) He jumped on a ship going the opposite direction and ignored God.

2. Derailed by bad priorities

🔊 Another strong possibility is that Demas chose temporary stuff over his long-range goal of living for Jesus. Paul says Demas left him because of his "love for the world."

🔊 This is extremely common for young adults, especially those who go away to college and put their faith on the back burner for a few years while pursuing other priorities.

🔊 Personal illustration: My Shortsighted Friend (see sidebar)

🔊 Biblical illustration: Samson (see sidebar)

My Shortsighted Friend

Share another personal illustration of a friend who chose a love of worldly stuff over a pursuit of God. Again, this may be best told as a part of your own story, if that's the case in your life. Be careful here not to glorify the sin your friend (or you) pursued at that time and to communicate that this path robs a person of the fullness of life God desires for us.

My story involves a friend named Steve who was more interested in partying and sex than in following Jesus. When I asked him about this in college, his answer was clear: "I only have a few good party years left. After that, I'll get more serious about following Jesus." To this day (20 years later) Steve is still saying the same thing.

Samson

Read Judges 16:4-21, then retell the story, starting with some background information. Samson had made a promise to God to be set apart. As part of this special thing he had going, God gave Samson superhuman strength. As a sign of his commitment to God Samson was never to cut his hair (kind of a weird sign, huh?).

But Samson had the hots for a woman named Delilah. It was one of those destructive relationships—she didn't really care about him at all. But he was very interested in the relationship he had with her. She kept pestering him to reveal the secret of his strength. The first two times she did this, Samson made up a fake answer. But when each of Delilah's attempts to remove his power failed, she just bothered him more and more to get him to reveal his secret to her.

The guy should have known better—especially after those first two times. But he was more interested in his short-term goal to stay with Delilah, so he sacrificed his long-term goal to stick with his commitment to God. After she whined and manipulated some more, he finally gave in and told her the truth about the true source of his power. Sure enough, later that day she cut off his hair while he was sleeping, and he lost his strength.

3. The slow fade

- This seems to be the most common form of falling away from Christ.
- This is a series of seemingly small choices, each not very far from the last, that slowly lead us away from the path of following God.
- Visualization: Turning Slowly (see sidebar)
- Personal illustration: My Slow-Fade Friend (see sidebar)
- Biblical illustration: David (see sidebar)

Turning Slowly

Help your students visualize this process by explaining it as a path of trajectory. Point straight ahead and say that this direction represents following God in my life. Then explain that you might make a small bad choice, like gossiping one time or watching a movie you know isn't a good choice for you. Turn to the left about 10 degrees and point in that direction. Point out that this choice doesn't seem like a big deal because it seems so easy to get back on the right path.

But then you make another bad choice (turn another 10 degrees and point in that direction), which isn't really that far off from the first choice. This second choice may be something as simple as not dealing with the first choice. And then you continue to make small adjustments, seemingly small choices that point you farther and farther away from God's path for your life (continue to turn as you explain).

Before you know it, you're heading down a path that is completely opposite from God's design for your life. (Now you should be facing backward; if you're not using a microphone, be sure to speak up, or students won't be able to hear you!) It's not that you deliberately set out to turn and run from God—it was a whole series of small choices, an incremental turning, a slow fade.

Personal illustration

My Slow-Fade Friend

Again, share a personal illustration of a friend of yours who slowly turned away from God like this. Make sure to point out that wherever the friend ended up is certainly not where they intended to be—it just happened over time with a series of smaller decisions.

Biblical illustration

David

Read 2 Samuel 11:2-17. Then retell the story. David, one of our greatest biblical examples of a man of faith, started out very innocently—just walking around on the roof of his palace. But then he noticed Bathsheba, a gorgeous woman who was bathing outside her home. It's likely that this was an innocent thing to notice—he just happened to see her. But at that point he made his first choice—to continue watching her. It didn't seem like a really big deal at the time. Then he made the additional choice to think about her, to fantasize about her. Next he makes a pretty big choice—he has her brought to him so he can sleep with her. Bad news: She gets pregnant. He tries to cover up his sin with a series of lies and manipulation. He brings her warrior husband home from battle, hoping the husband will sleep with her, which could explain her pregnancy. But the husband doesn't sleep with her. So David takes more drastic measures and has the husband killed.

Now, David didn't just wake up one day and decide he felt like committing murder. It was a series of smaller decisions that got him to that point—which didn't seem all that far from the path he'd already chosen.

closing

The Grand Finale

🔊 Ask—Which one of these biblical scenarios is most likely to happen to you?

🔊 The good news: It's possible to come back! We don't know what happened to Demas, but the men in the other three illustrations (Jonah, Samson, and David) all realized where they'd ended up and chose to fix where they'd gone wrong and return to God. This outcome is possible for any of you who have already faded from God.

🔊 The best fade prevention is:

- Pursuing a close, daily relationship with Jesus.

- Being aware of your own weaknesses and the possibility of "fade" in your life.

- Being accountable to friends who will help you see this stuff in your life.

discussion
Encore

Get It?	Middle School

- 📣 Who was Demas? What happened in his story?
- 📣 What are the three ways that people tend to fall away from God?
- 📣 What was the deal with Jonah? How was his story an example of "wimping under the heat"?
- 📣 What was the deal with Samson? How was his story an example of being "derailed by bad priorities"?
- 📣 What was the deal with David? How was his story an example of "the slow fade"?

Get It?	High School

- 📣 What's the basic storyline of Demas' life—at least the part we know?
- 📣 What are some of the possible reasons why Demas faded from the faith?
- 📣 What does "wimping under the heat" look like? What might it look like for a teenager today?
- 📣 What does being "derailed by bad priorities" look like? What might it look like for a teenager today?
- 📣 What does "the slow fade" look like? What might it look like for a teenager today?
- 📣 Which of those three do you think was the most likely scenario for what happened to Demas?

What If?	The Big Picture

- 📣 How would you react if people in your life started mocking you for your beliefs? What would you do?
- 📣 What if it was pointed out to you that your priorities aren't in the best order? How can you discern if that's true or not? How can you reorder your priorities?
- 📣 What kinds of things tend to be "slow-fade" decisions for students you know?
- 📣 How would it impact your life if you followed Demas' example and walked away from your faith?

So What?   It's Your Life

🔊 In what ways are you like Jonah—wimping under the heat and avoiding the stuff God is calling you to do?

🔊 In what ways are you like Samson—with messed-up priorities? Where are your priorities out of whack? How, specifically, can you reorder them?

🔊 In what ways are you like David, making small decisions that will lead you away from God? Think of some of those small decisions you've made in the past week and discuss them (if you're comfortable doing that).

🔊 If you're going to be a sucker for the world, like Demas, which of these three ways of exiting your faith would be most likely for you? Why?

🔊 Which of the prevention steps are in place in your life? How can you increase their effectiveness?

The Rules of Real Life

Contributed by **Mark Oestreicher**

Primary theme passionate living	
Themes discipleship, lordship, priorities, rules, behavior, evangelism	
Scripture Luke 5:18-20; Matthew 22:37-39; Galatians 2:20	
Approximate length through The Grand Finale 15-20 minutes	

You'll need

- A personal story about a time when you misunderstood a situation and it created an embarrassing situation for you

- Pictures of the Zilwaukee bridge (see note in the sidebar)

This is a short, punchy talk about living. It's a bit hyperbolic, pushing students to radical living. But today's students are ready for a radical life; they're ready to be challenged to give themselves completely to a cause or a truth. And we know the ultimate cause and the ultimate truth. This talk can easily be used as a call to action for Christian students or as an evangelistic talk, calling students who aren't Jesus followers to real living. The final point ("die") sets up a good opportunity to present the gospel and life in the upside-down kingdom of God.

intro

The Opening Act

🔊 Ask—Have you ever misunderstood a situation and created an embarrassing moment? (Allow enough time for students to share a couple examples.)

🔊 Personal illustration: My Misunderstanding (see sidebar)

🔊 Background: Rules Are Part of Life! (see sidebar)

🔊 Illustration: The Zilwaukee Bridge (see sidebar)

🔊 Transition by saying something like—I want to talk about three little rules—one small set of rules—that come from the Bible. And this set of rules will give you the best life possible.

Personal illustration

My Misunderstanding

Tell a story from your own life about a time when you misunderstood a situation (what someone was talking about, the rules of a game, what was expected of you) and it created an embarrassing situation for you.

For example, a couple I could share would be loudly singing lyrics to a popular song, only to find I was totally singing the wrong words—or the time I told a group of junior highers on a mission trip that "the hole in my butt was getting bigger" when I really meant that the hole in my pants was getting bigger.

End this illustration by mentioning what a bummer it is when we misunderstand things. Sometimes it only creates humorous or embarrassing situations, but something the results can be more extreme.

Background

Rules Are Part of Life!

Everyone lives by a set of rules. Some rules are imposed on you—like school rules and rules at home. Other sets of rules are ones you choose. For example, most friendship groups have spoken or unspoken rules, and all faith systems—even atheism!—have rules.

Some of the rule sets people choose are

• "Be a good person"—This says that the best way to live life is to be good, then hopefully your "good stuff" will outweigh your "bad stuff."

• "Live for yourself" or "Go for the gusto"—this more selfish set of rules says to do anything that pleases you.

• "Be a safe Christian" or "Be like us"—this is a lousy set of rules found in a lot of churches: play it safe, don't take risks, don't rock the boat, and above all act and look just like us.

The Zilwaukee Bridge

North of Detroit, Michigan, the I-75 freeway spans a long, high bridge over a now-unused shipping channel. It's called the Zilwaukee Bridge. When the freeway was first built, they put a drawbridge over the channel. It seemed like a good idea at the time, but it turned out to be ridiculous because both directions of freeway traffic would have to come to a complete stop for long periods of time to allow the bridge to raise up and ships to pass through. This created nightmarish traffic jams.

Eventually plans were laid to construct a new superbridge that would take traffic high enough over the channel that ships could easily pass underneath. After years of construction, the bridge was close to completion. Only the section out over the water itself remained to be completed. It was then that a miscalculation in the weight of a section caused it to tip slightly on its pilings. The result, though it seemed so minor at the time, was disastrous. There was no way to complete the bridge as it was; there was no simple way to correct this error or compensate for it.

Construction stopped, and the unfinished bridge sat there for a couple more years. Finally, at enormous additional expense, most of the bridge had to be torn down and the project started over.

Unfortunately, many people live their lives this way! They go through life committed to a set of rules or to a way of living. And in the end, they realize they were living with a misunderstanding, a wrong calculation, the wrong set of rules—and they've missed out on life!

(Note: while giving this example, it would be ideal if you could show pictures of the bridge. There's a government Web site that contains a history of the project (http://www.michiganhighways.org/indepth/zilwaukee.html) with pictures of the old bridge, the new bridge under construction (with the unfinished gap), and the completed new bridge. If your group is small, print a few of these photos and show them while you talk. If your group is larger, download them to a computer and show them on a TV or project them onto a screen using PowerPoint or MediaShout.)

heart of the talk

The Main Event

1. Live dangerously.

🔊 This isn't about doing stupid stuff or even about living an adrenaline-filled, X Games life. This is about taking risks—living out of your comfort zone.

🔊 Scripture: Luke 5:18-20 ("Some men came carrying a paralytic on a mat and tried to take him into the house to lay him before Jesus. When they could not find a way to do this because of the crowd, they went up on the roof and lowered him on his mat through the tiles into the middle of the crowd, right in front of Jesus. When Jesus saw their faith, he said, 'Friend, your sins are forgiven.'")

> • This was a radical, dangerous, risky course of action. It was no more appropriate in Jesus' day to tear a hole in someone's roof than it would be to do so today.

🔊 The kind of "dangerous living" we're talking about here is a "dangerous pursuit of Jesus." Don't settle for wimpy living. Get out of your comfort zone and take a chance on God.

2. Live passionately.

🔊 We're not talking about romantic passion! The "rule" here is to live life to its fullest—to be passionate about whatever you do. This is the life God wants for you!

🔊 Scripture: Matthew 22:37-39 ("Jesus replied: '"Love the Lord your God with all your heart and with all your soul and with all your mind." This is the first and greatest commandment. And the second is like it: "Love your neighbor as yourself."'")

🔊 Jesus sums up passionate living in these verses—love God and love others. According to Jesus these are the two greatest commandments. Give your life over to these two pursuits, and you will really experience life!

The third rule may surprise you! In order to really live, you have to—

3. Die.

🔊 We're not talking about physical death here. We're talking about giving up our lives. (Note: If you're speaking to young teens, you need be extra careful on the "die" point. With their often-weak ability to think abstractly, you'll want to make sure they understand what you mean by this. Also, be sensitive if a student recently lost a loved one to death—that's not the point of this talk.)

🔊 Scripture: Galatians 2:20 ("I have been crucified with Christ and I no longer live, but Christ lives in me. The life I live in the body, I live by faith in the Son of God, who loved me and gave himself for me.")

🔊 Paul says this so well: we have to give up our lives in order to really live.

🔊 This is a daily process—a choice to give God leadership in our decisions, our plans, and our priorities. When I choose to live for myself, I forfeit my real opportunity to live!

closing

The Grand Finale

- 🔊 Remind students of the Zilwaukee Bridge illustration.

- 🔊 Remind them that many people live their lives by the wrong set of rules; in doing so, they give up the opportunity to live passionate, wild, and wonderful lives.

- 🔊 God gives us these three radical rules: Live Dangerously, Live Passionately, and Die!

discussion

Encore

Get It?	Middle School

- 🔊 Do you agree that everyone lives by "sets of rules"?

- 🔊 What sets of rules do you see students in your school living by?

- 🔊 What are some of the unspoken rules of certain friendship groups?

- 🔊 What does it mean to "live dangerously"? How is this different than being someone who takes physical risks, such as crazy skateboard moves or walking on the edge of a cliff?

- 🔊 What's passion? What does it mean to live passionately? What does that look like in the life of a teenager?

- 🔊 So, to live we have to die? What does that mean? What does that look like in the life of a teenager?

Get It?	High School

- 🔊 How are some people living their lives like the construction of the Zilwaukee Bridge? What does that look like in the life of a teenager?

- 🔊 What does "living dangerously" look like in the life of a student? How is that a spiritual thing?

- 🔊 What does passion look like in the life of a teenager?

- 🔊 When can passion be a harmful thing? When is it a good thing?

- 🔊 How could passion be a spiritual thing?

- 🔊 So, we're supposed to die. What does that mean? What does that look like?

149

What If? | The Big Picture

- How might your family respond to you if you suddenly start living with passion and risk?

- How might your friends and classmates respond to you if you suddenly start living this way?

- What do you give up if you choose not to live this way?

So What? | It's Your Life

- In what ways are you living by the wrong set of rules? How can you identify that and change it?

- What are some practical ideas for living dangerously this week?

- What risks might God be asking you to take?

- How can you find more passion for the things that honor God? What would that look like this week?

- If you were to choose to "die to yourself" tomorrow, what would it look like? Are you willing to do that?

A Few Things You Don't Have to Do

Contributed by **Mark Oestreicher**

Primary theme grace	
Themes salvation, forgiveness, rules, evangelism, church, freedom, assurance	
Scripture Matthew 22:37-39; 1 John 5:12-13; Matthew 10:29-31	
Approximate length through The Grand Finale 20-30 minutes	

You'll need

- Whiteboard
- Marker

Often students hear two primary sets of things about what it means to live the Christian life: all the things you can't do and all the things you have to do. Of course this leads to legalism—which is exactly what Jesus slammed the Pharisees for preaching and living. This talk is intended to provide some space, to communicate what we don't have to do. It identifies three common things students try to do that waste their energy on wrong assumptions about what it means to live in God's story. Since it's an assumption-overturning talk, it works well as an evangelistic talk also.

intro
The Opening Act

🔊 Brainstorming: "Have to Do" and "Can't Do" (see sidebar)

🔊 Transition by saying something like—We often spend too much time in church talking about all the things you have to do and all the things you can't do. The truth is, there are many things you just don't have to do. We're going to talk about three of those things, and my hope is that they will free some of you from living in a way that God didn't intend for you to live.

Brainstorming

"Have to Do" and "Can't Do"

Using a whiteboard or a flip chart, brainstorm two lists with your group. First, write THINGS YOU HAVE TO DO and ask your group to name the things people say they have to do in order to be a "good Christian." If your kids are wise to you and start explaining about grace and how we don't have to do much, push them to list things people think of when they think of Christians. The list might include things like: go to church, read your Bible, pray, do good things, memorize Scripture, or follow the Ten Commandments.

After you've developed a good list, create a second list with the heading, THINGS YOU CAN'T DO. This list might include things like: partying, sex, drugs, and all those other no-no's we always talk about.

heart of the talk
The Main Event

1. You don't have to live by a huge set of rules.

🔊 When people spend all their time talking about how we "can't do this and can't do that," it's called "legalism."

🔊 Jesus constantly nailed the Pharisees (the religious leaders of his time) for this kind of thinking.

🔊 Scripture: Matthew 22:37-39 ("Jesus replied: '"Love the Lord your God with all your heart and with all your soul and with all your mind." This is the first and greatest commandment. And the second is like it: "Love your neighbor as yourself."'") Jesus gives us two simple rules: Love God and love others.

🔊 Illustration: Loving God

🔊 Does this eliminate the need to address sin in our lives? Of course not—if we focus on loving God, we'll want to address those areas of our lives. But our motivation changes.

Loving God

Some junior high students were on a mission trip. They were at a camp for handicapped kids and were doing physical work to prepare the camp for its summer programs. One of their tasks was to drain and clean the pool, which was half-filled with disgusting water that had been sitting over the winter months. The pump broke, and the pool had to be emptied by hand—with buckets. It was hard work and totally gross.

One day the students were really struggling and having a very difficult time maintaining a good attitude while they emptied the pool. Their youth worker encouraged the kids to think about doing this work for Jesus. Then it started raining, and the work got even more frustrating.

After lightning caused them to leave the pool area, the youth worker noticed one boy, Jim, was still down in the deep end scooping up buckets of stagnant water and throwing the water up over the edge of the pool. Jim was working really hard! The youth worker went over in the rain to call Jim out of the pool. He noticed that Jim had a huge, messy smile on his face.

The youth worker asked, "Jim, what's going on?" Jim replied with great excitement, "I'm just showing Jesus how much I love him!"

2. You don't have to wonder about your place in heaven.

🔊 If you've chosen to be a Jesus follower, your future is sealed!

🔊 Scripture: 1 John 5:12 ("He who has the Son has life; he who does not have the Son of God does not have life.") Heaven starts now! It's not just a place "out there" where we go "someday."

🔊 Say—The next verse says, "I write these things to you who believe in the name of the Son of God so that you may be pretty sure that you have eternal life." (Then correct yourself and reveal that's not what the verse says.)

🔊 Scripture 1 John 5:13 ("I write these things to you who believe in the name of the Son of God so that you may know that you have eternal life." (emphasis mine))

🔊 Ask—How many things in life can you be totally, 100-percent sure of? (Not much—even death isn't really a given since Jesus could return before we die!) But this truth—that we can know we have eternal life—is sure.

🔊 Illustration: The $100,000 Gift (see sidebar)

Illustration

The $100,000 Gift

If someone gave me a gift of $100,000, and I was to say, "Wow, I was thinking of buying this pack of gum; would that be okay?" they'd answer, "Of course, it's your money! It was a gift!"

And if I were to put it in a safety deposit box at a bank, then return a week later and ask the clerk, "Is it really okay for me to see the money?" the clerk would look at me like I'm an idiot and say, "Of course, it's your money."

To treat the $100,000 as if it has strings attached to it is to insult the gift giver! The same is true when we question the undeserved gift of life God gives to us.

3. You don't have to earn God's approval.

📢 You already have God's approval!

📢 Have students repeat these phrases after you:
- There's nothing I can do to make God love me more.
- There's nothing I can do to make God love me less.

📢 Illustration: Earning God's Love (see sidebar)

📢 Scripture: Matthew 10:29-31 ("Are not two sparrows sold for a penny? Yet not one of them will fall to the ground apart from the will of your Father. And even the very hairs of your head are all numbered. So don't be afraid; you are worth more than many sparrows.")

📢 Explanation: Sparrows and Numbered Hairs (see sidebar)

Illustration

Earning God's Love

Tell students to pay attention as you read the following story and notice how similar—yet different in one way—this true story is from the earlier true story about Jim in the pool.

A group of students was on a mission trip in northern Minnesota working alongside a small Native American church. Other than a wood-burning stove in the basement, the church building didn't have heat. So they needed a large stock of wood to make it through the winter. The students on the trip spent a good amount of their time in the woods, picking up logs cut by the youth worker, stacking them in a truck, and bringing them back to the church.

One hot and humid afternoon, the group decided to go swimming at a nearby lake to cool off. When they left the woodpile, one girl kept working. The youth worker went back to get her. He yelled to her, "Jackie, come on!" But she kept working, picking up logs that weighed almost half her own weight and heaving them down off the pile onto the ground.

When the youth worker climbed the pile and tapped Jackie on the back, she spun around and he noticed she was crying.

He asked, "Jackie, what's going on?"

She answered, "I just want God to love me!"

Jackie sadly thought she was unlovable, but if she worked hard enough, maybe God could love her.

Sparrows and Numbered Hairs

At first, these words of Jesus' might seem a bit strange. First, it's important to realize that when coming to the temple to offer sacrifices, the Jewish people could purchase animals in the temple courtyards. The most inexpensive animals for sale were small birds, such as sparrows. They sold "two for a penny." Jesus is making the point that they're almost worthless; but they're still highly valued by God.

Then Jesus goes on to mention that our head hairs are numbered! He's not making the point that God knows more trivia than anyone else. He's saying that God knows more about us than we even know about ourselves. God knows everything about us: our hopes, our fears, our dark secrets, everything.

Then Jesus brings it back to the sparrows and communicates an amazing truth: God's love for us isn't at a distance. God knows everything about us, and he still loves us!

closing

The Grand Finale

◀ᴵᴵ Review the three things we don't have to do.

◀ᴵᴵ Introduce the wonderful spiritual concept of freedom: that God wants us to live free lives without burdens and legalism.

◀ᴵᴵ Close your time in prayer, thanking God for these incredible truths.

discussion

Encore

Get It?	Middle School

◀ᴵᴵ Why don't we have to live our lives by a big set of rules? If that's true, what about all the stuff like the Ten Commandments?

◀ᴵᴵ So, no one has to worry about their place in heaven? Who doesn't?

◀ᴵᴵ Explain the $100,000 gift example.

◀ᴵᴵ How come we can't make God love us more or less? Why doesn't our sin make God love us less and our good deeds make God love us more?

◀ᴵᴵ Explain the verse about sparrows and numbered hairs. What does it have to do with God loving us?

Get It?   High School

- What are the two rules Jesus gives us? What about all the other rules?

- Aren't there still other things we're supposed to do and not do? Where do they fit?

- How can our place in heaven be locked in? How come we don't lose that if we screw up?

- Why is there nothing we can do to make God love us more or less? Does that make good deeds a waste of time and sin not a big deal? (Discuss.)

What If?   The Big Picture

- What would it look like for you to totally give yourself to living by those two rules Jesus gave us (love God, love others)? What would change in your life? What might some of the implications be? How would people in your life respond to you if you started living this way?

- What if you did have to earn your way to heaven? What would life be like?

- What if God were fickle—if he would love us more or less based on our behavior? How would that affect our lives?

So What?   It's Your Life

- Which of these three truths did you most need to hear today? Why?

- What needs to change based on your reminder or new understanding of this truth? What will that look like this week?

- What's the "cost" of ignoring these truths?

Lessons
on
Righteousness
from a Kid

Contributed by **Mark Oestreicher**

This outline is saved as GTO2_18 on the CD-ROM.

Lessons on Righteousness from a Kid

Primary theme righteousness	
Themes discipleship, temptation, standards, obedience, influence, peer pressure, focus, priorities	
Scripture 2 Kings 21–24	
Approximate length through The Grand Finale 30-40 minutes	

King Josiah is one of the more amazing case studies in the Bible: a kid king who passionately lived for God in the middle of evil. His life story is rich with application for us today, and especially for teenagers, since Josiah was a young adult when he did most of this stuff.

You'll need

- A pair of horse blinders would be great, if you can get your hands on a pair (otherwise, just describe them)

- Two personal stories about a time when you either influenced someone else or were influenced by someone else—one major and one minor

- A professional camera with a telephoto lens (one you can focus manually) or a pair of binoculars with a focus wheel

- Blank paper and pens for journaling (optional)

intro

The Opening Act

🔊 Say—Today we're going to talk about righteousness. What's that? (Field some responses; try to land on a working definition that includes right living and a heart given to God—right living alone isn't a whole definition.)

🔊 Ask—Does it ever seem like being righteous is tough because of all the bad or evil stuff surrounding us every day? (Discuss.)

🔊 Say—We're going to look at a guy who was also surrounded by evil. His name is Josiah.

🔊 Scripture: 2 Kings 21:1-18 (Manasseh did evil in the eyes of the Lord.)

🔊 Scripture: 2 Kings 21:19-26 (Amon did evil in the eyes of the Lord.)

🔊 Josiah comes next in the lineup, but we'll come back to him.

🔊 Scripture: 2 Kings 23:31-35 (Jehoahaz did evil in the eyes of the Lord.)

🔊 Scripture: 2 Kings 23:36-24:7 (Jehoiakim did evil in the eyes of the Lord.)

🔊 Scripture: 2 Kings 24:8-17 (Jehoiachin did evil in the eyes of the Lord.)

🔊 Scripture: 2 Kings 24:18-20 (Zedekiah did evil in the eyes of the Lord.)

🔊 So, two kings who reigned before Josiah and four kings who reigned after Josiah are all remembered with the phrase, "He did evil in the eyes of the Lord."

🔊 Scripture: 2 Kings 22:1-2 (Josiah did right in the eyes of the Lord.)

🔊 Transition by saying something like—We're going to look at Josiah's action plan—four steps that helped him in his pursuit of righteousness.

heart of the talk

The Main Event

1. Wear blinders.

🔊 Scripture: 2 Kings 22:2 ("He did what was right in the eyes of the Lord and walked in all the ways of his father David, not turning aside to the right or to the left.")

🔊 Object lesson: Horse Blinders (see sidebar)

🔊 Of course, you're not suggesting that students strap horse blinders to their heads! The idea is to live like Josiah did, not turning to the left or the right—keeping focused on the goal of living for God.

🔊 In our lives, standards can act like blinders—predetermining our behavior. For example, if you have a standard that you will not, under any circumstance, be involved in sexual activity before you get married, that will function like a pair of blinders in your life. You can't set that standard when you're in the middle of a passionate moment; it has to be set ahead of time.

🔊 Brainstorming: Ask the students to name more examples of "life standards" that would be good to have in place before any temptations arise.

🔊 Illustration: Carding 30-Year-Olds (see sidebar)

Object lesson

Horse Blinders

It'd be great if you could get your hands on a pair of horse blinders. But if you can't find a pair, then just describe them to the group. Racehorse owners put these blinders (little pieces of leather that block the animal's side view) on their horses to keep them looking forward during a race. They prevent the horse from seeing what's on their left or right and from being distracted by the other horses. They're essential to a racehorse because without them the horse would be easily distracted from its goal.

Illustration

Carding 30-Year-Olds

Some convenience stores (like 7-Eleven®, Circle K®, and the like) have a small sign posted near their cash registers that expresses a simple policy: WE CARD ANYONE WHO LOOKS 30 OR YOUNGER. Carding people who wish to buy alcohol (which means asking them to prove they're at least 21 years old by showing some form of identification with their picture on it) is something the store clerks have to enforce.

Prior to the creation of this policy, store clerks had to guess if someone looked 21 or not. If they didn't look old enough, then the clerk would ask them to show their ID. This involved too much guesswork. So the storeowners wanted to create a simple "blinder"—an easy way to help the store clerks stop guessing. And the 30-year-old age barrier accomplished this task. Unless you're obviously older than 30, you're gonna get carded if you try to buy alcohol at one of these stores.

In the same way, we—like Josiah—can create "rules" for ourselves that will act as blinders to keep us from making bad choices.

2. Radical obedience

- Explanation: No Bible (see sidebar)

- Scripture: 2 Kings 22:3-11 ("When the king heard the words of the Book of the Law, he tore his robes.")

- Explanation: Obedience Spree (see sidebar)

- Radical obedience = doing whatever is right, no matter what the cost.

- Obedience is often considered a "bad" word in our world—it sounds like oppression. But obeying God is really in our best interests since God knows what's best for us and loves us perfectly.

- Illustration: Schoolyard Restraint (see sidebar)

Explanation

No Bible

Josiah wanted to live for God and lead his people to do the same. But this was difficult because during the years of evil kings before him, the Scripture (the "Book of the Law" or Deuteronomy in our Bibles) had been lost in the temple. The high priest didn't even know it existed! It was lost on a shelf in a dusty closet. So Josiah had no instructions, at least not good ones, regarding what God wanted from him.

He decided it would be a good thing to fix up the temple a bit, and then goes about the task of getting that going. In the midst of this cleaning and renovation work, the high priest finds this scroll, the book of Deuteronomy, and gives it to Josiah's assistant, who brings it back and reads it to Josiah.

Explanation

Obedience Spree

When Josiah tore his robes after hearing the Scripture, it was the ultimate sign of sorrow or grief. At that moment he realized just how far he and his people had strayed from God's desires for them.

So Josiah went on an obedience spree. The next chapter-and-a-half of 2 Kings describes the work he did, which included tearing down and burning the temples that were used to worship other gods and purging the land of idols. This obedience spree is costly, time consuming, and difficult—but Josiah goes the distance.

(Note: If you want to read this part of the story to your students (the rest of chapter 22 and 23:4-30), feel free—but there are many things in the description that will require some explanation.)

Schoolyard Restraint

This is a true story: Nathan was a missionary kid from Africa. His mom and dad worked with a small tribe there, and he'd lived with his parents his whole life. He'd even been home-schooled by them.

Then he moved to suburban Chicago when his parents started working for the mission board. Several weeks later, Nathan started attending a public middle school with more students than the entire population of the African tribe he'd lived with his whole life so far. He was picked on constantly because of his funny way of saying things and his lack of understanding about current fashion trends.

Every day after school Nathan had to walk through a large field on his way home. A group of boys from school would hide in the field, surprise him, form a circle around him, and then beat him up. This went on day after day, and the school couldn't seem to stop it.

Nathan's youth worker was furious about the situation and wanted action! But at some point the bullying stopped, and nothing was ever done.

A few weeks later, Nathan's parents revealed something to the youth worker that was quite surprising. While growing up among the tribesmen, Nathan had been trained in a local form of fighting—kind of like an African version of martial arts. Over the years Nathan had progressed in his training until he was now able to simultaneously take on a number of grown men and defeat them.

In other words, Nathan could have wasted those guys in the schoolyard. But he was convinced that God didn't want him to fight back. During the next two years, Nathan brought many of those bullies to youth group events at his church, and a couple of them chose to become Jesus followers. Now that's radical obedience! What might God be calling you to do—something risky?

3. Influence

🔊 Scripture: 2 Kings 23:1-3 (The Israelites renew the covenant to follow the Lord and keep his commands with all their hearts and souls.)

🔊 Explanation: Me First, You Follow (see sidebar)

🔊 We influence people every day—sometimes positively, sometimes negatively, sometimes in small ways, sometimes in large ways.

🔊 Personal illustration: Influence (see sidebar)

🔊 Brainstorming: Ask—Who do you have the ability to influence?

Explanation

Me First, You Follow

There are a couple very important things to notice in this amazing piece of Josiah's story. First, when he decides to renew the covenant with God, he does so publicly—in front of all the people. It would have been perfectly acceptable for Josiah to formalize this covenant renewal in the temple with just the high priest or maybe a bunch of priests standing around. But the passage says he called together "all the people from the least to the greatest" (verse 2). Josiah wanted everyone in on this God thing. To him, this was not just a formality of government or religion.

Then Josiah does something quite amazing: he publicly states—all by himself—his intent to follow God with all his heart and soul. And after Josiah did this, "all the people pledged themselves to the covenant" (verse 3). Remember—Josiah was king. It would have been easy and acceptable in those days for him to issue a decree that the people of this land had to live in the covenant. Instead, Josiah models that renewal for the people. He used his influence to basically say, "Look, do what I'm doing."

Personal illustration

Influence

Share two personal illustrations of influence where you were either influenced or you were the influencer. It's important that one story shows a major influence (choosing a career, deciding to move) and the other shows a minor influence—something very "everyday." Kids tend to think of influence only in terms of the big stuff, so it's important to illustrate the small stuff too. They need to see that they are influenced and can be influencers every day.

4. Focus

🔊 Before revealing the final point, read the last Scripture passage—
2 Kings 23:25 ("Neither before nor after Josiah was there a king like him who turned to the Lord as he did—with all his heart and with all his soul and with all his strength, in accordance with all the Law of Moses.")

🔊 Point out the four "all" phrases in the passage:
  • "with all his heart"
  • "with all his soul"
  • "with all his strength"
  • "in accordance with all the Law of Moses" (commitment to Scripture)

🔊 Object lesson: Camera or Binoculars (see sidebar)

🔊 Ask—What are you focusing on? (For many, it could be getting into college, succeeding at a certain sport, or finding popular friends.)

🔊 The lesson on righteousness from Josiah's life is to make God our primary focus.

Object lesson

Camera or Binoculars

The best thing to use for this object lesson is a professional camera with a big telephoto lens you can adjust with your hand (not a little digi-cam!). Of course, being the crafty youth worker you are, you can certainly make do with something else. (Binoculars that have a focus wheel or lens will also work.)

Point the lens at someone in the front of your room but line it up so people seated at the back are also in the picture (if you're standing on a stage, you may have to step down to do this). Mention what you see: so-and-so is in focus, so-and-so in the back is also in the picture but isn't in focus, and so on.

Now change the focus without changing the perspective. Point out to your students how after you adjusted the focus the same two people are still in the picture, but the person in the back row is in focus, and the person up front is no longer in focus.

This is the lesson from Josiah's life! Josiah focused solely on God (with all his heart, soul, and strength). Being the king, he certainly had other things in his life that needed attention—but they were secondary. His primary focus was on God and on following God.

closing

The Grand Finale

🔊 Remind students that Josiah wasn't an old man. He's a great example for us—and especially for teenagers—because he set out on this course as a teenager and young adult.

🔊 Review the four lessons from Josiah's life: wear blinders, radical obedience, influence, and focus.

🔊 End your time in prayer, asking God to help everyone be more like Josiah. Invite students to choose one of the ideas from Josiah's life and spend some individual time in prayer about that one idea.

🔊 Consider having students spend 10 minutes journaling about what it would mean in their lives to follow Josiah's example in one of the four ways.

discussion
Encore

Get It?   Middle School

- Tell me everything you remember about Josiah, starting with the biographical stuff (how old he was, stuff like that).

- Why is it especially significant that Josiah did "what was right in the eyes of the Lord"?

- Why did Josiah tear his robe?

- How did Josiah influence other people?

- What's the difference between the four ways Josiah focused on God—the four "alls"?

Get It?   High School

- Retell the high points of Josiah's life story.

- What did "radical obedience" look like in Josiah's life? Why was it radical?

- Why was the way Josiah went about renewing the covenant significant? How did he influence people?

- Why can't we focus on lots of things at one time? What happens when we try to do that?

What If?   The Big Picture

- Josiah didn't have any Scripture to guide him until it was found in the temple. What would it be like to try to live for God if we didn't have the Bible?

- It's one thing for people serving in leadership roles to influence people. But how can normal, everyday students without positions of leadership influence others? How can shy people influence others?

- How can we rethink obedience as a positive word?

So What?   It's Your Life

- What's a standard you need to set in your life right now?

- What's one area where God is calling you to obedience but you've been resisting?

- Who can you try to influence for God this week? How will you do it?

- What one or two things tend to draw your focus away from God? Should that thing or things be eliminated from your life or just moved to a different level of focus in your life? How can you go about doing that?

Mo's Wild River Ride

Primary theme faith	
Themes God's provision, growth, courage, trust	
Scripture Exodus 2:1-10; Exodus 6:20; Numbers 26:59; Job 19:25-27; Jeremiah 29:11	
Approximate length through The Grand Finale 30-40 minutes	

You'll need

- A $1, $5, or $10 bill

- A personal story about a time when God provided a solution that was beyond what you were praying for

T his talk revolves around the amazing story of one of the Bible's heroes of faith— Moses' mother (Jochebed). Truly, she practiced more radical faith than most of us, especially in her somewhat crazy act of floating her son down the river. There are a few wonderful lessons on faith in this little 10-verse section of Scripture. Most of your kids have either heard the story or seen it portrayed in the animated movie, *The Prince of Egypt*. Don't let that be a distraction—instead, plunge in and bring some new life to this story.

Contributed by **Mark Oestreicher**

This outline is saved as GTO_01 on the CD-ROM.

intro

The Opening Act

🔊 Activity: Faith (see sidebar)

🔊 Explanation: Who's Jochebed? (see sidebar)

🔊 Explanation: Before Exodus 2 (see sidebar)

🔊 Scripture: Exodus 2:1-4 ("But when she could hide him no longer, she got a papyrus basket for him and coated it with tar and pitch. Then she placed the child in it and put it among the reeds along the bank of the Nile. His sister stood at a distance to see what would happen to him.")

🔊 Explanation: Mo's Wild River Ride (see sidebar)

Activity

Faith

Consider opening your time with some kind of crowd breaker or activity that is an illustration of faith. Check out *Ideas: Crowd Breakers & Mixers* (books one and two) (Zondervan/Youth Specialties, 1997 and 2003) or a book of team-building games like John Losey's *Experiential Ministry Handbook* (Zondervan/Youth Specialties, 2004). There are dozens of games and activities that could be used as an opener here.

Here's one simple idea: trust sit. Have a student come to the front of the room and blindfold her. Place a chair directly behind the teen and tell her you've done so. (It's key that you do this without the seat making any sound at all—the student can't have any evidence that the chair actually exists.) Ask her if she trusts you. Then ask her to sit down—without using her hands to feel if the chair is really there. If she's willing to sit down, she will undoubtedly do so with great trepidation, very slowly.

It's an easy segue into a discussion about why it's difficult to have faith when we can't see things (which is kind of the definition of faith). (Note: Don't be a bonehead youth worker and decide it would be funny not to place the chair behind her.)

Who's Jochebed?

I've asked this question dozens of times at youth groups, church services, and Christian schools: Who's Jochebed? (By the way, I've always pronounced her name JOE-sha-bed but have also heard JOCK-a-bed. And in the movie *The Prince of Egypt* they use the more Hebrew sounding yo-HEH-bed.) Very rarely has anyone I've asked, teen or adult, known who she is. So, if you have a group of church kids, it's fun to dangle a dollar or even a five- or ten-dollar bill (if you're feeling lucky!) and say you'll give it to the first person who tells you who Jochebed is. Acknowledge that it's someone in the Bible, but try not to reveal her gender (which would greatly narrow down the choices!).

If you feel like giving away your money anyhow, start giving clues at some point: Jochebed is a woman; you totally know her story, you just don't know her name; she had a very famous son; she was in the movie *The Prince of Egypt*. (By the way, her name is mentioned in two places in the Bible: Exodus 6:20 and Numbers 26:59).

Reveal the answer and introduce "Jo" as one of the most amazing women of faith in the history of the world—a great example to all of us.

Before Exodus 2

Take a moment to set the scene for this story. You'll need to modify this, based on the Bible knowledge of your group. But even the most Bible-familiar students could use a little review. I say something like this—many of you have heard the story of Joseph, the guy with the colorful coat whose brothers didn't like him much and sold him into slavery. He was taken down to Egypt, in Northern Africa. You might remember that God lifted him out of slavery, and he became the second in charge of the kingdom, working for the pharaoh. During a time of widespread famine throughout the region, he brought his entire family down to Egypt so they wouldn't starve, and things were going well.

Joseph's family (his father and 11 brothers) made up the whole Hebrew people at this point. We lose track of them for a bunch of decades, and when we pick up the story again, a few things have changed: they're still in Egypt, but now they're slaves, working on a new pharaoh's huge building campaign (things like the pyramids and the sphinx that are still there today); and, they're numbers have grown to thousands of people.

Pharaoh (like a king, but considered a god) decided there were too many Hebrew baby boys being born and that they might one day present a problem for him. So he issued a hideous decree—that all Hebrew baby boys under the age of two should be taken from their mothers and thrown into the Nile River to drown. This is the time when Moses was born.

Explanation

Mo's Wild River Ride

Retell the story—partly to keep it fresh for kids who've heard it a hundred times and partly to point out a few key things. Mention that normally the birth of a boy would be cause for great rejoicing; but in this context, it must have been cause for great fear. Jochebed lived every minute in the knowledge that at any moment the guards might invade her little slave hut and take her baby away to be drowned.

Talk about how newborns cry a lot but not very loudly. However, when babies are a few months old, their lungs are more developed, and their crying gets significantly louder. Undoubtedly, Jochebed realized she wasn't going to be able to keep Mo hidden any longer.

She was desperate for a solution. Surely, she was crying out to God to help her; she was thinking of every possible option and coming up with nothing. So she does this somewhat crazy thing: she waterproofs a paper basket and floats her son down the river! It was clearly an act of faith—like she was saying to God, "Look, I don't see any solutions here, and I'm desperate. I'm going to take this crazy step of faith and believe that you're going to do something with it."

heart of the talk
The Main Event

1. Sometimes faith is all you have to hold on to.

- Sometimes our lives feel totally out of control. If you haven't experienced this yet, you will at some point.

- Maybe things are really tough at home (parents fighting, divorce, living with a new stepparent), or maybe you've lost someone you love, or maybe you're having problems with friends or at school.

- Jochebed certainly felt out of control—as if there were no good solutions to her problem.

- Set up the passage from Job by mentioning that he was a guy who had lost everything: family, home, wealth, a profitable business, even his health. And his friends were giving him bad advice about why this had happened to him.

- Scripture: Job 19:25-27 ("I know that my Redeemer lives, and that in the end he will stand upon the earth. And after my skin has been destroyed, yet in my flesh I will see God; I myself will see him with my own eyes—I, and not another. How my heart yearns within me!")

- When our lives seem totally out of control, we have to (like Job) choose to believe that God is in control.

- Illustration: He Said What? (see sidebar)

He Said What?

Thirteen-year-old Blake was getting baptized in front of the entire church. He was asked to say something about what God meant to him, and he blurted out, "Well, when my dad died, it was hard; but God made it suck less." At first the congregation flinched because Blake had used a word that wasn't often said in church! But then, slowly, people began to spontaneously applaud because they realized Blake had said something very profound in his own way.

2. God wants you to put action to your faith.

◁)) Scripture review: Into the River (see sidebar)

◁)) Ask—Have you ever tried something you weren't sure about, but you took the risk anyway?

◁)) Illustration: Supreme Court (see sidebar)

◁)) Ask—Where might God be calling you to put some action to your faith? (Offer a moment of silence for students to think about this, then suggest the following options and give them a few seconds to ponder each idea.) Maybe—

    • Reaching out to a lonely kid at school or in our youth group?

    • Obeying and respecting your parents even when you don't want to, just because you believe God wants you to?

    • Opening your mouth and sharing with someone the hope you have in Jesus Christ?

Into the River

Remind students of the details of Jochebed's boat launch. Review how crazy it must have seemed at the time, even to her. Point out that it was an active step of faith. She was clearly communicating to God: I don't know what to do, and I see no good solutions, but I trust you can save my baby. So I'm floating him out in the river as an act of faith.

Illustration

Supreme Court

In the late 1980s, when many public junior high and high schools were struggling with what "separation of church and state" meant when it came to religious groups being allowed to meet on campus, one high school girl at Westside High School in Omaha, Nebraska, decided to take a stand.

She was a perfectly normal girl, by the way—not a student leader or the most popular girl on campus. She wanted to meet with her Christian friends once a week to have a time of prayer together—a Christian club of sorts. When the principal denied her request for permission, she took her request to the school board. When they denied her request, she sued them (not for money and not to be a jerk—just for the right to gather with her friends).

The local courts didn't know what to do with the case. The state supreme court didn't know what to do with the case. Ultimately, two years later, the girl stood in front of the United States Supreme Court and gave testimony as to why she wanted to meet with other Jesus followers. The Supreme Court agreed that it was her constitutional right to do so. And now, years later there are hundreds of thousands of Christian clubs on public school campuses. All because one girl was willing to take a risk, to get a little uncomfortable, to maybe fail, and even to look stupid. She put action to her faith.

3. God loves providing wild, surprising solutions to your problems.

- 🔊 Ask students to think about the problems they're facing. Give them a minute to reflect.
- 🔊 Scripture: Exodus 2:5-10 (God provides for Jochebed, and baby Mo is saved.)
- 🔊 Explanation: Baby Mo Is Saved! (see sidebar)
- 🔊 Personal illustration: The Wild Solution (see sidebar)

Explanation

Baby Mo Is Saved!

After reading "the rest of the story" from Exodus, rewind and review, filling in the details. Jochebed gives birth to Moses at the worst time in history to have a baby boy. She must have felt as if her life was out of control and there were no good solutions. She hid in the corner of her slave hut for three months, waiting for the guards to come take Mo away. Finally, she couldn't hide him any longer. She took a risky, almost crazy, step of faith—floating Mo out into the river.

God responds with a wild and surprising solution. Certainly, Jochebed's only prayer must have been, "God, please let my baby live!" But God does so much more! Not only does baby Mo live, but he is raised in total luxury—in the Pharaoh's palace, no less—and gets the finest education available (something that would never have been available to a regular Hebrew boy).

And with the help of Mo's quick-thinking sister, Miriam (who was standing nearby when Pharaoh's daughter found Mo), Jochebed gets to nurse Moses and raise him for the first couple years of his life. This is shocking, and we often miss this fact when we read this story: Jochebed floated Moses into the river with a hope and a prayer that he would live, and he was back in her arms in a matter of minutes!

Then God's sense of humor shows. Jochebed gets paid for taking care of Moses! Point out (with a bit of humor) that surely Jochebed, while desperately trying to hide Mo, didn't stand there in her slave hut and cook up a sneaky plan to make some extra cash! But God provided a solution that was so far beyond what Jochebed could even imagine. And God loves to do that for us too.

Personal illustration

The Wild Solution

Hopefully, you have an illustration you can share from your own life of a time when God provided a solution that was beyond what you were praying for. Share that. If you truly can't think of one, see if you have another adult leader who can share about a time like this.

closing
The Grand Finale

- 🔊 Scripture: Jeremiah 29:11 ("'For I know the plans I have for you,' declares the Lord, 'plans to prosper you and not to harm you, plans to give you hope and a future.'")

- 🔊 Close with something like—Like Mo's Mom, hold onto faith, put action to your faith, and don't be surprised when God shows up where you least expect him.

- 🔊 A great way to wrap this up is to have students pray this prayer with you, in unison: God, I'm open to whatever you want to do in my life, and in my problems.

171

discussion

Encore

Get It? — Middle School

- How did Jochebed end up as a slave in Egypt?
- Why was it such a big deal that Moses was born at that time?
- Why was Jochebed's action so risky?
- How did God's solution to Jochebed's problem go beyond her expectations?

Get It? — High School

- Summarize how the Hebrew people ended up as slaves in Egypt.
- Can anyone tell us how God used Moses in the years to come?
- Why was Jochebed's risky action important? Why couldn't she just wait for God to provide a solution while she was hiding Mo?
- How did God's solution to Jochebed's problem go beyond her expectations?

What If? — The Big Picture

- Put yourself in Jochebed's sandals: What would you have done in that slave hut?
- How might the history of the Hebrew people have been different if Jochebed hadn't chosen to put action to her faith?
- What does faith in action look like today in the life of a teenager?

So What? — It's Your Life

- When has your life felt out of control? What do you normally do in those circumstances? What can you do?
- What specific step of faith, what action step, can you take this week? Why would it be risky?
- How can this kind of faith in action become a lifestyle, not just a one-time thing?

Drop Your Nets

Contributed by **Will Penner**

This outline is saved as GT02_20 on the CD-ROM.

Primary theme discipleship	

Themes commitment, following Jesus, sin, temptation, choices, behavior, submission

Scripture Luke 18:18-30; John 8:1-11; Matthew 4:18-20; Matthew 5:1–7:29

Approximate length through The Grand Finale 90 minutes (see note below)

You'll need

- *An Insider's View of Jesus* (Youth Specialties/Zondervan, 2002) (optional)
- TV and VCR
- Paper and markers for each small group
- Large, decorative fishing net (displayed or hung up at the front of the room)
- Bibles
- Paper and pens for each student
- *Cruel Intentions* (Columbia Tri Star, 1999)
- *Jerry Maguire* (Columbia Tri Star, 1996)
- *Back to the Future* (Universal, 1995)
- TV and DVD player
- 3" x 5" cards for each student
- *Liar Liar* (Universal, 1997)
- A candle and a way to light it
- A clipboard, large piece of cardboard, or another object that will effectively block the candlelight
- One two-inch piece of yarn per person

This talk is a good way to dissect portions of the Sermon on the Mount. It's way too long "as is" to complete the whole thing in just one youth group session! But it can be broken up into pieces and then spread out over a weekend retreat or during a multiweek series. It can also be shortened into a 30-minute talk by taking out the movie clips.

When Jesus called his first disciples, they were already engaged in other occupations. But it's not just their jobs that he calls them to come away from—it's also their lives (as they knew them). Jesus is famous for this! He called the rich ruler to leave his wealth (Luke 18:18-30). He called the woman accused of adultery to leave her life of sin (John 8:1-11). And he calls us to leave behind things in our lives in order to follow him.

intro

The Opening Act

🔊 Drama: Choose a couple of your more dramatic students to act out the scene in Matthew 4:18-20 (the calling of the first disciples). They could act it out with the dialogue, or a narrator could read the passage while the actors play it out spontaneously.

🔊 Movie clip: *An Insider's View of Jesus* (available at ww.youthspecialties.com) (optional, see sidebar)

🔊 Discussion: Fishing for People (see sidebar)

🔊 When Jesus issued the invitation, Peter and Andrew immediately dropped their nets and followed him. Ask—What are our "nets"? What are those things that Jesus would have us drop in order to follow him better?

🔊 Activity: Our Nets (see sidebar)

🔊 Discussion or activity: Sermon on the Mount (optional, see sidebar)

Movie clip

An Insider's View of Jesus

Start 00:03:28 "Fish Tales" screen title
Stop 00:07:41 Peter says, "Okay."
In this clip two fishermen—and future disciples—named Peter and Andrew are bringing in their nets after a very unsuccessful night of fishing. They are tired, hungry, discouraged, and a little bit cranky. They've just discovered that their nets are full of large holes and muck, and it's going to take a lot of work to fix and clean them before they go fishing again. Then Jesus walks up to them and suggests they cast their nets just one more time. Peter and Andrew think he's nuts because they just spent the whole night casting their nets (66 times, to be exact) and didn't catch even one stinkin' fish. Plus, Jesus admits he's not a fisherman, so why should they follow his advice?

Fishing for People

Remind your group of Matthew 4:19 ("Come, follow me," Jesus said, "and I will make you fishers of men.") Then ask—What does it mean to fish for men? After you field a few responses, reveal that Jesus was talking about evangelism. Have your group brainstorm and come up with some more metaphors Jesus could have used if he was calling someone from a nonfishing profession. Give them a few examples, such as:

- To a farmer: "Drop your plow and follow me, and I'll give you a crop of people."
- To an accountant: "Drop your calculator and follow me, and I'll put people in the columns of your ledger."
- To a dishwasher: "Drop your dishrag and follow me, and I'll make you a cleaner of people."

Our Nets

To make this discussion more interactive, begin by getting kids into small groups (or triplets) and asking them to brainstorm some of the "nets" in their lives. Then ask them to choose one or two that are common to them and other Christian teens. Give them paper and markers and ask them to write down (in large writing) these various nets—one per sheet of paper. Using tape, students should attach these signs to the fishing net you've hung in the front of the room. (Note: If you don't have a fishing net, just have students use the signs to create a collage on a wall or banner for all to see.)

Sermon on the Mount

Ask your kids to break off into small groups and dissect the Sermon on the Mount (Matthew 5:1-7:29), looking for the different "nets" that Jesus refers to (those things that separate people from God).

Or just assign the seven Scripture references (one from each of the following main points) to a different small groups and ask the groups to read their Scripture passage and come up with a way to illustrate it to the rest of the group (through a drawing, skit, song, or a personal or made-up story).

heart of the talk

The Main Event

1. Jesus calls us from anger.

🔊 Scripture: Matthew 5:23-24 ("Therefore, if you are offering your gift at the altar and there remember that your brother has something against you, leave your gift there in front of the altar. First go and be reconciled to your brother; then come and offer your gift.")

📣 Ask—How might life be different if we all took these verses seriously? Would it be difficult if, before we were allowed into our place of worship, we had to go and take care of any relationships in our lives that weren't right? How many people would be in church the next Sunday? Would you be there?

🔊 Activity: But I Hate Him! (see sidebar)

Activity

But I Hate Him!

Pass out sheets of paper and pens to each student. Ask them to take some time and write a letter to someone they've been angry with, offering that person a word of forgiveness. Tell them they won't have to send these letters (although they're certainly welcome to do so). They're just for practice.

And if they're so angry with the person that they can't even write a fake letter of forgiveness, then they should write a letter to God and ask him to change their hearts and provide the willingness they need in order to forgive the other person.

---

2. Jesus calls us from focusing on popularity.

🔊 Scripture: Matthew 6:3-4 ("But when you give to the needy, do not let your left hand know what your right hand is doing, so that your giving may be in secret."), verses 6-8 ("But when you pray, go into your room, close the door and pray to your Father, who is unseen…do not keep on babbling like pagans, for they think they will be heard because of their many words. Do not be like them, for your Father knows what you need before you ask him."), and verse 16 ("When you fast, do not look somber as the hypocrites do.")

🔊 Movie clip: *Cruel Intentions*

🔊 Discussion: Popularity Motivation (see sidebar)

Movie clip

Cruel Intentions

Start 00:10:31 Kathryn says, "Do you remember Court Reynolds?"
Stop 00:11:23 Kathryn says, "Everybody loves me, and I intend to keep it that way."
(Note: This is a fairly raunchy movie, so choose your scenes wisely!) Sebastian (Ryan Phillippe) and Kathryn (Sarah Michelle Gellar) are stepbrother and stepsister. They are both spoiled and rich, and they are often left to their own devices by parents who allow them to do pretty much whatever they please. As a twisted form of amusement, these teenagers enjoy playing cruel games with other people's lives. In this clip Kathryn has just begun to tell Sebastian about her latest plot for revenge.

Optional Additional Clip

Start 01:30:28 While addressing the student body, Kathryn says, "However dark the cloud, there's always a silver lining."
Stop 01:33:21 The school headmaster just shakes his head.
This clip shows the end result of Kathryn's schemes to humiliate others as everything backfires on her. (Note: Use some discretion for language here.)

Discussion

Popularity Motivation

Explain that during Jesus' time it was common for religious people to be involved in these activities: giving to the poor, praying, and fasting. In fact, we're still supposed to do all of them today too! But it had become common for people to use these practices as ways of bringing attention to themselves. They had the wrong motivation.

Ask—How much time do each of us spend trying to be popular at school through the way we dress, talk, and act? It's in our churches too. What kinds of religious stuff might people in our church do in order to be accepted or to get positive attention?

3. Jesus calls us from our love of money.

🔊 Scripture: Matthew 6:24 ("No one can serve two masters...You cannot serve both God and money.")

🔊 Movie clip: *Jerry Maguire* (see sidebar)

🔊 Explanation: Many of us get so caught up in wanting more money that we lose sight of other things that are more important. We'll risk our health, our families, even our happiness—all in order to make more money. When we do that, we're worshiping money instead of God.

Movie clip

Jerry Maguire

Start 00:02:57 Jerry says, "Inside that building, that's where I work."
Stop 00:04:50 Steve Remo says, "I've gotta get the bonus."
In this clip Jerry (Tom Cruise) reveals why he doesn't feel good about his career as a sports agent anymore. Where professional athletes used to serve as positive role models for kids, now contracts and, ultimately, the Almighty Dollar, control an athlete's decisions regarding everything from what autographs they'll sign to whether or not they'll continue to play after they've been injured. It's enough to inspire Jerry to impulsively strike out on his own and start his own agency.

4. Jesus calls us from worrying about the future.

🔊 Scripture Matthew 6:34 ("Therefore do not worry about tomorrow, for tomorrow will worry about itself. Each day has enough trouble of its own.")

🔊 Movie clip: *Back to the Future* (see sidebar)

🔊 Discussion: Stop Worrying (see sidebar)

Movie clip

Back to the Future

Start 01:14:23 Doc says, "Are you sure about this storm?"
Stop 01:16:33 Marty slips the envelope into Doc's coat pocket.
Marty (Michael J. Fox) is trying to tell Doc (Christopher Lloyd) about what will happen to him in the future so he can prepare for it. However, Doc really believes it's important not to know too much because it might disrupt the natural order of things.

Optional additional clip

Start 01:31:24 Doc says, "You're late! Do you have no concept of time?"
Stop 01:33:59 Doc says, "Great Scott!"
If you have time, show this second scene as well. Doc discovers the letter from Marty and adamantly refuses to read it—he even goes so far as to tear it up into small pieces and throw it in the gutter. This scene really shows how passionately Doc feels about not knowing what's going to happen in the future and not worrying about it.

Stop Worrying

Say something along the lines of—Almost all of us wonder what's going to happen to us in the future. In fact, we're encouraged to think about it from the time, like when we're small and someone asks us, "What do you want to be when you grow up?" (If you have time, have students share how they would have answered that question when they were little kids.) Even in church we continue that conversation, we just wrap it up in churchy jargon: "What do you think you're called to do?" or, "Where do you think you'll go when you die?" Jesus is asking us not to worry about it. God is in control, and we can rest assured that everything will work out according to God's purpose.

5. Jesus calls us from judging others.

🔊 Scripture Matthew 7:3 ("'Why do you look at the speck of sawdust in your brother's eye and pay no attention to the plank in your own eye?'")

🔊 Brainstorming: Say—One of the things we all yearn for is to have people in our lives who accept us for who we are—people who won't judge us. Yet, we can often be so judgmental toward others. What might be some reasons for that?

🔊 Activity: I, Judge (see sidebar)

I, Judge

Pass out 3" x 5" cards, one to each student, along with something to write with (if students don't already have a pen or pencil from a previous activity). Ask them to privately think about the people they tend to judge: friends, family members, other youth group participants. Have them write down a list of names and a word or two next to each name that briefly describes how they judge that person. For example:
- Susie—the way she dresses and tries to get attention
- Pastor Phil—that voice he uses when he prays
- My dad—how he seems so clueless sometimes

Explain that this should be done with an attitude of wanting to identify their own judgmental ways so they can turn them over to Jesus. Don't have kids share these with the group after they're finished. (That's the last thing you need—"I think Susie only dresses that way to get guys' attention!")

Wrap up this exercise with prayer, asking God to both forgive us and free us from our judgmental attitudes.

6. Jesus calls us from timidity about our faith.

- 🔊 Scripture: Matthew 5:14 ("You are the light of the world. A city on a hill cannot be hidden.")
- 🔊 Object lesson: Light under a Bushel (see sidebar)
- 🔊 Ask—What causes us to be timid about our faith? Why did Jesus even need to bring this up?

Object lesson

Light under a Bushel

Light a candle and hold it up for all to see. (The darker you can make the room, the more powerful this will be.) Say something like—For a candle to effectively illuminate anything, it must be out there shining brightly, sometimes even in the midst of the darkness. And to whatever extent the candle is hidden (place an object in front of the candle), it's no longer useful to enlighten anything. Jesus created us to be light in a dark world. When we choose to hide our faith, our joy, or even our struggles from others, we diminish how useful we can be to them.

7. Jesus calls us from lying.

- 🔊 Scripture: Matthew 5:37 ("'Simply let your "Yes" be "Yes," and your "No," "No."'")
- 🔊 Movie clip: *Liar Liar* (see sidebar)
- 🔊 Explanation: It's Just a Little White Lie (see sidebar)

Movie clip

Liar Liar

Start 00:39:03 Max and his dad walk to a picnic table on the playground.
Stop 00:41:22 Max says, "But you're the only one that makes me feel bad."
Fletcher Reede (Jim Carrey) lies a lot, so his son, Max (Justin Cooper), made a birthday wish that his dad wouldn't be able to tell any more lies. In this clip Fletcher is telling Max why he wants the boy to take back his birthday wish.

It's Just a Little White Lie

Not telling the truth is as popular in our culture today as it was in Israel 2,000 years ago. In fact, deep down, most of us don't really trust each other, and we have a lot of reasons not to. Even as little kids we learn to qualify the important things we promise with an, "I swear" or "cross my heart; hope to die," or other similar oaths, as if to say, "Sometimes I don't always tell the truth, but this time I am—I promise!" Jesus says we're better off if we say yes when we mean yes and no when we mean no. This is less about "swearing to God," and more about being a person of your word—telling the truth at all times.

closing

The Grand Finale

🔊 People have always struggled with the "nets" we've been talking about, and they always will.

🔊 Summary: Jesus' Sermon on the Mount provides us with a plan for how we should act. Just as he called Peter and Andrew to drop their nets and follow him, he says the same to us: Drop the stuff that's occupying your lives right now and follow me—leave that stuff behind.

🔊 Prayer exercise: Preparing the Net (see sidebar)

Preparing the Net

Either hand out pieces of yarn to your group members or have them take a piece from a bucket that's positioned near the large fishing net you used earlier in your talk. Explain that the yarn represents the "nets" in their lives.

Tell students to spend a couple minutes in silence, asking God to further reveal more "nets." What are the things Jesus is calling them to leave behind? This could be one of the seven things you've just talked about from the Sermon on the Mount, one of the "nets" they wrote out at the beginning of the talk, or something else.

Then ask students to come to the fishing net, in an attitude of prayer, and tie their piece of yarn onto the net to represent their desire to drop the thing that is preventing them from following Jesus completely. Play some soft music during the response time and close with prayer. For added effect, you could have the net rigged so that it drops during a closing benediction as you tell the kids to drop their nets and follow Christ out into the world.

discussion

Encore

Get It?	Middle School

- 🔊 What were the names of the first two disciples Jesus called?

- 🔊 What did he offer them? What was their response?

- 🔊 Why was it a big deal for them to "drop their nets"?

- 🔊 What were the "nets" that Jesus talked about in the Sermon on the Mount—those things that keep us from following him more closely?

- 🔊 What does it mean for us to "drop our nets"? Obviously, we're not carrying around actual nets—so how does this apply to our lives?

Get It?	High School

- 🔊 What were the "nets" that Jesus talked about in the Sermon on the Mount, and which one do you think is the most difficult to drop?

- 🔊 Why do you think Jesus cares about this?

- 🔊 How did the disciples respond to Jesus' invitation?

- 🔊 Do you personally know anyone who "immediately dropped their nets" to follow him? What did that look like in their lives?

- 🔊 What effect does it have on your life if you follow Jesus while you're still "dragging around your nets"?

What If?	The Big Picture

- 🔊 If Jesus were giving his Sermon on the Mount right here to this group, what kind of "nets" would he describe in our group?

- 🔊 How would our group be different if we all dropped our nets and totally followed Jesus?

- 🔊 If Jesus were standing before you now to issue an invitation to follow him:
  - What would he offer? (like making you fish for people)
  - What would he ask of you? (like a fisherman dropping his nets)

So What?	It's Your Life

◄» Given what we've discussed about what it means to be a disciple of Jesus, we need to continually watch for those "nets" in our lives that we need to drop. Discuss some ways to stay aware of those nets (mentors, accountability groups, Bible study, prayer, written character inventories).

◄» Let's examine the evangelism strategy we have in this youth group.
  • How do we share the gospel with people?
  • How do we call students to be disciples?
  • Are we asking too much? Too little?
  • Are we setting realistic standards?

◄» What net will you drop today? How will you do this? What difference will it make this week? How can you keep from picking it up again?

Facing Our Demons

Facing Our Demons

Primary theme temptation	
Themes sin, evil, Satan, self-reliance, peer pressure, power, Scripture, self-control	
Scripture Matthew 4:1-11; Psalm 119:105	
Approximate length through The Grand Finale 40 minutes	

Contributed by **Will Penner**

You'll need

- 🔊 *The Devil's Advocate* (Warner Brothers, 1997) or *Bedazzled* (20th Century Fox, 2000)

- 🔊 *A Christmas Story* (MGM/UA, 1983)

- 🔊 TV and DVD player

- 🔊 A personal story about doing something stupid on a dare

- 🔊 A copy of *The Screwtape Letters* by C. S. Lewis (Harper, San Francisco, 2001)

- 🔊 A copy of the Amy Grant song "Thy Word" and a way to play it (optional)

Throughout the Bible there are stories about people being tempted. The whole book of Job recounts Satan's fierce battle to turn Job's heart away from God. Many decent men and women in Scripture succumbed to the temptations offered them. Even Jesus was tempted—but, of course, he didn't sin. Just before Jesus began his public ministry, he went into the wilderness to be tempted by Satan. This talk looks at three common areas of temptation through Jesus' experience.

This outline is saved as GT02_21 on the CD-ROM.

intro

The Opening Act

🔊 Movie clip: *The Devil's Advocate* or *Bedazzled* (see sidebar)

🔊 Say something like—It sure would be easier to stay away from temptation if we saw a little guy dressed in red and carrying a pitchfork—or at least then we'd know where the temptation was coming from. But temptation is usually sneakier than that.

🔊 Reading: *The Screwtape Letters* (see sidebar)

🔊 Transition with something like—Let's examine the three temptations of Jesus and see how each of them relates to our own lives.

Movie clip

The Devil's Advocate

Start 01:58:50 Kevin says, "Because you're my father?"
Stop 01:59:28 Satan says, "Call me Dad."
In this clip Kevin (Keanu Reeves) finally realizes that the man who's been serving as his mentor is actually his father—and he's also the devil (Al Pacino). (Note: Be careful about language and adult content before and after the clip.)

Bedazzled

Start 00:12:56 The devil asks, "How would you like to make one simple decision that'll change your life forever?"
Stop 00:14:01 Elliot says, "Night-night!"
A beautiful woman (Elizabeth Hurley) approaches Elliot Richards (Brendan Fraser) in a bar, which never happens to him. And she makes him an offer that seems too good to be true. When he keeps putting her off, she tells him who she really is. (Note: This is a milder clip than the one from *The Devil's Advocate*, although not as powerful.)

The Screwtape Letters

Begin by saying something like—All of us are tempted by things in our lives. And many of us bring habits into our Christian lives that provide an easier in-road for those particular temptations. What are some of the habits you carry with you in your Christian life that still tempt you?

Here is some background information about The Screwtape Letters, a fictional story written by C.S. Lewis. It's a collection of letters written from Screwtape, a high-level agent of the underworld, to Wormwood, his nephew who is new to the job of tempting humans. They refer to the humans who are being tempted as "patients."

Start reading the second letter at the beginning: "My Dear Wormwood, I note with grave displeasure that your patient has become a Christian..." and stop reading at the end of the first paragraph: "All the habits of the patient, both mental and bodily, are still in our favour."

heart of the talk

The Main Event

1. The temptation to not rely on God

🔊 Scripture: Matthew 4:3 ("The tempter came to him and said, 'If you are the Son of God, tell these stones to become bread.'")

🔊 Discussion: Eat This Bread (see sidebar)

🔊 Scripture: Matthew 4:4 ("Jesus answered, 'It is written: "Man does not live on bread alone, but on every word that comes from the mouth of God."'")

Eat This Bread

Who among us doesn't want to have his basic needs met? When we're hungry, we want to eat; when we're tired, we want to sleep; when we're cold, we want to warm up; and when we're wet, we want to get dry. So, what would've been the problem with Jesus turning just one little pebble into a biscuit?

2. The temptation of the double dare

🔊 Personal illustration: My Double Dare (see sidebar)

🔊 Movie clip: *A Christmas Story* (see sidebar)

🔊 Scripture: Matthew 4:6 ("'If you are the Son of God,' [the devil] said, 'throw yourself down.'")

🔊 Illustration: Off a Cliff? (see sidebar)

🔊 Ask—What's the real temptation that Jesus is facing here? (The temptation to "prove it.") How does that temptation show up in the lives of students today? (It's the root of all peer pressure— "C'mon, prove you're one of us," "It's no big deal to do this," or "Everybody does this.")

🔊 Scripture: Matthew 4:7 ("Jesus answered him, 'It is also written: "Do not put the Lord your God to the test."'")

Personal illustration

My Double Dare

Tell a story from your own childhood (or teenage years) when you did something really stupid on a dare. Then talk about how kids would up the ante (every kid does this, right?)—"I double-dare ya!" and even "I double-dog-dare ya!" (Who knows what that really means?)

Movie clip

A Christmas Story

Start 00:16:12 The camera pans down a flagpole to a group of arguing kids.
Stop 00:18:21 Ralphie says, "I don't know. The bell rang!"
It's a cold winter day, and a group of grade schoolers are outside in the snow for recess. Flick (Scott Schwartz) and Schwartz (R.D. Robb) begin arguing over whether or not it's true that a person's tongue will stick to a frozen flagpole. (Flick says it won't; Schwartz says it will.) So in the heat of the moment, Schwartz triple-dog-dares Flick to stick his tongue against the flagpole and prove it. After a moment of consideration, while his classmates look on in amazement, Flick does it—with some painful and embarrassing consequences.

Off a Cliff?

Have any of you ever done something really stupid on a dare? What would possess someone to actually follow Satan's dare on this one? I mean—throw yourself off a cliff? When we were kids and we tried to use the excuse "Timmy did it first" or "Timmy dared me to do it—I had to!" most moms replied, "If Timmy threw himself off a cliff, would you do that, too?"

3. The grand temptation of power

🔊 Scripture: Matthew 4:9 ("'All this I will give you,' [the devil] said, 'if you will bow down and worship me.'")

🔊 Discussion: I Got the Power (see sidebar)

🔊 Ask—What are some other forms of power that you see in yourself, your family, your school, and our youth group? Why would this be any real temptation to Jesus?

🔊 Scripture: Matthew 4:10 ("Jesus said to him, 'Away from me, Satan!'")

I Got the Power

Everyone wants some degree of power—even timid and shy people do. You can see it in two-year-olds when they first learn that they can say no. Many girls learn early on that they hold some power over guys (and over other girls who are their competition for these guys) through the way they look, the way they dress, and who they hang out with. Many guys learn that they can have power over other guys (often in competition for the girls) through physical strength and athletic prowess. Teenagers and adults continue to play power games with intellect, money, and titles. Even church people like to "out-spiritualize" others sometimes. All of these are forms of power.

closing
The Grand Finale

🔊 Discussion: The Overarching Temptation of Christ (see sidebar)

🔊 All people get tempted during their lives, and all of us fail at times.

🔊 Explanation: Thy Word (see sidebar)

🔊 Scripture: Psalm 119:105, KJV ("Thy Word is a lamp unto my feet, and a light unto my path.")

🔊 Song: "Thy Word" by Amy Grant (see sidebar)

Discussion

The Overarching Temptation of Christ

Ask if students can see any theme or central issue in Satan's three attempts to tempt Jesus. Talk about their responses for a bit. If they don't get there on their own, explain to your group that all three of Satan's tries were meant to get Jesus sidetracked from his mission, to give up his servant-savior role, and just take charge of things.

Explain that most Jews during Jesus' time were looking for a Messiah (a savior) who would come in strong and powerful and become both a political and a religious leader. Jesus' mission was very different from that—but Satan was tempting him to take charge, to go against his Father's plan for saving the world.

Explanation

Thy Word

Even Jesus was tempted in the areas of self-reliance, following a dare, and taking power. He left us a model to follow for resisting temptation: Scripture. In each of the three temptations, Jesus responded with Scripture! Studying Scripture is the best defense against temptation. When we know God's heart, which we can find in God's Word, we are more likely to be able to see temptation for what it really is (even without seeing the little red guy with horns and a pitchfork).

Song

"Thy Word" by Amy Grant

Yup, it's an oldie, but not too moldy. Consider playing Amy Grant's song, "Thy Word" (a simple song containing the words of Psalm 119:105). Admittedly, this would not work in some youth groups and might just get you dismissed as an ancient goober—so gauge your group!

discussion
Encore

Get It?	Middle School

- 🔊 What was the first thing Satan tried to get Jesus to do? The second? The third?

- 🔊 How did Jesus respond to the temptations?

- 🔊 Where do you see the temptation not to rely on God show up in the lives of middle schoolers?

- 🔊 How does peer pressure show up in the lives of middle schoolers?

- 🔊 What does power look like in the middle school world?

- 🔊 What does power look like in the lives of people who aren't up-front, leader-type people?

Get It?	High School

- 🔊 What was Jesus' first temptation and how did he respond? Second? Third?

- 🔊 Why did Satan try to use these three temptations on Jesus?

- 🔊 Why did Satan tempt him at this point in Jesus' life (just before he started his public ministry)?

- 🔊 How can you distinguish between a normal impulse and a temptation to sin?

What If?	The Big Picture

- 🔊 What are the three areas of your life in which you are most easily tempted? (examples: sex, drugs, lying to parents, cheating on tests, stealing.)

- 🔊 What areas of temptation are not so obvious (people may not see the results right away if you gave in to the temptation)?

- 🔊 Jesus was out in the wilderness when Satan tempted him. What are some of the places, people, or circumstances that constitute the "wilderness" areas for teenagers—places where teenagers are most easily tempted? (examples: Internet pornography, music with explicit lyrics, expensive department stores, desire for popularity.)

- 🔊 What difference might it have made if Jesus had given in to one of Satan's temptations?

So What?   It's Your Life

🔊 What can you do this week to resist a temptation in your life? What difference will it make if you do? If you don't?

🔊 Pick one or two temptations that you (or someone you know) has to deal with regularly. Find a Scripture verse or two that you might find helpful when confronted with that situation. Write it down, repeat it over and over, and memorize it so it becomes "hidden in your heart."

🔊 What can you do to draw on Jesus' strength to resist temptation? If Jesus wants to help us make good choices, how does that work? How can it work in your life this week?

The Other Brother

Primary theme grace
Themes anger, righteousness, forgiveness, jealousy, selfishness, exclusivity, God's sovereignty
Scripture Luke 15:11-32; Jonah 3:3-5, 10; Jonah 4:1-4; Matthew 25:40; Mark 10:17-22; John 2:13-16; Luke 6:1-5; Matthew 18:21-22
Approximate length through The Grand Finale 20-30 minutes

You'll need

- Whiteboard
- Marker
- Copy of *Messy Spirituality* by Michael Yaconelli (Zondervan, 2002)
- *Big* (20th Century Fox, 1988)
- TV and DVD player

The story of the prodigal son is most often told from the viewpoint of the prodigal himself where we are given a sense of God's love and mercy. But, of course, there's some back story and another important storyline besides that of the bad boy returned home. There's also the good boy—the brother who did everything right. How did he feel? This talk is an exploration of the feelings that "good kids" often have when "bad kids" don't seem to get what they deserve. As children of God we have the opportunity to be extensions of God's grace to others, but we sometimes have difficulty getting beyond our anger, arrogance, and jealousy.

Contributed by **Will Penner**

This outline is saved as GTO2_22 on the CD-ROM.

intro
The Opening Act

🔊 Scripture: Luke 15:11 (The Parable of the Prodigal Son) Read this passage aloud, ending with the part that says, "The older brother became angry and refused to go in." It might be helpful to get a couple kids to act out the parable or mime it while a narrator reads the passage.

🔊 Brainstorming: Ask the group to come up with some reasons why the older brother gets angry when he finds out why his father is hosting the feast. Write these ideas on a whiteboard.

🔊 Activity: Ask kids to describe some situations from their own lives when they have felt angry for these same reasons. This could be done in small groups, or you could do it all together in one large group.

heart of the talk
The Main Event

1. Anger keeps us from being grace givers.

🔊 The word used to describe the anger the older brother feels is the same one Jonah used when he got upset with God for not destroying Nineveh.

🔊 Talk about the phrase "righteous indignation" (the idea that we can be angry-with-a-purpose, ticked-but-holy.)

🔊 Scripture: Jonah 3:3-5, 10 and Jonah 4:1-4 (Jonah prophesies, Nineveh repents, God relents, Jonah gets angry).

🔊 Discussion: Weird Anger (see sidebar)

🔊 Reading: Kingdom Monitors (see sidebar)

Discussion

Weird Anger

Say something like— Isn't it interesting how we can get upset with God for being compassionate toward the people we don't like? If you were to be really honest right now, are there people you would like to see God smite? Have you ever been so angry with someone else that the thought of God having mercy on them makes you sick? What would Jesus have to say about that?

Kingdom Monitors

Read a selection from Michael Yaconelli's book *Messy Spirituality* (Zondervan, 2002). Pages 47 and 48 describe this tendency we have to try to "help" God understand who should receive his grace and who should not.

2. Exclusivity keeps us from being grace givers.

◀» Transition by saying something like—There's another danger when we're operating in the role of the older brother—the tendency to compare ourselves to others in unhealthy ways.

◀» Discussion: Our Group Is Better (see sidebar)

◀» Scripture: Luke 15:31-32 (the father's explanation to the older son)

◀» Ask—How did the older brother show exclusivity?

◀» Explanation: "Everything I Have..." (see sidebar)

Our Group Is Better

If you have time, ask your group to brainstorm a list of ways that teenagers in their schools break off into different groups. Or, if you're feeling gutsy, talk about what this looks like in your own youth group.

There are all sorts of ways we define ourselves (both individually and collectively)—by clothing styles, favorite music, athletic talent, extracurricular interests, geography (where we live), race, gender, belief systems, and more. Sometimes these are productive and even helpful ways to define ourselves. For instance, in some churches people say affirmations of faith (like the Apostles' Creed) in each worship service as a way of declaring who they are by what they believe.

But other times we add value to these definitions of who we are—and it becomes judgmental and exclusive. (Note: If you're speaking to young teens, you may want to define exclusivity for them.) Teenagers are especially good at defining who they are based on a counterresponse to how adults try to define them, or in response to other groups in their schools or church group. When this thinking becomes "our group is better than other groups," we become exclusive—and that's both dangerous and hurtful to ourselves and to others.

Ask a few pointed questions:

• In our group, do we ever try to define ourselves in exclusive, rather than inclusive, terms? If so, how? (Examples: our theology or doctrine, our denomination, our cool programs and trips.)

• Do we say or do things that exclude the "prodigals" from our group?

• Do we define ourselves over and against other people or groups?

• Or do we look for more inclusive ways to define who we are?

"Everything I Have…"

The father reaffirms his love for the older son, along with his place in the family, yet he insists that this kind of love does not exclude the younger brother. In this part of the parable, Jesus is speaking directly to the attitude of the Pharisees and teachers of the law who were of the mindset that God's love was reserved exclusively for a select group of chosen Israelites who kept the commandments.

3. Jealousy keeps us from being grace givers.

🔊 Transition by saying something like—Sometimes our reaction, just like that of the older brother, is as simple as good, old-fashioned jealousy. We all struggle with jealousy. It's the ugly little monster in all of us that screams, "It's not fair!" and, "I deserve better!"

🔊 Activity: Jealousy Commercials (see sidebar)

🔊 Scripture: Luke 15:28-30 (The older son is whining.)

🔊 Discussion: What About Me, Me, Me? (see sidebar)

🔊 Movie clip: *Big* (see sidebar)

🔊 After the clip, say something like—Here's a guy who'd done everything he was asked to do. He did all of his homework and put together a nice presentation for the meeting. Tom Hanks's character was new to the company and he hadn't done any prep work, but he's the one who wins the admiration of the boss. Those of us who come to church regularly, pray every day, and read our Bibles may feel a little ripped off by others who seem to be able to get away with anything. But God still calls us to be instruments of his love and forgiveness to these people.

Jealousy Commercials

Divide students into groups. (The size can vary—a large youth group could break up into smaller groups of 10; a smaller group could divide into groups as small as three.) Tell the teams you want them to create a 30-second commercial for "Jealousy" (which they will act out for the rest of the group). They should treat "Jealousy" as if it were a positive product, but they should include a list of product warnings or possible side effects at the end of their commercial (as if being read by the company's legal department). Give the groups about five minutes to put together their commercials. Then have them all perform the commercials.

What About Me, Me, Me?

"I've done everything you've ever asked of me, and you've never thrown a party for me," says the whiney older brother. Discuss the following questions with your students:

• Are there areas in your life where you feel that way?

• Do your parents ever treat your siblings differently?

• How about at church? Do you ever feel like more attention is given to "the lost" than to the kids who follow the rules?

Big

Start 00:42:33 "These tests were conducted over a six-month period…"
Stop 00:45:44 "Did you see the look on MacMillan's face?"
A group of toy company executives is meeting to look over the designs for a new toy. Paul (John Heard) is leading the meeting, and he's done all the research and behind-the-scenes work to get this one particular toy ready for production. So when Josh (Tom Hanks) keeps asking questions like, "What's fun about a building?" and pointing out the flaws in this new toy design, Paul is more than a little upset—especially when their boss, MacMillan (Robert Loggia), loves Josh's ideas.

closing

The Grand Finale

🔊 Exercise: Church Board (see sidebar)

🔊 Explanation: That may have seemed a bit awkward if you recognized the Josh character to be Jesus. But don't we judge people like that every day? Let's not forget that what we do to the least of our brothers and sisters, we do to Jesus (Matthew 25:40). So this story may not be as far-fetched as you think.

🔊 Discussion: Look at each of the Scriptures that correspond with the examples in the Church Board exercise. Instead of looking for the moral in each story or viewing those situations through the eyes of the prodigal, try looking at it from the viewpoint of the person or people whom Jesus is criticizing:

• Mark 10:17-22 (the rich young man)

• John 2:13-16 (money changers in the temple)

• Luke 6:1-5 (the disciples plucking grain on the Sabbath, and Jesus' reference to David eating the bread of the presence)

🔊 Wrap up by saying something like—Often we are reminded of our own personal need for God's grace and forgiveness. None of us has to look very far into our own heart before we discover that if we always got what we deserved, we'd be in trouble. As children of God, we have the unique opportunity to be extensions of that kind of grace toward other people, as well. As we go out into the world, let us write a different storyline when we find ourselves in the role of "the other brother."

Exercise

Church Board

Explain to your group that they have recently been elected to your church board. It is their job to make decisions that are in the best interests of this church. Of course there are other churches out there, but some of them teach things that you don't find compatible with Scripture. (If you have too many kids for one discussion, divide into smaller groups.)

Explain the situation—You like to see people in your congregation work hard because when they make a lot of money, they tithe more. This is good because it helps you pay for rent, utilities, staff salaries, and so on. You also like seeing the youth group sell muffins in the lobby between worship services because it helps them offset the costs of their ski trips. One thing that's well-known about your church is that everyone who's a member takes the day off from work once a week and comes to a worship service. At this service they take communion, but whatever bread is left over after communion gets thrown away. Nobody is supposed to eat it.

This meeting has been called to order because Josh, a young man who's not even a member of this church, has been creating problems.

First of all, he told one the largest contributors that he couldn't be a good Christian unless he sold everything he had and gave it to the poor. Now we had been counting on that money to buy new carpeting for the church! Second, he knocked over the muffin table, saying something about "Dad's place." Third, he not only was working last week when he was supposed to take the day off, but then he came in and told the kids it was okay to eat the communion bread that no one is supposed to eat!

Now tell the students their job is to figure out what to do with this troublemaker. (Encourage the kids to stay in character and come up with the kind of solution(s) their church board might develop based on these scenarios.) Give them a few minutes to come up with a proposed course of action. If you have more than one "church board" working on this, allow time for all the groups to share their solutions with the rest of the group.

discussion

Encore

Get It?	Middle School

- 🔊 How did the older brother feel after his father received the younger brother so warmly? Why?
- 🔊 How does anger keep us from being a part of God's grace to other people?
- 🔊 What is exclusivity?
- 🔊 How does exclusivity impact our lives and God's desires?
- 🔊 What does jealousy do to us? How can our jealousy impact other people?
- 🔊 What was Jonah's response to God's mercy toward Nineveh?

Get It?	High School

- 🔊 Sure, the older brother sounds whiny. How are we like him?
- 🔊 What roles do anger, exclusivity, and jealousy play in our lives?
- 🔊 How do they keep us from experiencing the fullness of life that God wants for us?
- 🔊 When they show up in our lives, how do they impact other people?
- 🔊 Why does Jesus throw this extra bit of storyline onto the end of his parable of the prodigal son? Who's he speaking to?
- 🔊 What's his message? Why is this also a message for us, not just for the Pharisees?

What If?	The Big Picture

- 🔊 How are you like the other brother? (In what ways do you hold back from extending grace and forgiveness to others?)
- 🔊 Who are the "other brothers" in your life (the people from whom you most often need to receive grace and forgiveness)?
- 🔊 Who are the "prodigals" in your life (the people to whom you most often need to extend grace and forgiveness)?
- 🔊 What would you really have done if you'd been in the older brother's shoes?

So What?   It's Your Life

🔊 We not only have individual "prodigal" and "other brother" tendencies, but we also have these collectively. In what areas is our youth group "prodigal," and in what areas are we the "other brother"?

🔊 In what areas is our church "prodigal," and in what areas are we the "other brother"?

🔊 In what practical ways can you combat anger, exclusivity, and jealousy in your life?

🔊 Which of those three do you struggle with the most? What specific step of action will you take this week to make some changes in that area?

🔊 How can we take seriously the responsibility Jesus gave his disciples (in Matthew 18:21-22) to forgive people over and over again?

Through the Roof!

Primary theme commitment	
Themes discipleship, social status, humility, embarrassment, death	
Scripture Mark 2:1-12; John 3:1-13; Mark 5:25-34; Mark 10:46-52; Matthew 16:13-19, Acts 6:8-7:60	
Approximate length through The Grand Finale 30-35 minutes	

You'll need

- A personal story about an embarrassing situation
- *10 Things I Hate about You* (Touchstone, 1999)
- TV and DVD player
- Paper and pencils

The gospels are full of stories about people who desperately wanted to get to Jesus. Some wanted to learn from him because they heard he was a great teacher. Some wanted him to heal them. Others wanted to try and trick him. Some went to great lengths to meet Jesus, despite what it might cost them socially. One thing is for sure, though. None of the people in the Bible who chose to follow Jesus always had it easy, and no one who chooses to follow him today always has it easy, either. Sooner or later, if we truly want to follow Jesus, it's going to cost us something. So what are we willing to pay? These are some of the stories from the Bible about the costs of discipleship.

intro

The Opening Act

🔊 Storytelling: Setting the Stage (see sidebar)

🔊 Scripture: Mark 2:1-12 (healing the paralytic who gets lowered through the roof)

🔊 Discussion: How many of us would be willing to cut through someone's roof in order to see Jesus? What might the results be—other than a healed friend—if we ripped a hole in someone's roof?

Storytelling

Setting the Stage

In your own words, tell most of the Scripture story—without the final bit. Add some explanation to fill in the background. Here's an example: Two thousand years ago most of the houses in Israel had roofs made of thatch. Thatch is a mixture of clay, mud, sticks, and grass. And most of these houses were relatively small, too, with only two or three rooms. They had few windows, which meant they could get awfully stuffy inside.

So imagine being packed into one of these homes—so packed that it's already beyond standing room only. A group of people that wants to get inside—can't. There's simply no more room. They've all come to hear some guy talk, just like you. He's more than a teacher, really; he's a healer, too. His sermons are outstanding, but his miracles are legendary. News of his deeds is spreading all across the land, and that's why the house is so packed.

He's preaching like crazy, saying some revolutionary stuff. You're trying to pay attention, but it seems like pieces of the roof are falling on you. There's a hunk of mud. Ouch! Then a huge block of sticks and grass falls to the floor. Somebody's cutting a hole in the roof! You wonder if it's the Romans—or maybe an assassin. Or maybe just some crazy beggar who thought he'd get a chance to be blessed by the Master. (You've heard he's got a soft spot for people like that, which you find a bit odd.)

Either way, you know the host is going to be pretty ticked off. He already seemed irritated by the folks sitting in the windowsills, twice too many people at the kitchen table, and several of the younger ones seemingly camped out in the middle of the family room.

The hole is getting bigger. Jesus is still talking, although fewer people are paying attention to what he's saying. They're starting to look up as they notice the hole, too. Before long you can see a few men up on the roof, standing around the opening and looking down into the room below. Now they look like they're lowering something through the hole—something that looks a lot like a person.

Jesus has stopped talking, and everyone is completely focused on the man being lowered into the room. Once you see him, it becomes obvious why this man is here—he can't walk. Immediately, whispers are heard all around the house. You strain your ears to hear what Jesus and the guy are saying to each other.

heart of the talk
The Main Event

1. The risk of status loss

🔊 A passion for following Jesus might cost you social status—it might make you less popular. People might think you're odd.

🔊 Scripture: John 3:1-13 (the story of Nicodemus coming to Jesus in the night)

🔊 Ask a couple questions to clarify why Nic came to Jesus in the middle of the night. (He didn't want his fellow Pharisees to know he was there!)

🔊 Transition by saying something like—It might be popular these days to be "spiritual," but following Jesus still kinda freaks people out. If you truly live your faith, you'll risk the loss of acceptance from your peers.

2. The risk of embarrassment and vulnerability

🔊 Personal illustration: My Embarrassment (see sidebar)

🔊 Scripture: Mark 5:25-34 (Jesus healed the bleeding woman.)

🔊 Explanation and discussion: Exposed! (see sidebar)

🔊 Transition by saying something like—No matter how badly this woman felt, she knew Jesus was the answer. She was willing to endure anything for the opportunity to be healed.

Personal illustration

My Embarrassment

Share a story from a time when you were made more vulnerable than you'd intended (either emotionally or physically) and how it embarrassed you. The sillier the story, the better. This will get the students thinking about how they feel about their own embarrassing moments and set the stage for the Scripture story.

Exposed!

Jewish law said that when a woman was having her period (her monthly menstrual cycle), she was considered unclean and must stay separated from other people. After her period was over, she had to go through a ritual cleansing at the temple. The woman in this story, however, had been a hemophiliac for 12 years! It was amazing she hadn't died already! If the people in the crowd had known about her condition, they would have cleared away from her as though she had a highly contagious disease. And they would have been mad at her for entering the crowd.

Ask a couple content questions:
• How did the woman approach Jesus to be healed?
• What did the disciples think when Jesus said, "Someone touched me"?

Help your students think through the implications of this story by asking them a few reflection questions like:
• Why was it risky for the woman to sneak into the middle of the crowd?
• Why do you think she chose to approach Jesus this way?
• How do you think she felt when, just after realizing she had been healed by touching Jesus' cloak, he turned around and asked, "Who touched me?"
• How might all-out living for Jesus create situations in the life of a teenager today that could force vulnerability or embarrassment?

(Note: if you have many young teen boys in your group, you'll have to think about their maturity level (possibly nonexistent?) and your ability to keep this Scripture story from devolving. You never know how 12-year-old boys will respond to a story about a woman with a 12-year-long menstrual cycle. If you do have several young teen boys in your group, you might consider using another Scripture story where someone risked embarrassment in order to get to Jesus, such as blind Bartimaeus in Mark 10:46-52.)

3. The risk of death

◀» Scripture: Matthew 16:13-19 (Peter's confession)

◀» Explanation: Blasphemy (see sidebar)

◀» Explanation and discussion: Death? (see sidebar)

◀» Ask—If you were called by God to move to a more dangerous place to live in order to be a "light in the darkness," would you be willing to do it?

Blasphemy

There was a lot of speculation about who this Jesus guy really was, which prompted the discussion between Jesus and his disciples. Really, his disciples were just starting to figure out who he was! Anyone who declared Jesus to be anything more than a teacher or healer risked being laughed at by his peers—but hopefully that wouldn't happen among the disciples.

Saying that Jesus was a prophet would have probably gotten you in trouble with the religious authorities because that would have given Jesus credibility, which could go against the teachings of the authorities. (Remember—the religious authorities could put you in jail or worse!)

But to say he's the Son of God, the Messiah? In Jewish law there was no greater sin than blasphemy, and the punishment was death. Remind your students that even after Jesus' time on earth, Saul (who later became the apostle Paul) was tracking down Christians and having them put to death. Stephen's death is one example of this—and Saul was there when Stephen was stoned by the religious leaders! (Acts 6:8—7:60)

So having Peter call Jesus the Son of God is a big deal! This was the first time any of them had made this statement out loud (as far as we know). Peter wasn't always the most solid example of a faithful disciple, but Jesus was impressed by his willingness to go out on a limb.

Can you imagine what the other disciples might have been whispering to each other about Peter when he first said it, even if they were thinking the same thing? And then can you imagine their surprise when Jesus said Peter would be the foundation of his church?

Death?

Explain to your group that there are still places all over the world where people are killed or imprisoned for declaring themselves followers of Jesus. If you want more information on this so you can talk intelligently about the issue with your group, check out: Open Doors, USA via www.opendoors.org. The Open Doors Web site has a section designed for teenagers called "Student Underground" that has some great resources for youth groups.

Another good source of information about the persecuted church can be found at the National Day of Prayer for the Persecuted Church Web site: www.persecutedchurch.org. Or go to the Youth Specialties resource, Student Underground, at www.youthspecialties.com.

Talk about what an equivalent would be in our own country—not physical death but something similar. Have students brainstorm on this.

closing

The Grand Finale

🔊 Movie clip: *10 Things I Hate about You*

🔊 Wrap up by saying something like this—We all have it in us to go the extra mile for people or ideals we believe in or desire strongly. We value it in sports, business, and romance. What a difference we could make, though, if we were to develop that quality in our faith! What an impact we could make for the kingdom of God if, when called upon to do so, we were willing to go "through the roof!"

Movie clip

10 Things I Hate about You

Start 00:53:21 A car pulls up in front of the house.
Stop 00:55:07 Cameron says, "And I'm back in the game!"
In this short clip, Cameron (Joseph Gordon-Leavitt) shares about all the things he was willing to do to try to win Bianca's (Larisa Oleynik) affection, despite the fact that she never showed him any interest at all. Of course, Jesus is more than willing to pay attention to us, unlike this self-centered girl! Mention that, but use this clip as a means of illustrating a passionate pursuit of someone.

discussion

Encore

Get It?	Middle School

🔊 What two things did Jesus do for the man who was lowered through the roof?

🔊 What did Nicodemus want to know from Jesus? Why was it a big deal for Nicodemus to want to know this?

🔊 What real risk did the bleeding woman put herself in? What was the result of her risk taking?

🔊 When Jesus asked his disciples who they said he was, what did Peter say?

🔊 Why was his response such a big deal and not just the obvious answer?

Get It?   High School

🔊 What did Jesus first say to the man after he was lowered through the roof?

🔊 How did the Scribes respond? What did Jesus do next?

🔊 What was the risk, for Nicodemus, in coming to Jesus? What did he want to know?

🔊 What was Jesus' response to the bleeding woman? How did that differ from the disciples' response?

🔊 What did Jesus ask Peter?

🔊 Why was his response so radical and risky?

What If?   The Big Picture

🔊 All of the people in today's lesson were highly motivated to risk all sorts of things for Jesus' sake. What deep need could lead you to take that kind of risk?

🔊 Why do you think it's not always easy to be a Christ follower?

🔊 Do you think God intended it to be that way? (If God really wants all people to know him, why didn't he make it a supereasy life with no risks?) Why or why not?

🔊 If Jesus were in this room now, how would you respond in each of the scriptural situations presented today? Could you risk your social status like Nic? Could you risk embarrassment and vulnerability like the bleeding woman? How about death?!

🔊 Which of these risks is the most real in your life? In what ways have you already experienced these?

So What?   It's Your Life

🔊 Think about the people in your life who exhibit "through the roof" faith. What kinds of qualities do they have that you would like to imitate in your own life? Pick one of these people and write a thank-you letter to him, expressing your appreciation for his example in your life. (Whether you give it to this person or not, the letter writing will help you think through this person's qualities that you want to imitate.)

🔊 What's one area of risk you can take this week? What might the result be?

🔊 Are you willing to try it? Why or why not? If you are willing, what's your plan of action?

🔊 When your friends ask you about your faith, are you wishy-washy, or are you willing to endure ridicule, laughter—even social death?

🔊 Peter was able to clearly answer that Jesus was the Son of God. Over the years the church has routinely asked itself the same question: Who do we say God is? They have affirmed their faith through creeds and confessions that define who they are and what they believe. Hand out paper and pencils to the group and give everyone about five minutes to write out a statement of faith that encompasses what they believe (about God, Jesus, the Holy Spirit, the church, the responsibilities of a Christian, and so on).

Major Metamorphosis

Contributed by **Kara Powell**

Primary theme contentment	
Themes dedication, change, evangelism	
Scripture Luke 4:38–5:11	
Approximate length through The Grand Finale 25-30 minutes	

According to Pascal, within every human there is a "God-shaped void." You and your students have a God-shaped hole in your heart that only he can fill. Trying to fill that void with achievements, relationships, or possessions is about as effective as trying to cram a square peg into a round hole. Not only does it fail, but you also end up pretty frustrated. This talk helps students realize that the friends, clothes, and grades they look to for happiness fall short. The only lasting contentment comes from the change that Jesus brings. And as Jesus showed Peter—once he changes you, he wants you to change the world around you.

You'll need

- A personal story about something BIG that happened to you that changed your life
- Pictures of yourself as a teenager (the geekier, the better) (optional)
- *Veggie Tales: Madame Blueberry* (Warner Home Video, 2003)
- TV and DVD player
- *Seventeen* magazine (or another secular girls' teen magazine) (optional)
- Three hearts cut out of construction paper (one red, one yellow, and one green) (optional)
- A personal story about something God has done for you to help you experience his peace and contentment
- A stack of green construction paper hearts (optional)
- Pens or pencils for each of the students (optional)
- Traffic signal or stoplight (optional)

intro
The Opening Act

🔊 Personal illustration: A Big Change (see sidebar)

🔊 Being a teenager is all about changes. Maybe not as big as the change you just described, but teenage life is full of all sorts of new choices and options.

🔊 Illustration: This Is My Life (optional, see sidebar)

🔊 Transition by saying something like—When I was a teenager, I was looking for things to change me. When I looked in the mirror, I wasn't all that impressed. When I saw what I was doing, it didn't seem to matter very much. When I looked at my life, it seemed pretty boring and humdrum. To be honest, I really didn't like myself very much. Everybody else seemed so much better off than I was. So I was looking for anything to change me. Or at least change how I felt about myself.

Personal illustration

A Big Change

Open by sharing a story about something BIG that happened to you that changed your life. It could be going away to college, meeting your spouse, getting married, having children, or maybe even purchasing this very book. Contrast how you felt before it happened with how you felt after it happened. The more specific you make the details in your story, the better.

Illustration

This Is My Life

Show three to six pictures of yourself as a teenager. Ideally, you would show them as part of a MediaShout (or PowerPoint) presentation. However, if your church's technology level is still hovering somewhere near 1978, then use your photocopier to blow up and copy the pictures onto color overhead transparencies so everyone can see them. As you flip through each of your teenage snapshots, comment on how awkward, lonely, and insecure you felt.

heart of the talk

The Main Event

1. The "if only" syndrome

🔊 Continue by saying—Lots of times I told myself "If only—." If only I had, if only I was, if only I knew—then everything would be so much better. Here are some of the "If onlys" that I chased after, and I bet you can relate to some of these too.

- "If only I had FRIENDS" (especially the right friends, meaning popular friends)
- "If only I had the right THINGS." (If you own the right shoes, clothes, computer games, or CDs, then you'll feel better about yourself.)

🔊 Movie clip: *Veggie Tales: Madame Blueberry* (see sidebar)

- "If only I had the RIGHT LOOK"

🔊 Illustration: *Seventeen* magazine (optional, see sidebar)

🔊 Brainstorming: Have students suggest other "if only" statements teenagers might have. Some more possibilities are—

- "If only I had the RIGHT BOYFRIEND or GIRLFRIEND"
- "If only I had DRUGS or ALCOHOL"
- "If only I had the right GRADES"
- "If only I were great at SPORTS"

🔊 Explain by saying something like—There are a couple of problems with all of these "if onlys." First, they're temporary. Even if you can get these things, they usually don't last. Which means you'll be scrambling for another "if only" in no time. Also, they never completely satisfy. They might change things on the surface for a while, but at the end of the day, you're still looking at the same old you in the mirror. Let's look at someone who found a better kind of change.

Movie clip

Veggie Tales: Madame Blueberry

Start 00:01:45 "There's never ever ever ever ever been a show like *Veggie Tales!*"
Stop 00:03:16 Larry says, "I don't know. How much stuff is there?"
(Note: By starting the clip a few seconds before the actual dialogue, you give students a chance to cheer and clap for their beloved *Veggie Tales* and not miss out on the conversation between Bob the tomato and Larry the cucumber.)

Bob (voice of Phil Vischer) and Larry (voice of Mike Nawrocki) are talking about one of Larry's cool new possessions: a brand-new action jeep. But Larry says he's still not completely happy. Soon he admits that he won't really be happy until he has it all—the camper, dirt bike, jet ski, action hang glider, and on and on.

211

Seventeen magazine

Use this illustration if you have a lot of girls in your group. If your group is predominantly guys, it won't have the same impact—and guys' magazines don't usually make the same point. Buy a copy of *Seventeen*—or some other secular mag for teen girls. Flip through its pages, showing the titles of the articles—especially the ones about physical appearance. There's a subtle and sometimes not-so-subtle message that the right look will give you a perfect life.

2. Stoplight changes

◁») Scripture: Luke 4:42 ("At daybreak Jesus went out to a solitary place. The people were looking for him and when they came to where he was, they tried to keep him from leaving them.") Jesus was getting more popular, and like a rock star or sports hero he was drawing quite a crowd.

◁») Scripture: Luke 4:38-39 (Jesus heals Peter's mother-in-law of a fever.) Peter had seen Jesus in action.

◁») Scripture storytelling: Gone Fishin' (see sidebar)

◁») Illustration: Stoplight Hearts (see sidebar) (optional)

Gone Fishin'

Retell the story of Luke 5:1-11 in your own words but with a bit of additional explanation along these lines:

- Luke 5:1—Jesus was teaching at the Sea of Galilee, which is located in the midst of some rolling green hills in Israel. He probably looked around and could tell that some of the people couldn't hear him very well since they didn't have microphones in the first century.

- Luke 5:2-3—At the Sea of Galilee, fishermen generally worked in pairs and fished at night because fish were more likely to swim into their nets and be caught in the dark. But in the morning, after the men were done fishing, they would have to wash, stretch out, and repair their nets. Jesus stepped into Peter's boat and got Peter to stop fixing his net. He asked Peter to put his boat out a little from shore and started speaking from the boat.

- Luke 5:4-5—Next Jesus asked Peter to cast his nets out in the deep water. Peter had already tried fishing (even at night, which was the preferred time to fish) and had come up empty. So why in the world should he, an expert fisherman, obey Jesus? Peter resisted a bit; he was tired, dirty, and probably smelly. But because of the way Jesus had healed Peter's mother-in-law, Peter knew enough about Jesus that he obeyed him.

- Luke 5:6-7—Peter and his buddies put down their nets and caught so many fish that their nets began to break. In the original Greek the verb *signaled* meant using their heads to get attention. Their hands were so full of fish and bursting nets that they had to use their heads to signal for help.

- Luke 5:8-11—Peter had an understandable reaction as he saw Jesus' power: Get away from me! But Jesus told Peter that he was changing him. He wouldn't just catch fish now. He would catch people. He would be used by Jesus to draw others to Jesus.

Stoplight Hearts

(Note: The construction-paper-hearts illustration will likely work best with younger teens than older ones. If you're speaking to high school students, consider modifying this illustration by just explaining it—refer to a stoplight and Peter's heart without holding up the cut-out hearts, which older students will likely find cheesy.)

Say something like—Like Peter, each of us is on a journey with God. I've got three different colored hearts here that represent the stoplight you might be sitting at right now.

(Hold up the red paper heart as you explain the following.)

Originally, we are born with a heart that is red. That's the color of our hearts before we understand anything about God or Jesus. That was the color of Peter's heart before he met Jesus. He was resistant to Jesus.

(Now hold up the yellow paper heart as you continue.)

Then Peter saw Jesus heal his mother-in-law. Peter's interest was heightened—his openness to Jesus grew a bit. But just like cars at a yellow stoplight, he was cautious. He hesitated when Jesus asked him to cast his net.

(Finally, hold up the green heart as you explain the last part.)

And then Peter saw more of Jesus' power and ended up following Jesus wholeheartedly and without hesitation. Like a car at a green light, he was going forward in his journey. Peter ended up leaving everything to follow Jesus, including his job as a fisherman (which netted him a better-than-average income). But Peter knew that the money, the job, and all of the comforts of home were nothing when compared to Jesus.

3. The best change

◀») Even though we look to all sorts of "if onlys" to change us, the change Peter experienced is the best change. And it's a change that you can experience.

◀») Unlike everything else being changed by Jesus is a change that lasts. Sure, Peter had his ups and downs (after all, he was an emotional guy), but he was a fundamentally different person. The same can be true of you 2,000 years later.

◀») Personal illustration: It's Good for You (see sidebar)

It's Good for You

Take a few minutes to share about something God has done for you that has helped you. Try to connect your story to some of the fears and anxieties that plague your students. Point out that it's your relationship with Jesus that gives you true peace and contentment.

closing

The Grand Finale

🔊 Say something like—Some of you are sitting here with red hearts (or "at red lights"). You've haven't seen much of God yet on your spiritual journey. Others of you are yellow hearts (or "at yellow lights"). You have been changed some in the past, but now you're cautiously moving forward toward God. Some of you are already green hearts (or "cruising through green lights") and are truly moving forward in your journey with Jesus.

🔊 Activity (for younger teens): Green Hearts (see sidebar) (optional)

🔊 Object lesson (for older teens): Stoplight (see sidebar) (optional)

🔊 Close in prayer, asking God to change your students and use them like he used Peter.

Activity

Green Hearts

Invite students to choose to "be green" and move forward in their walk with God. Whether they are red or yellow, they can now choose to be changed by Christ and change the world around them. And unlike everything (and I mean everything) they have tried in the past to change, God's changes last, are good for them, and will spill out onto others.

Place a stack of green construction paper hearts in the center of the room. Play some closing worship music and give students the chance to pick up a green heart as a symbol of the decision they're making today. Or a more subtle approach would be to pass a stack of green hearts throughout the students and anyone who wants to be green in their walk with God can take one. You also might consider having students write out a prayer or some kind of action plan on their hearts.

Object lesson

Stoplight

See if you can borrow an actual traffic signal from a traffic control company. (It's amazing what you can get when you simply ask—especially on behalf of a church.) It would be even better if you could figure out how to power it. Have students spend time looking at the light, praying, and contemplating where they are in relationship to Jesus. Ask them to consider whether they're willing to move up to the next light color.

discussion
Encore

Get It?   Middle School

🔊 What kinds of changes do junior highers tend to experience?

🔊 Today we talked about things teenagers "use" to try to change themselves: friends, stuff, a certain look, sex, drugs, and alcohol. Which of these things do you see other kids at school using or desiring with the hope that they'll feel better about themselves?

🔊 Can you think of some other things that people look to in order to feel better about themselves that we didn't mention today?

🔊 How have you been impacted by others who were "green hearts"? What did they do or say that was different than what other people tend to do or say?

Get It?   High School

🔊 Why do we tend to look to things to change us?

🔊 Of all the "if onlys" we talked about today, which one is the most dominant at your school?

🔊 Why do you think Jesus drew such a crowd?

🔊 Peter had seen Jesus heal his mother-in-law, yet he still hesitated when Jesus asked him to do something. What have you seen Jesus do?

🔊 Why do you tend to hesitate before doing what Jesus asks you to do?

🔊 How does choosing the "green light" impact others?

🔊 What do you have to lose by choosing the green light? What do you have to gain?

What If?   The Big Picture

🔊 If you had been a stowaway on Peter's boat and seen what happened, what would you have told your friends about it later? How would you have felt?

🔊 What do people with "red hearts" (or who are stopped at red lights) tend to do—how do they tend to act?

🔊 How about those with "yellow hearts" (or who are hesitating at yellow lights)?

🔊 What about the greenies with the "green hearts" (or those who choose to cruise on through green lights)?

🔊 How much of being changed by God is our job? How much of it is his job?

🔊 Will God change the color of our hearts, if we don't want him to? Why or why not?

So What? | It's Your Life

🔊 Which of the "if onlys" do you use to try to feel better about yourself?

🔊 What color best describes your heart before we met and talked about all this (or best describes the traffic light of your relationship with Jesus)?

🔊 What color is it now?

🔊 Has the color of your heart changed? If so, why? If not, why not?

Alone or Accountable?

Contributed by **Kara Powell**

Primary theme accountability	
Themes friendship, choices, truth, humility	
Scripture Judges 16:4-22	
Approximate length through The Grand Finale 20-30 minutes	

You'll need

- Pennies (or scraps of paper), seven per student
- A cheap pair of sunglasses with large lenses
- Masking tape
- A copy of the Samson Skit, page 224
- A copy of The Truth and Nothing but the Truth, page 223 for every student
- Pencils

Throw a rock and you'll hit a teenager who knows he needs friends (that throw-a-rock part is just metaphorical, of course). Friends are a teenagers' lifeblood. They spend all day with them at school; they call them as soon as they get home; they email them while they do their homework; and they hang out with them in the evenings. But how purposeful are these friendships? Are a teen's friends just some people to pass the time with so he doesn't get too bored? Or do a teen's friends make him a better person? This talk brings a new twist to the story of Samson and Delilah by inviting students to develop intentional accountability friendships. By giving others the freedom to walk around in their lives, your students will be less likely to trip and fall flat on their faces.

intro

The Opening Act

🔊 Activity: Have You Ever? (see sidebar)

🔊 Say something like—Some of you have done some pretty unusual things. And some of you have gone through some unusually difficult times. Sometimes our problems are out of our control. But other times they're a result of bad choices that we've made. That's because we all constantly blow it. Today we're going to look at a guy who learned the hard way what can happen when you make bad choices and how you need others to help you before it's too late.

Activity

Have You Ever?

Split your students into groups of six to eight students. Give each student seven pennies (or seven scraps of paper, if that's easier for you to get your hands on). Say something like—In this game, you'll take turns in your groups. Go around the circle and each person will share one strange thing they've done by asking a "Have you ever?" question. For example, if you've gone skydiving, you could ask the rest of the group: "Have you ever gone skydiving?" If their answer is yes, they don't do anything. If their answer is no, they have to put one penny in the center of the circle. Then the person who asked the question collects all of those pennies before the next person shares their "Have you ever?" question. The goal is to come up with somewhat bizarre or unusual things you've done so you get the most pennies. If you run out of pennies, you can still play the game by recapturing some pennies the next time it's your turn to ask a "Have you ever?" question.

Let students play in their own groups for four or five minutes. At that point, tell students it's the final round, and this time they are to share about problems or tough things that have happened to them (still in the form of a "Have you ever?" question).

Finally, have everyone count up their pennies and then give the person with the most pennies a prize—all the pennies!

heart of the talk
The Main Event

1. Why do we need others?

🔊 Object lesson: Temporary Blindness (see sidebar)

🔊 Many times we try to keep our sins and problems hidden from others, but inside they haunt us. We end up feeling like we're living double lives: the external life everyone else sees and the internal life only we can see with our private sins and struggles.

🔊 Illustration: Catch Me if You Can (see sidebar)

🔊 Whether it's a blind spot or a sin we've kept secret, we shouldn't deal with it on our own. We need to talk to someone about it.

🔊 Melodrama: Samson Skit (see page 226). You play the part of the narrator and choose nine students to act out Judges 16:4-22. Encourage them to ham it up. The more they get into their parts, the better.

🔊 Say something like—Let me ask you this: Where were Samson's friends? Where were the people he could go to and say, "My girlfriend Delilah is doing some pretty strange stuff. What do you think I should do?" And, come on, love doesn't just make us blind. Sometimes it makes us stupid. Even if Samson wasn't wise enough to go to his friends, where were the buddies who could have come to him and said, "Hey, we need to talk to you about your girlfriend—dude, she's serious trouble!" You see, too many times we are like Samson. Our vision is clouded, and we make the same costly mistakes over and over again without someone to stop us. There's no one to warn us, "Mayday, mayday, you're doing down in flames. Eject! Eject!"

Object lesson

Temporary Blindness

Ask for a student volunteer to stand in front of the group wearing a cheap pair of sunglasses with large lenses. Tell the group how this person can see pretty normally now, but then they start to make bad choices (you should name specific types of bad choices that relate to the struggles and problems your own students face). As you list each of the bad choices, put small pieces of masking tape over the lenses of the glasses so the student can't see. (Just lay them lightly on the lenses because you're going to want to pull them off in a few minutes.)

When the glasses are almost covered, have the student try to walk to a particular spot in the room. Point out how difficult it is since the student is more likely to stumble over things. Tell the students that the same is true with us. As we make bad choices, our vision is blocked, and we are in for all sorts of problems.

Illustration

Catch Me If You Can

Sir Arthur Conan Doyle, the author of the Sherlock Holmes series, was apparently a real prankster. One week he decided to play a joke on 10 of his closest friends. He sent an anonymous telegram to each person that said, "Your secret is out. All is known." After receiving the telegram, every one of his 10 friends fled town. They just hit the road. They would rather leave everything behind than have their secrets found out.

2. How can others help us?

🔊 Say something like—We don't want to be the kind of people who have hidden secrets that block our vision and lead us to make bad choices. Instead, we want to have friends who love us enough to help us see our errors. (Start pulling some of the masking tape off the sunglasses as you continue to speak.) Those kinds of friends are called accountability friends. Accountability is a fancy word that means inviting others to speak into your life. And if you want accountability, there are a few steps you can take:

- Get committed people. It can be one other person or three people, but find people who are committed to you and to your growth.

- Get consistent. Set up a time and place to meet, such as every other Tuesday at a coffee shop or in front of your school.

- Get a core set of questions.

🔊 Illustration: The Truth and Nothing but the Truth (see sidebar and page 225)

Illustration

The Truth and Nothing but the Truth

Distribute a copy of The Truth and Nothing but the Truth (see page 225) to each student. The handout gives examples of questions to ask in an accountability session. Mention to the students that when they meet with their accountability friends, they don't have to ask all of the questions. They should just choose a few that are the most relevant.

closing
The Grand Finale

🔊 Distribute a pencil to each student. Say something like—On the handout I just gave you, I want you to circle the two questions that you most need someone to ask you these days.

🔊 Depending on the vulnerability level and size of your group, you can choose from a number of different ways to finish the talk:

- Ask students to write down the name of one person they could go to this week to talk about those two questions.

- Or (for a more vulnerable group) ask the students to turn to the person sitting next to them, share one of the questions they circled, and explain why that question is relevant to them.

- Or (if you have the most vulnerable youth group around) ask students to divide up into smaller groups (each with an adult leader) and share which questions they circled and their answers to each of them.

discussion
Encore

Get It?	Middle School

🔊 Describe accountability in your own words.

🔊 How would Samson's life have been different if someone else had held him accountable?

🔊 Think of a Christian you really admire. Does she still need accountability? Why or why not?

🔊 What problem have you had in the last few weeks? How would you have been helped if someone were holding you accountable through that experience?

Get It?	High School

🔊 How do our bad choices block our vision?

🔊 If you had received that telegram from Arthur Conan Doyle, what would you think? How would you feel?

🔊 What kind of qualities would you want in someone who was holding you accountable?

🔊 Looking at those qualities, what qualities do you see in yourself? What qualities are lacking? How can you work on those qualities?

What If? The Big Picture

🔊 What do you have to lose by inviting people to walk around in your life? What do you have to gain?

🔊 Are there ever times when you should keep your problems to yourself? Give some examples.

🔊 Is it possible to be so perfect and sinless that you don't need someone to hold you accountable? Why or why not?

So What? It's Your Life

🔊 What are some problems you have had recently?

🔊 Are they consequences of your choices or someone else's choices, or are they just random?

🔊 What two questions on the handout did you circle?

🔊 How would having someone hold you accountable help you?

🔊 Who do you know who could hold you accountable?

🔊 When could you meet with them?

🔊 What would you talk about?

The Truth and Nothing but the Truth

Accountability = inviting others into your life.

Accountability Questions

1. How has your relationship with Christ been changing?

2. What's going on in your prayer life?

3. How have you encountered God's Word recently?

4. How have you served other people this week?

5. How have you been treating your family?

6. What was your biggest disappointment? How did you decide to handle it?

7. What was your biggest joy? How did you handle it?

8. How have you been tempted recently? How did you respond?

9. How have you done controlling your tongue?

10. How have you been doing in your thought life? Are you spending time thinking about things that distract you from God?

11. How have you worshiped God recently?

12. How are you doing at letting non-Christians know about your faith?

13. What do you see as your number-one need for next week?

14. Have you lied in your answers to any of the above questions?

15. How can we pray for you?

Samson Skit

Characters:
> Samson
> Delilah
> 2 Philistine rulers
> 2 Philistine soldiers
> 7 strings (to be played by one person)
> New rope (yup, played by one person)

Our hero (at least sort of), Samson, fell head over heels in love with Delilah. Life with Delilah seemed so good that he skipped around with a big dopey smile on his face. Delilah was a Philistine, and was thus an enemy of the Israelites. So two Philistine rulers crept to see her and said, "See if you can lure Samson into showing you the secret of his great strength so we can tie him up and beat him up. We'll pay you big bucks."

So Delilah said seductively to Samson, "Hey big boy, tell me the secret of your strength and how you can be tied up and subdued."

Samson said, like a good little boy scout, "If anyone ties me with seven fresh strings that have not been dried, I'll become a weakling."

So the two Philistine rulers brought Delilah seven fresh strings and, while Samson was sleeping, she tied his hands with them.

In the meantime, two Philistine soldiers hid in the room. Delilah yelled loudly, "Samson, the Philistines are upon you!" But he broke the strings and beat up the two soldiers.

Delilah cried and moaned. "Samson, you lied to me and have made me look foolish. You'd better tell me the secret of your strength."

Samson said, "If anyone ties me with new rope, I'll become a weakling."

So when Samson was sleeping again, Delilah took new rope and tied him with it. Then, with the same two soldiers hidden in the room (who were still limping from their first meeting with Samson), she called to him, "Samson, the Philistines are upon you!"

But he snapped the ropes off his arms and beat up the Philistine soldiers.

Delilah huffed and puffed and stomped about. Still stomping, she said to Samson, "Stop making me look foolish! Tell me the secret of your strength!"

Samson sighed, "All right, woman. If you weave my hair, I'll become a weakling." So while he was sleeping and snoring loudly, Delilah wove his hair. And guess what she yelled? "Samson, the Philistines are upon you!" He awoke and flexed, showing how strong he still was.

Delilah knew she really had to pour on her womanly wiles. She batted her eye lashes and said sweetly, still batting her eyelashes, "Samson, how can you say 'I love you' when you lie to me? Tell me your secret."

Samson finally sighed loudly and admitted, "If anyone shaves my head, I will become weak."

The two rulers and the two limping soldiers came and hid in Samson's room. Delilah shaved his head while Samson was asleep and snoring.

Then Delilah yelled, "Samson, the Philistines are upon you!" But this time Samson was weak and stumbled around the room. The four Philistines jumped on top of him and blinded him.

The two Philistine rulers jumped for joy because they finally got their man. They paid Delilah her reward, and she then strutted off the stage and headed down to the local shopping mall to spend the money. The blind Samson was put in handcuffs and led away by the two still-limping soldiers.

Death Vader

Primary theme death	
Themes serving others, sacrifice, making a difference	
Scripture James 4:13-17	
Approximate length through The Grand Finale 20-30 minutes	

You'll need

- ◀» A local newspaper
- ◀» Videotape of local or national news broadcast (optional)
- ◀» A water mister
- ◀» An inflatable children's swimming pool
- ◀» Some children's floaty toys
- ◀» A rock or a brick
- ◀» *Pay It Forward* (Warner Brothers, 2000)
- ◀» TV and DVD player
- ◀» Paper and pencil for each student
- ◀» A list of things you'd like to have said about you at your funeral

One morning the Swedish chemist, Alfred Nobel, woke up to a startling obituary in the newspaper. A newspaper reporter had accidentally mixed up some details and had written an obituary for Alfred when it was actually Alfred's older brother who had died. The result? Alfred decided to start giving out the Nobel Prize to scientists and writers who fostered peace. James (in the Bible!) would applaud such midlife evaluation. This talk invites students to take the teachings of James 4 seriously and make sure that their life, however long it is, counts for something.

Contributed by **Kara Powell**

intro
The Opening Act

🔊 Illustration: Death Images (see sidebar)

🔊 Say—There are people in our town who will die today. They didn't wake up this morning thinking that this would be their last day alive, but nonetheless, it is.

🔊 Transition by saying something like—Odds are good that you don't often think about your own death. After all, you're teenagers. You have your whole life ahead of you, right? Regardless of how long you're going to live, the Bible has some things to say about death. And because of what it says about death, we're going to want to do some things differently.

Illustration

Death Images

Students are surrounded by images and stories about death. They're so surrounded by them that they often grow numb to both the reality of death and to the questions about what happens after someone dies.

Bring in a copy of your local newspaper and point out the stories about people's deaths (from the obituary section or others). Or better yet, tape the news (local or national) the day before you give this talk and cue the tape to a story or two about death.

After you've shared these stories with students, ask questions like:
• Who do you think is affected by this person's death?
• How do you think they might be feeling?
• Do you think much about your own death?

Depending on the size and dynamics of your group, you can either let students answer these questions in large or small group discussions or make them rhetorical questions. (Note: Be sensitive to any students who may have recently lost someone close to them.)

One more thought: This would be a great "location" talk—consider taking your students to a cemetery for all or just parts of this talk.

heart of the talk
The Main Event

1. Do good today.

🔊 Scripture: James 4:14 ("Why, you do not even know what will happen tomorrow. What is your life? You are a mist that appears for a little while and then vanishes.") James was writing to businesspeople (see James 4:13) who had big goals about their future careers.

🔊 Ask—What kinds of careers do you want to pursue?

🔊 Verse 14 gives us a penetrating question: What is your life?

🔊 Object lesson: Mister, Mister (see sidebar)

🔊 Object lesson: Ripples (see sidebar)

Object lesson

Mister, Mister

Ahead of time, fill a mister with some water. Squeeze the handle so that some mist appears. Point out to students how the mist appears for a little while and then vanishes. The same is true with our life (see James 4:14). We're not around for all that long.

Object lesson

Ripples

Ahead of time, fill a child's inflatable swimming pool with water. Toss some children's bath toys into the pool. Explain that the pool represents the students' school, and the floating toys are their friends.

Hold up a heavy object, such as a rock or a brick, and explain that it represents each student here. Now toss the rock into the pool. (Note: You should probably practice this ahead of time to make sure your rock or brick is big enough to shake up the floaty toys.) Point out how the rock causes all sorts of movement in the pool. The same is true with us. What we do impacts others. And when we do good, not only will others be affected, but the whole school could also look different.

2. Doing good will cost you.

📢 Say something like—Although I want you all to do good things and impact others, I respect you too much not to be honest with you. Doing good will cost you. It might cost you some popularity, your reputation, your time, your friends, and even some bigger things.

📢 Movie clip: *Pay It Forward* (see sidebar)

Movie clip

Pay It Forward

Start 01:51:47 Trevor says, "See you later, guys!" as he walks to a bike rack.

Stop 01:59:07 The scene fades to black at the end of the movie.

Set up the clip by explaining that as part of a school project, Trevor McKinney (Haley Joel Osment) is challenged by his social studies teacher, Mr. Simonet (Kevin Spacey), to find a way to change the world during the coming school year. So Trevor decides to "pay it forward" by doing good deeds for people. Then those people are supposed to do good deeds for others, and so on. This clip shows how Trevor decides to step in to help another kid at school. The ending is very sad, so be prepared for students (and leaders!) to reach for some tissues. That's okay. Death is sad, and yet James believes it's the tragic finality of death that should motivate us to do good.

Optional Additional Clip

Start 00:07:35 Mr. Simonet says, "Now this class is social studies…"

Stop 00:12:34 A close-up camera shot of the chalkboard

If you have time, first show your group this five-minute clip, which gives some good background information about the school project. In this clip, the point is made that the world doesn't expect much from kids because they're young. Thus, the teacher challenges these preteens to show the world that they can make a difference.

closing

The Grand Finale

📢 Activity: Live So They Won't Have to Lie at Your Funeral (see sidebar)

📢 Personal illustration: Your Own Funeral (see sidebar)

📢 Close in prayer, asking God to give his grace to help us live the kinds of lives he wants us to live.

Live So They Won't Have to Lie at Your Funeral

Distribute papers and pencils to your students. Explain that there's a bumper sticker that says, "Live So They Won't Have to Lie at Your Funeral." Have students write down the kinds of things they would want said at their funeral. Then have students write down the kinds of things that might be said about them if they died today. After they've had some time to work on this, ask them to go over the two lists and consider what the two lists have in common and how they are different. Now ask students to write down one thing they'd like to do differently this week in order to be the kind of people they want to be. Encourage them to pick something that involves doing good to others, even though it might cost them.

Your Own Funeral

Whenever you have the chance, it's good to share with students your own answer to a tough question that you've asked them to think about. Use this as an opportunity to share about the kinds of things you'd want said about you at your funeral. Then be honest about how you're not living up to a few of those qualities. Share a few specific things you'd like to do differently to be the kind of person you want to be.

discussion

Encore

Get It?	Middle School

🔊 Who do you know who has died? What was the funeral like?

🔊 How is your life like a mist?

🔊 What was the point of the swimming pool and floaty example?

🔊 What kind of kid was Trevor in *Pay It Forward*?

🔊 How did you feel as you watched the *Pay It Forward* clip?

Get It? High School

- What kind of future do you want to have?

- How much do you think about your own death? What tends to make you think about your own death?

- Do you talk with your friends much about death? Why or why not?

- In what ways have you been impacted by others who have done good to you?

- What are some potential costs of doing good?

What If? The Big Picture

- If Trevor had known that helping that other boy would cost him his life, do you think he still would have done it? Why or why not?

- If you were Trevor's mom, would you have wanted him to help the boy even if it cost him his own life, or would you have wanted him to let the boy get beat up? Explain your answer.

- If you knew you were going to die tomorrow, what would you do today?

- If you knew you were going to die in a year, what would you do in the next year?

- Should we try to live as if we're going to die soon? Is that realistic? Why or why not?

So What? It's Your Life

- What kind of things do you want people to say about you at your funeral?

- Which of those things are you already doing or are you already like? Which of those do you think you should work on?

- What can you do this week to do good for others? What might that cost you?

Jingle Yells

Contributed by **Kara Powell**

Primary theme advertisements	
Themes the media, friendship, self-image, emotions, desire, contentment	
Scripture 1 Thessalonians 2:8; Philippians 4:11-13; Romans 12:1-2	
Approximate length through The Grand Finale 25-30 minutes	

You'll need

- Three large pieces of butcher paper
- A marker
- Rolls of tape, one per small group
- Several teen magazines (like *Seventeen*, *Teen People*, *Rolling Stone*, and so on), two or three for each small group
- *Rudy* (TriStar Pictures, 1993)
- TV and DVD player

What was the last major purchase you made? Why did you make it? Did you really need the item? Even if you did need it, why did you choose the particular brand that you did? Was it because you wanted to be more of something? More trendy, more impressive, or more attractive? Regardless of your age, admit it: You're influenced by advertising. The students you work with aren't just influenced; they're immersed in the jingles and slogans of TV, radio, and Internet ads. This talk helps students realize how their lives are marinating in advertisements and asks them to evaluate whether the messages behind the ads reflect reality.

intro

The Opening Act

🔊 Activity: Slogan Sing-Off (see sidebar)

🔊 Activity: Bible Verse Shout-Out (see sidebar)

🔊 Transition by saying something like—We're surrounded by slogans, labels, and advertisements. We see thousands of them every day. Look around now. How many labels or logos do you see? (Have students share what they see around the place where you're meeting, ranging from the Sony DVD player in your room to the Levi's the guy sitting next to them is wearing.) How do these labels, logos, and advertisements influence us? Do they give us a true picture of what life is like, or do they distort the picture to make us want what they're selling? Let's compare the messages of advertisements today to the message of the apostle Paul in his letters to the first-century church.

Activity

Slogan Sing-Off

Ask your students to yell out slogans or jingles from various advertisements. They can be TV jingles, magazine slogans, or radio ads. If you want to make it more competitive, you can divide your room in half and have a slogan sing-off. One side of the room sings five to ten seconds of a song or jingle, and then the other side sings five to ten seconds of a different one. Then the first side sings again, and so on. The sides cannot repeat a song or slogan that has already been said or sung. The first team that can't think of a slogan loses. If you want to make it even more difficult, you can designate different themes for each round (for example: cars, food, clothing).

Activity

Bible Verse Shout-Out

Ask students to yell out any Bible verses they know. If you used teams during the Slogan Sing-Off, you can keep your students in the same teams and continue the competition. Unless your students are abnormal Bible scholars, they'll know way more slogans and jingles than they will Bible verses.

heart of the talk

The Main Event

1. True or false: relationships

🔊 Activity: Mad, Glad, or Sad (see sidebar)

🔊 Scripture: 1 Thessalonians 2:8 ("We loved you so much that we were delighted to share with you not only the gospel of God but our lives as well, because you had become so dear to us.") We share our whole lives with the people we care about, not just the happy stuff.

🔊 Movie clip: *Rudy* (see sidebar)

Activity

Mad, Glad, or Sad

Ahead of time, tape three large pieces of butcher paper to a wall. Write one word—MAD, GLAD, or SAD—at the top of each piece of paper.

Divide your students into groups of four to six and distribute teen magazines and a roll of tape to each group. Give students three to five minutes to flip through the magazines and look for pictures of relationships. It can be same-sex friendships or opposite-sex relationships. After a few minutes have students tape their pictures onto the piece of butcher paper that best describes the feelings of that relationship. Are they mad? Glad? Or sad?

You're almost certain to have more "glad" pictures than mad or sad pictures. Advertisements typically portray only one dimension of friendship—the dimension that says if you buy what they're selling, then your relationships will be all sweetness and light.

Movie clip

Rudy

Start 01:33:11 A view of the interior of the coach's office door
Stop 01:34:47 A close-up shot of a pile of football jerseys
Based on the true story of Rudy Ruettiger, Rudy (Sean Astin) worked hard to accomplish his dream of playing football for the University of Notre Dame. His hard work at football practices earned him the respect of the other players. But since Rudy wasn't as big or as good as his teammates, the head coach (Chelcie Ross) didn't want him to play. But his friends on the team showed the true nature and meaning of friendship by their own willingness to sacrifice their spots on the team so Rudy could play in a game. Unlike what we see in advertisements, real friendship means hard choices and serving others, not just big smiles at fun parties.

Idea from *Videos That Teach* by Doug Fields and Eddie James (Youth Specialties, 1999)

2. True or false: happiness

🔊 Illustration: Sappy Happy (see sidebar)

🔊 Activity: Say Cheese (see sidebar)

🔊 Scripture: Philippians 4:12 ("I have learned the secret of being content in any and every situation.")

Illustration

Sappy Happy

Stand in front of the piece of "glad" butcher paper with all of its happy, smiling faces. Say something like—These people are all smiles, but they're only smiling because they want you to buy their product. If you buy their jeans or wear their cologne, you'll have great friendships and smile from ear to ear like they are.

Activity

Say Cheese

Ask students to smile as if they were having their picture taken. Now have them hold that smile. After about 15 seconds, their cheeks will probably start to ache. Have them hold their smiles for at least 30 seconds before letting them relax. Point out that the kinds of smiles you take for pictures aren't sustainable. Life is not just a bowl of cherries. It's more like the ups and downs of a roller coaster, but it's a rich ride.

3. True or false: bodies

🔊 Illustration: Picture Picture (see sidebar)

🔊 Scripture: Romans 12:1 ("Offer your bodies as living sacrifices, holy and pleasing to God—this is your spiritual act of worship.") How our bodies look doesn't matter all that much to God. He wants our bodies to be living sacrifices.

🔊 Illustration: The Verdict Is In (see sidebar)

Picture Picture

Most guys think Michelle Pfeiffer is pretty hot. She can go from baseball-hat-wearing cute to way sexy in seconds.

Several years ago, the cover of *Esquire* magazine had her picture on it. It said, "What Michelle Pfeiffer Needs Is Absolutely Nothing." She looked gorgeous. She was wearing this red dress and had her head tipped back with her mouth open in this huge (and, of course, sexy) smile. But we got our hands on a copy of the bill from a friend of a friend of a friend (of a friend of a friend…) of the photographer who not only took that picture, but then also touched it up. Here are the touch-ups listed on the bill:

"Clean up complexion, soften eye lines, soften smile line, add color to lips, trim chin, remove neck lines, soften line under earlobe, add highlights to earrings, add blush to cheek, clean up neckline, remove stray hair, remove hair strands on dress, adjust color and add hair on top of head, add dress on side to create better line, add dress on shoulder, clean up and smooth dress folds under arm and create one seam on image of right side, add forehead to create better line, remove red dress at corner of neck, add dress on shoulder to sharpen and create a better line, soften neck muscle a bit, and soften neckline on image on left side."

He added forehead. That's gotta hurt!

No wonder we get bummed that we don't look like Michelle Pfeiffer in the picture. Even Michelle Pfeiffer doesn't look that way!

Adapted from *Mirror, Mirror* by Kara Powell and Kendall Payne (Youth Specialties, 2003).

The Verdict Is In

Whether you know it or not, magazine advertisements and articles influence the way you feel about your body. Some people did a test to see if there was any connection between magazines and how girls feel about themselves. One at a time they brought 39 different female college students into a room to wait several minutes before taking a test to see how satisfied they were with their bodies. Half of the women viewed *Vogue, Harper's Bazaar, Wile,* and *Allure* while they waited; the other half looked at news magazines like *Time, Newsweek, U.S. News* and *World Report,* and *BusinessWeek.*

The women who viewed the fashion magazines ended up more bummed about how they looked. They wished they weighed less, were more frustrated about their weight, were more preoccupied with the desire to be thin, and were more afraid of getting fat than the other half of the women who looked at news magazines. And get this—there were no significant differences between the weights and heights of the two groups. The major difference was in the type of magazine they flipped through before taking the test.

From *Mirror, Mirror* by Kara Powell and Kendall Payne (Youth Specialties, 2003).

closing

The Grand Finale

🔊 Say something like—The goal isn't to hide from all advertisements. The goal is to be more wise when we see or hear them, realizing that they don't capture life as it really is.

🔊 Close in prayer by giving students 30 seconds to pray silently about struggles they have when it comes to the images of friendship they see in advertisements. If they don't have any struggles with those false images of friendships, have them pray silently for friends they know who do.

🔊 Similarly, give students 30 seconds to pray about their issues related to happiness, and then a final 30 seconds for issues related to body image.

discussion

Encore

Get It?   Middle School

🔊 What are some of your favorite ads? Why do you like them?

🔊 What ads can you think of that specifically target teenagers?

🔊 What have you bought recently? How did ads play a part in your purchase, if at all?

🔊 We talked about false images of friendship, happiness, and perfect bodies. What other inaccurate messages have you seen in ads?

Get It?   High School

🔊 Did you know more advertisement jingles or Bible verses? (Discuss.)

🔊 What are some of the most effective ads you've seen? What makes them effective?

🔊 What did you think about what the photographer did to the picture of Michelle Pfeiffer? What does that tell you about the pictures you see in magazines?

🔊 How is new technology changing the influence of advertisements?

What If?   The Big Picture

- Is it possible to avoid advertisements? Why or why not?

- One of advertisers' biggest targets is the teenage market. Why do you think that is?

- If you were going to design an ad to target teenagers, what kinds of messages would you include in it?

So What?   It's Your Life

- Given what you've heard today, how do you think you have been influenced by advertisements?

- What do you want to do about that?

- What do you have to lose by doing what you just described?

- What do you have to gain?

Pizza Parlor Grace

Primary theme grace	
Themes sin, serving others	
Scripture Ephesians 1:1-14	
Approximate length through The Grand Finale 25-30 minutes	

You'll need

- 🔊 Enough pizza (or another food that teens love) for your whole group
- 🔊 Bibles
- 🔊 *Les Misérables* (TriStar Pictures, 1998)
- 🔊 TV and DVD player
- 🔊 A candle
- 🔊 A match or lighter
- 🔊 A piece of paper
- 🔊 Thank you notes and pencils for each student

Duck, duck, goose. It's a game you and your students loved when you were six years old, but unfortunately, it still influences your theology today. If you sit up really straight and smile really big, then God will choose you. And he doesn't choose everyone; he only chooses the good boys and girls. The reality is that God chose everyone 2,000 years ago at Calvary. This talk helps students realize how great it is to be chosen by God and how much greater it is to say yes to his rescue. Then it invites students to view their lives as big thank-you notes back to God.

Contributed by **Kara Powell**

intro
The Opening Act

📢 Object lesson: Who Wants Some? (see sidebar)

📢 Object lesson: Some for All (see sidebar)

📢 Say something like—Notice the difference between the two times I brought out the pizza. First I only chose a few of you. But then I brought out enough for everyone. When it comes to our relationship with God, I have good news: He has chosen EVERYONE.

Object lesson

Who Wants Some?

Bring out a nice, hot pizza and ask, "Who wants some pizza?" Choose only a few students to come forward and get a slice. Comment on how tough it is when you want to be chosen but aren't. Whether it's receiving a piece of pizza, choosing teams in P.E., or waiting for someone to ask you to dance, being skipped over can be agonizing.

Object lesson

Some for All

Once the "chosen" students have finished their slices, bring out more pizza—enough for every student to have a piece this time. Play some rowdy music for a few minutes and let the students enjoy a slice or two.

heart of the talk
The Main Event

1. Why would God choose me?

📢 Scripture: Ephesians 1:1-14 ("For he chose us in him before the creation of the world.") Since it's such a long passage, you may want to choose a few students (ahead of time) to read it out loud in front of the group. To make it more interesting, have them read alternating verses.

📢 The word *chosen* used by Paul resembles the word for *chosen* that's found in the Old Testament and refers to God's choice of Israel. Before the foundations of the world were laid, God chose to love us.

- 🔊 Ask—Why did God need to choose us in the first place? (Because of our GUILT, meaning our sin.)
- 🔊 Illustration: Cheesy Sin (see sidebar)
- 🔊 Because of our guilt, we couldn't rescue ourselves. God gives us GRACE so we can have a relationship with him. God's grace is one of the things that makes Christianity different from all other religions.
- 🔊 Movie clip: *Les Misérables* (see sidebar)
- 🔊 As a result of God's grace, we want to serve him with GRATITUDE.
- 🔊 Object lesson: Thank-You Note (see sidebar)

Illustration

Cheesy Sin

Because of Adam and Eve's choice in the Garden of Eden, all humans now sin. It's not just something we do; it's part of our nature. We are sinners. Every part of us is distorted by sin. It's like the cheese that covered the pizza you just ate. Imagine you're the crust, and the cheese is sin. Every one of us is covered in our sin.

Movie clip

Les Misérables

Start 00:03:00 An old woman says, "You can't sleep here."
Stop 00:09:52 The bishop says, "And now I give you back to God."
Jean Valjean (Liam Neeson) was arrested for stealing food to feed his sister and her family, and he served time in jail for 19 years. He's now been released, but since he is a former convict, he has to show his yellow passport to every potential employer and landlord so they know he's an ex-convict before they decide to hire him or to let him stay at their place. As you might imagine, most people don't want a former convict staying in their house or working for them, so Jean Valjean's options are rather limited. When a bishop (Peter Vaughan) lets Jean stay with him, Jean experiences some extravagant grace—the same extravagant grace that God shows us.

Object lesson

Thank-You Note

Show your group a thank-you note. It can be blank, one that you have written to someone, or one that you have received. Point out that when someone does something nice for us, we want to thank that person. God has done the nicest thing ever for us by giving us his grace as an escape from our sin. Our whole lives should be big thank-you notes back to him. We should want to do what he says because of all he has given to us.

2. What is the mark of being chosen?

- Scripture: Ephesians 1:13 ("You were marked in him with a seal.") The Holy Spirit is a mark, or seal, of being chosen.
- Object lesson: Marked with a Seal (see sidebar)
- Illustration: Wedding Ring (see sidebar)

Object lesson

Marked with a Seal

Before the creation of the post office people sent letters with seals on them. The seals were usually made of wax and reflected the identity of the sender of the letter.

Demonstrate how a seal works by lighting a candle. (Note: You might want to practice this ahead of time because different candles produce different amounts of wax at different speeds. And don't use a no-drip candle! You may even need to light the candle before you start speaking in order to produce a sufficient amount of wax to make a seal.) Then tilt the candle to the side and let some of the wax drip onto a piece of paper. Fold the paper, showing how the wax seals or closes it. Explain how, in the same way, we are now sealed and sent with the Holy Spirit. He is with us as a sign of our ultimate sender—God.

Illustration

Wedding Ring

As the Holy Spirit is a sign of our relationship with God, a wedding ring is a sign of your relationship with your spouse. If you're married, hold up your wedding ring (if you can get it off your finger) and talk about its meaning and how looking at it reminds you of your relationship. If you're not married, then either borrow a wedding ring or use this as an opportunity to let another adult volunteer share for a few minutes about his wedding and wedding ring.

closing
The Grand Finale

🔊 Say something like—Although we've talked about God choosing us, we have to say yes to him. Just like you had to actually say yes when I offered you the piece of pizza, you also need to say yes to God's grace.

🔊 Activity: 3-G Notes (see sidebar)

🔊 Close in prayer, asking God to help you realize your great guilt, be aware of the way he chose you through his grace, and serve him in gratitude.

Activity

3-G Notes

Distribute blank thank-you notes and pencils to the students. Have them write a note to God. The note should have three parts. First, they write a few sentences about their guilt and sin. Second, they thank God for his grace. Third, they write down specific ways they want to serve him out of gratitude for all he has done for them. Depending on the size and dynamics of your group, you might want to have students read their thank-you notes to one another.

discussion
Encore

Get It?	Middle School

🔊 What was the difference between the first time I brought out the pizza and the second time?

🔊 For those of you who got the pizza the first time, how did you feel?

🔊 What about those who didn't get pizza the first time?

🔊 Why should we be grateful to God?

🔊 If we've said yes to being chosen, are we better than those who haven't said yes yet? Why or why not?

Get It? — High School

- What's the difference between saying that a person's actions are sinful and that a person's nature is sinful?

- How would you describe grace in your own words?

- Given what you know about other religions, how are they different than the guilt, grace, and gratitude of Christianity?

- If I've already said yes to God and been sealed by the Holy Spirit, can I do whatever I want? Why or why not?

What If? — The Big Picture

- What can we do to earn the privilege of being chosen? Explain your answer.

- If we say yes to being chosen and yes to God's grace, why do we still sin?

- What would you say about someone who received a great gift from someone (like a cure for their cancer), but they didn't want to do even a small thing to thank her for it (like wash her car)? How is that like what God has done for us and how we respond to him?

- Are there other reasons we should want to serve God other than our gratitude?

- What difference does the Holy Spirit make in a person's life?

- So if God has chosen everyone, does that mean we're all going to heaven? Why or why not?

- If we're sealed by the Holy Spirit, can we ever lose that seal? In other words, can we lose our salvation?

So What? — It's Your Life

- On a scale of 1-10 (1 being oblivious and 10 being very aware) how aware are you of your guilt?

- In what ways do you try to earn being chosen?

- What do you think you could do this week as a big thank-you note back to God?

A Day of Good News

Primary theme evangelism	
Themes hope, the gospel, witnessing	
Scripture 2 Kings 6:25-30; 2 Kings 7:3-9	
Approximate length through The Grand Finale 25-30 minutes	

You'll need

- *City Slickers* (Castle Rock Entertainment, 1991)
- TV and DVD player
- A personal story about a time when you felt hopeless and despairing, like there was no way out of a certain situation

In a postmodern world, philosophies of pluralism and relativism impact our students in a very real way. We exist in a culture that preaches that it is okay to believe in anything you want and live any way you please as long as it is right for you. The subliminal impact that this worldview has on our Christian students is very powerful. In a world where it is no longer acceptable to share one's faith, many people are asking the question, "Why should we reach out? Why should I be a witness to the saving grace of Jesus?" This talk is designed to give our students a reason why they should be proactive in sharing the Good News of Jesus. In a world full of despair we have been given a great and precious gift. It is our God-given responsibility to share this Good News in a world crying out for hope and belonging.

intro

The Opening Act

🔊 Movie clip: *City Slickers* (see sidebar)

🔊 After the laughter subsides, begin by saying something like—The reality is that many people will live their lives exactly the way this video describes. Perhaps you know people just like this. They get to the end of their lives and look back to see only hopelessness and no meaning. You may not know it yet, but if you are a believer in Jesus Christ, you have been given an incredible gift. That gift is an abundant life—a life full of meaning and hope. You have been given Good News, and we all have a responsibility to share that Good News with others.

🔊 Mention the somewhat-unknown Old Testament story that describes a bleak time for the people of Israel and how you'll be looking at it to dig up some motivation for sharing our faith with others and answering the question, "Why do we reach out?"

Movie clip

City Slickers

Start 00:15:19 The teacher says, "Daniel, would you introduce your father please, and tell us what he does."

Stop 00:17:58 Mitch says, "Any questions?"

Mitch Robbins (Billy Crystal) is going through a midlife crisis. In this scene he is attending career day at his son's school, but he doesn't really enjoy his job anymore. So when it's his turn to talk to the class, he goes on and on about all the negative things they can expect from life as they get older.

(Note: One of the other characters in this scene makes a crude hand gesture while Mitch is talking, so use your discretion. You may wish to start the clip a little later, in which case you can begin showing the clip at 00:16:40 instead, when Mrs. Green (Jane Alden) says, "Mr. Robbins?" The clip should still make sense from this starting point.)

heart of the talk

The Main Event

1. Cannibals and calamity

🔊 Scripture: 2 Kings 6:25-30 ("There was a great famine in the city...As [the king] went along the wall, the people looked, and there, underneath, he had sackcloth on his body.")

246

◄)) Kind of a gross story. The people of Samaria, who were living in a walled city, woke up one day to find themselves besieged by a foreign army. This army cut off all supplies to the city, which brought a great famine upon them. It got so bad that some people were reduced to awful acts of desperation in order to survive. The people of Samaria had never known such despair.

◄)) Highlight verse 26 (a woman cries out, "Help me, my lord the king!"). Just as the people of Samaria were crying out for help, so are many people in our world crying out for help today.

◄)) Quote: Not Quite Nirvana (see sidebar)

◄)) Continue by saying—Do you know anyone in this kind of pain? Are there people in your life who are crying out for help like this? Maybe they are turning to drugs and alcohol to help them through their pain, but these are just short-term solutions to a long-term problem. And that problem is sin.

◄)) Personal illustration: My Experience of a Broken World, Part 1 (see sidebar)

◄)) Acknowledge that the world is full of despair and pain, and sometimes it seems as though there is no way out.

◄)) Transition by saying something like—But the good news I want to share with all of you is that God is bigger than our greatest hurt and pain.

Quote

Not Quite Nirvana

Kurt Cobain, the leader of the 1990s rock group, Nirvana, was a guy about whom most people would have said he had everything. This quote was written just after the birth of his new baby, at a time when Nirvana was the most popular band in the world and literally millions of people would have done nearly anything just to spend 15 minutes with this man. Yet here he is, just three months before he killed himself, crying out for help:

> All I want is friends that I can talk to and hang out with, just like I've always dreamed, we could talk about books and politics and vandalize at night, want to? I can't stop pulling my hair out! Please! God, Jesus Christ Almighty, love me, love me, we could go on a trial basis, please I don't care if it is the out of the in crowd, I just need a crowd a gang, a reason to smile. I won't smother you, please isn't there anybody out there? Somebody, anybody, God help, help me please. I want to be accepted. I have to be accepted. I'll wear any kind of clothes you want! I'm so tired of crying and dreaming. I'm soo soo alone. Isn't there anyone out there? Please help me, help me.

—Kurt Cobain

From *Heavier Than Heaven: A Biography of Kurt Cobain* (Hyperion Press, 2001)

Personal illustration

My Experience of a Broken World, Part 1

Take some time to share about a time in your life when you felt hopeless and despairing, when you felt like there was no way out of a certain situation. At this point hold back so you don't conclude with how God led you out of this difficult time—we'll save that for later!

2. Lepers and life

- Scripture: Continue this story by reading 2 Kings 7:3-8 ("Now there were four men with leprosy at the entrance of the city gate. They said to each other, 'Why stay here until we die?'") Stop before you read verse 9.

- Recap and explanation: Those Who Need Hope the Most (see sidebar)

- Illustration: The Slave Trader (see sidebar)

- Christian history is full of people like John Newton who (just like the lepers in the passage we just read) were full of hurt and pain; but because of God's goodness, they have been forgiven and given new hope for life.

- Personal illustration: My Experience of a Broken World, Part 2 (see sidebar)

- Continue by saying—All of us can see ourselves in the lepers in that Bible story. All of us have a disease that the Bible calls sin. Our sin separates us from a life of goodness, joy, love, and meaning. But just like those lepers, some of us have stumbled onto a great mass of riches. All of a sudden our lives have been blessed beyond our understanding. And now we have a choice—Do we share this Good News that we have been given, or do we keep it to ourselves?

- Encourage your group to imagine what life would have been like for these lepers. They had lived a long time as outcasts of their society. Now all of a sudden they found themselves rich beyond their wildest imaginations. And they now have a choice. Do they keep all this good stuff to themselves, or do they share it? Ask students what they would have done.

- Scripture: 2 Kings 7:9 ("Then they said to each other, 'We're not doing right. This is a day of good news and we are keeping it to ourselves. If we wait until daylight, punishment will overtake us. Let's go at once and report this to the royal palace.'")

- The lepers looked at each other, and they came to a conclusion. They said, "Hey, guys, it isn't right to keep all this good stuff and this good news to ourselves. There are people in that city eating their own children. We have to go and share what we have found."

Those Who Need Hope the Most

Explain this part of the story by retelling it—Four guys were sitting outside the city. They were outcasts; nobody would even go near them for fear of catching their incurable and disfiguring disease. Finally, they get to a point of complete hopelessness and they say to each other, "If we stay here outside the city, we will die; if we go into the city we will die—why don't we go and surrender to this army? Perhaps they will allow us to live." So they enter the camp of the invading army and find it abandoned. But they did find silver, gold, horses—you name it, they found it. The four people in the city who were the most hopeless and most despairing were the ones to stumble upon great riches.

The Slave Trader

John Newton was a bad man. The worst of the worst. Several hundred years ago, he made a living by stealing people from their homes and villages and selling them into a life of slavery. Decent, respectable people would not have anything to do with the man—in their eyes he was the scum of the earth.

Then one day, when his life was full of despair, hurt, and pain, he stumbled onto an amazing truth: There is a God who could forgive him of any sin, no matter how bad his life had been. Not only could God forgive John Newton, but he could also give John hope and meaning for his life.

Not long after he discovered this amazing fact, John Newton sat down and wrote the words to one of the most well-known hymns in history, "Amazing grace! How sweet the sound that saved a wretch like me! I once was lost, but now am found; was blind, but now I see."

My Experience of a Broken World, Part 2

Return to the story that you began telling your students in the first part of this message—about the time when you felt completely abandoned and hopeless. Now finish that story by sharing about how God met you in that place and how he restored hope and meaning to your life.

closing
The Grand Finale

🔊 Transition by talking about the amazing Good News we have that can change people's lives and rescue them from despair. Ask your students if they are willing to share the news, or will they keep it to themselves?

🔊 Conclude by saying something like—In this world there is a lot of pain. It is full of people who are crying out for help. We need to understand that we are just like the lepers in this story—we have stumbled onto amazing goodness. Now it is our responsibility to share this Good News with all those people in our families, our schools, our neighborhoods, and our lives who need the same hope and meaning that we have found.

discussion
Encore

Get It?   Middle School

🔊 In your life right now who are the people you see crying out for help in their lives?

🔊 If you are a Christian, describe how your life is better because you have made a decision to be a believer in Jesus.

🔊 What are some of the things that stop you from sharing the Good News with others?

Get It?   High School

🔊 Where do you see examples in our world of real hurt, pain, and brokenness?

🔊 Describe your life before you met Jesus.

🔊 How has your life changed as a result? What hope and meaning has God given to you now that you have decided to follow him?

🔊 Why do we sometimes fail to share the Good News?

What If?	The Big Picture

- What if you had never stumbled onto the Good News of Jesus Christ? Think as far forward as you can. What might your life look like now?

- What regrets do you think you might have at the end of your life?

- Even though some of us have decided to become Christians, does this mean that we are immune to pain and hurt? If not, how might having a relationship with Jesus better equip us for dealing with pain and disappointment?

So What?	It's Your Life

- How can we become more aware of the good things we've received since becoming Christians?

- What is your biggest stumbling block in sharing with others about Jesus?

- What is your greatest motivation for sharing with others the Good News?

- What are some things you can do to make you more willing and able to share your faith with others?

A Place of Sanctuary

A Place of Sanctuary

Primary theme grace

Themes justice, safety, church, kingdom of God, family, salvation, community

Scripture Joshua 20:1-9; Luke 4:18-19; Proverbs 28:5; Matthew 7:7-8; John 10:10

Approximate length through The Grand Finale 30-35 minutes

You'll need

🔊 *The Hunchback of Notre Dame* (RKO Radio Pictures Inc., 1939) (You can use any version of this film except the animated Disney one, which doesn't contain the necessary scene.)

🔊 TV and DVD player

🔊 Your testimony of salvation

Contributed by **James Prior**

Many years ago I was watching *M★A★S★H*, one of my favorite shows. In one episode a soldier, who had gone AWOL, ran into the mess tent where weekly church services were held and claimed the right of sanctuary to the resident priest. Being a young child, I didn't understand the pretense of this entire show because the concept of sanctuary was foreign to me. Some years later I did an intense study on the history of sanctuary throughout Christian times. I was surprised to discover that the right of claiming sanctuary, protection in the house of God, went all the way back to the Old Testament. Our students live in an unsafe world. The longing to find a place of rest and refuge is as strong in their hearts as it was in times of old. In this talk we will discuss the history of sanctuary and what the implications of a place of refuge are for us today.

intro

The Opening Act

📢 Movie clip: *The Hunchback of Notre Dame* (see sidebar)

📢 Ask your students if they have any idea what Quasimodo was crying out. What did he mean by "sanctuary"?

📢 The history of claiming a church or a place of worship as a place where people are safe from the arm of the law is very old. We have examples of it throughout the middle ages and even in America. In 1980, people who were fleeing the death squads of El Salvador and Guatemala claimed sanctuary in a Presbyterian church in Arizona.

📢 Illustration: Muslims Seek Sanctuary (see sidebar)

📢 The concept of claiming sanctuary, a place of safety, goes even further back than Western history.

📢 Scripture: Joshua 20:2 ("'Tell the Israelites to designate the cities of refuge'".)

📢 Explanation: Cities of Refuge (see sidebar)

📢 Illustration: Running to Sanctuary (see sidebar)

📢 Transition by saying something like—What does that sanctuary look like? What are you feeling as you finally make it through those doors and are finally safe? What do you feel? (Give your students some time to reflect on what it would be like.)

Movie clip

The Hunchback of Notre Dame

There are quite a few versions of this old movie, and in every one of them (except the animated Disney version) there is a great scene where Quasimodo swings down from his room at the top of the cathedral to save the woman from hanging. After rescuing her from certain death, he cries out at the top of his voice, "Sanctuary, sanctuary—I claim sanctuary!"

Illustration

Muslims Seek Refuge

On April 2, 2001, a standoff began at the Church of the Nativity in Bethlehem when militant Muslims sought refuge from invading Israeli forces. As the political situation unfolded, most questions were focused upon the end of the standoff and finding a peaceful solution. Yet rarely did a commentator ask the intriguing and theological question, "Why did Muslims seek refuge within the confines of a Christian church?"

The Church of the Nativity is considered the traditional site for the birthplace of Jesus Christ. Actually, the church is built over a cave that many Christians believe is the manger where Jesus was born. Ironically, the Palestinian gunmen did not seek refuge at the Mosque of 'Umar, located directly across the street from the church, since it was under fire from the Israeli army. When one of the men inside the church was asked why they chose the church over the mosque, he answered, "We here understand our history and that the Church of the Nativity [has been a sacred] place to the people during all wars."

Explanation

Cities of Refuge

In the time of Joshua, there was very little law. It was kind of like the Old West, only worse. If someone was murdered, the family of the murder victim would get together and appoint someone to avenge the killing. If the murderer was caught and executed, justice was considered done. Unfortunately, there was no provision for the people who accidentally killed someone (what we call "manslaughter" today). So God steps in and says to his people, "I want you to set up a bunch of cities that people can flee to if they accidentally kill someone." These places became known as "cities of refuge."

Illustration

Running to Sanctuary

Just imagine you've accidentally killed someone. Your family stuffs some food into your hands for the long journey ahead, pushes you out the door, and commands you to RUN! So you run and run and run—all the while you're looking over your shoulder to see if you are being pursued. Then just on the horizon you see it: that strong tower—that fortress of refuge. You know that if you can just make it there, you will be safe, you will have arrived.

heart of the talk

The Main Event

1. Sanctuary is a place of salvation.

🔊 Illustration: The Soldier and His Son (see sidebar)

🔊 The word *salvation* in the Bible has many interesting meanings that we don't think about very often.

🔊 We tend to think of salvation as being saved from something. In the Bible the understanding was a little different. They believed that salvation was also about being saved to something. But to what?

🔊 Scripture: Luke 4:18 ("The Spirit of the Lord is on me, because he has anointed me to preach good news to the poor.") This is the very first message of Jesus that's recorded in the Bible. Here he sets forth the entire theme of his life. It isn't about going to heaven, though he does speak of that later. Right at the beginning of his ministry Jesus stands up in front of all the religious leaders and says I have come—

- so you no longer have to live in the prison of sin, but you can live a life of freedom. (Jesus didn't just mean literal "prisoners"—like of the jail variety!)
- so people can see the truth. (Jesus didn't only mean people who literally couldn't see—but all of us!)
- so people don't have to be oppressed anymore. (Jesus meant real earthly oppression and the oppression of sin!)

🔊 This is not just about being saved from something, but also about being saved to something—an abundant life.

🔊 Personal illustration: Your Story of Salvation (see sidebar)

Illustration

The Soldier and His Son

A few years ago an American soldier and his son were hiking in the Italian Alps when a huge blizzard began to blow in. They found a small bluff, dug in, and stayed there for 11 days. When all hope of ever finding the two alive was lost—they reappeared as if from nowhere! That bluff became to them a sanctuary of salvation.

Your Story of Salvation

Take some time to share with your students the story of your salvation, about that very first time you cried out to God. You don't need to have the best testimony in the world—simply describe what life was like before Jesus and now what it is like since he saved you to, not just from.

2. Sanctuary is a place of truth and justice.

🔊 Continue by saying something like—The city of refuge was set up not only to be just a place of salvation, but God also instructed that these cities be chosen so that there might be justice in the land. Think of what it would be like to live in a place with no justice, with no law.

🔊 Illustration: The Godfathers Are Crazy (see sidebar)

🔊 Justice is defined as "the quality of being just; fairness; the principle of moral rightness, equity."

🔊 Scripture: Proverbs 28:5 ("Evil men do not understand justice, but those who seek the Lord understand it fully.")

🔊 Illustration: The Simple Way (see sidebar)

The Godfathers Are Crazy

History records that in Italy there was a 400-year period in which 600,000 people died due to vengeance killings (like the ones we are reading and talking about today). The only real form of justice in Italy at this time was these revenge killings. This is what it is like to live in a place where there is no true justice.

Illustration

The Simple Way

In 1997, a group of students from Eastern College in Philadelphia heard about the plight of 80 homeless people in their inner city. In seeking refuge from the bitter winter of that city, these people had sought refuge in an abandoned church. When the owners of the building discovered that homeless people were living inside, they immediately moved to have them evicted. So this group of college students decided to leave school and move into the church as a form of protest to this injustice. Why should homeless mothers and children have to live on the street when a church is sitting empty?

During the three months that these students lived with this community, such a deep bond was formed that some of them decided that God was calling them to begin a community right in the heart of that neighborhood.

Many years later God has used these pursuers of justice to feed thousands of homeless people, run after-school programs for at-risk children, and be witnesses to the love of Jesus in this neighborhood. Their houses in this poor and downtrodden community have become places of sanctuary—places of justice.

3. Sanctuary is a place of family.

📣 Continue by saying something like—When you find sanctuary, not only do you find salvation and justice, but you also discover family. You are surrounded by many other people just like you, people in the same predicament that you are. You find brothers and sisters. We all need sanctuary.

📣 Refer back to Joshua 20:4. The city fathers in these "cities of refuge" were to give the fugitives a place "to live with them"—in community.

📣 Acknowledge that many of your students may come from families where there is lots of pain, so it may be difficult for them to think about their own families as safe places. But we can all experience family the way God intended.

📣 The New Testament uses the words *brothers and sisters* over 100 times. It's not evoking just an image, but a great reality. When you find sanctuary in the community of faith, you find a true family.

closing

The Grand Finale

◄») So where is this place of sanctuary today? Where is this city of refuge? Good question. This place of salvation, of justice, and of family is right here in our midst.

◄») Jesus called it the kingdom of God or the kingdom of Heaven. Jesus said he came to earth to make this type of community a reality. No longer do we need to run to a church or to a city to find these things—Jesus died so we can experience that sanctuary in him!

◄») If you are longing for salvation, for freedom from sin and oppression, if you don't want to be a prisoner anymore, but you want a place of justice and family—Jesus wants to be that for you.

◄») Scripture: Matthew 7:7-8 ("'Ask and it will be given to you; seek and you will find; knock and the door will be opened to you. For everyone who asks receives; he who seeks finds; and to him who knocks, the door will be opened.'") Jesus isn't talking about giving us "stuff"—but about giving us life!

discussion

Encore

Get It?	Middle School

◄») Where is the safest place in the world to you?

◄») Describe what it would be like for you to lose that place.

◄») Describe in a few sentences the word *salvation*.

◄») Describe the perfect family. Do you think it exists?

Get It?	High School

◄») What does it mean to be saved not only from something, but also to something?

◄») What does the word *justice* mean to you?

◄») Is finding a place of sanctuary as simple as just asking God for it? Explain.

What If? — The Big Picture

🔊 After hearing this message, what does the word sanctuary mean to you?

🔊 What does a life of freedom from sin and oppression look like? Is such a life really available to us? How?

🔊 What did Jesus mean when he said, "I have come that they may have life, and have it to the full" (John 10:10)? What does this have to do with a place of sanctuary?

So What? — It's Your Life

🔊 How can you allow God to use you as an agent of justice in this broken world?

🔊 If the kingdom of God that Jesus so often describes really is the place of sanctuary that many are looking for now, what are some things that you can do to make this kingdom a reality in your life and in the lives of others?

🔊 Is it possible to see other Christians as your true family? How?

🔊 How can you allow Jesus to be this sanctuary for you?

Stand Up and Don't Bow Down!

Contributed by **James Prior**

This outline is saved as GTO2_31 on the CD-ROM.

Primary theme courage	
Themes passionate living, temptation, accountability, faith	
Scripture Daniel 3:1,13-27	
Approximate length through The Grand Finale 30 minutes	

You'll need

- 🔊 A copy of *The Worst-Case Scenario Survival Handbook* (Chronicle Books, 1999)
- 🔊 A personal worst-case scenario situation
- 🔊 Paper and pencils for each student
- 🔊 A large piece of butcher paper and markers (optional)

Ever wonder what you would do if you were faced with a life-or-death situation? Say, for example, you saw a child drowning in a river that would likely take you also—would you jump in? What if that life-or-death situation was directly related to your faith in Jesus Christ? Do you think your conviction would give you the courage to make the right decision at the right time? In this talk we examine a situation just like this for three teenage boys. They were strangers in a strange land, yet their faith remained unwavering—even in the face of sure death. These boys were about the age of many of our students: What do we have to learn about the strength of their conviction?

intro
The Opening Act

- 📢 Illustration: *The Worst-Case Scenario Survival Handbook* (see sidebar)

- 📢 The authors, Joshua Piven and David Borgenicht, said their reason for writing the book was, "You never really know what curves life will throw at you, what is lurking around the corner. You never really know when you might be called upon to choose life or death with your actions. But when you are called, you need to know what to do. That's why this book is written."

- 📢 Illustration: My Worst-Case Scenario (see sidebar)

- 📢 Several thousand years before Jesus lived, the people of Israel were attacked and many of their brightest students were taken to a strange and feared country called Babylon. God had told the people of Israel that if they worshiped idols, this would happen—and it did.

- 📢 Continue by saying something like—Today we are going to look at a story describing the worst-case scenario for three of these teenage guys taken from their homeland. They found themselves in a life-or-death situation, and they didn't need a handbook to help them survive. They knew what they had to do because they had conviction. They knew what they believed to be right. As we look at this passage, I want to challenge all of us to consider this question: "Do we have this same type of conviction?"

Illustration

The Worst-Case Scenario Survival Handbook

In 1999, two authors by the names of Joshua Piven and David Borgenicht got together to write a manual about what to do if the worst should happen. Entries in this book include how to escape from quicksand, how to land a plane in the event of an emergency, how to perform a tracheotomy, how to escape from killer bees, and so on.

Here are some examples:

- How to escape from a mountain lion attack: don't run; open your coat so that you seem bigger; if you have small children, pick them up and place them on your shoulders so that you appear larger; wait until the animal moves away.
- What to do if a bull charges: don't antagonize the bull. (That's very helpful, thank you.)
- How to survive if your parachute fails to open: find a jumping partner, lock your arms in his or her chute, then open the chute—"the force of the opening of the chute will be severe, probably enough to dislocate or break both your arms." If your friend's canopy is slow and big, you may hit the ground slowly enough to only break a leg…However, if it is a fast one—"

From *The Worst-Case Scenario Survival Handbook* by Joshua Piven and David Borgenicht (Chronicle Books, 1999)

My Worst-Case Scenario

Ahead of time think about what your own worst-case scenario would be. Share it with your group. Stuck in a pit with rats? Locked inside a small box? Think of something creative to share with your group, then invite a few of your students to share theirs as well.

heart of the talk
The Main Event

1. Idols all around us

◀꣠ Scripture: Daniel 3:1-7 (the description of Nebuchadnezzar's big ol' statue)

◀꣠ In the first chapter in the book of Daniel, we find that God is blessing some of the Israelite boys because of their faithfulness. Even though they find themselves in a place where people hate or mock the God they serve, these boys refused to allow their surroundings to dictate to them how they would worship their God.

◀꣠ Continue by saying—In the midst of what seems to be not such a bad life for these guys the king of Babylon decides to erect a massive monument to himself, and he commands that everyone must worship it. Uh-oh—worst-case scenario alert!

◀꣠ Illustration: The Fall of Saddam (see sidebar)

◀꣠ Nebuchadnezzar's statue was huge! Made of pure gold, it was close to nine stories high!

◀꣠ Explanation and reflection: Idols in the Ancient World (see sidebar)

◀꣠ Idols are just as real in our world as they were in Babylon—we just don't see ones made of solid gold that stand nine stories tall anymore! We are all constantly faced with the temptation to bow down to things in our life that come before our relationship with God. It might be popularity, success, having lots of stuff, or other things. These things are idols in our world and they are BIG!

Illustration

The Fall of Saddam

Perhaps one of the most striking images so far in the 21st century is the sight of American tanks rolling into Baghdad to liberate the people of Iraq from the dictatorship of Saddam Hussein, the feared leader of that country for many decades. As the tanks rolled by city after city, we were all struck by images of the statues, pictures, and monuments that Saddam had erected to himself. The most powerful image of all was the fall of the huge statue in the center of Baghdad. But the statues of Saddam were nothing compared to the monument that King Nebuchadnezzar erected in Babylon.

Explanation and reflection

Idols in the Ancient World

So what's the big deal? All these guys have to do is bow down now, and then when they get home, they can ask God to forgive them. Or they could have bowed down and only pretended to worship the king—but really spent that time praying to God.

But they refused to do these things for a very specific reason. These boys knew the power of idols in their world. The temptation that constantly faced the people of God in the Old Testament was to give in to the idols of the countries around them. They had a belief that if they were to worship the idols of other countries, they too could have the military and economic power of those countries. But Shadrach, Meshach, and Abednego refused to bow down to this idol because they knew that to do so would be to reject the power of their God.

Take a moment and reflect on some of the idols people "bow down to" in our world today. Ask your students to share what they think some of the idols in our world are.

2. Commitment in the face of the worst-case scenario

🔊 Continue by saying—So thousands of people surround this idol, the music blows, and everyone falls on their faces before it. They know that there is a piping hot furnace right behind them, which is waiting to devour anyone who refuses to bow. So everyone falls down except for three Jewish boys. They stand strong when everyone else bows, even though they know it means certain death.

🔊 Scripture: Daniel 3:17-18 ("'If we are thrown into the blazing furnace, the God we serve is able to save us from it, and he will rescue us from your hand, O king. But even if he does not, we want you to know, O king, that we will not serve your gods or worship the image of gold you have set up.'")

🔊 Repeat the last words in this passage, pointing out their courage and faith.

🔊 Illustration: The Russian Sub (see sidebar)

🔊 Object lesson: Write Your Epitaph (see sidebar)

STAND UP AND DON'T BOW DOWN!

🔊 How we live each day determines not only how we will be remembered, but also the quality of our life while we're alive.

🔊 Thousands of years later we remember the conviction and the courage of Shadrach, Meshach, and Abednego and their courageous words because they refused to bow down to the idols of their world.

The Russian Sub

In 2000 a Russian nuclear sub called the *Kursk* suffered a series of explosions, which caused the death of 118 crewmen. Twenty-three of these men were trapped in a chamber for several hours, hoping to be rescued. One of them was a 27-year-old sailor by the name of Dmitri Kolesnekov. He wrote a note while he waited to die. It was displayed in a black frame on his coffin, and it simply read, "Must not despair."

It is not clear for whom those words were written—for his wife? His family? For himself? A strange thing happens when a person knows he is about to die. Something inside of him wants to record something personal and revealing to be left behind.

Object lesson

Write Your Epitaph

Hand out pieces of paper and something to write with. Or hang a large piece of butcher paper on a wall and provide markers for the students to use. Ask your students to think carefully and write out the words for their own gravestone—just one or two sentences. These shouldn't be witty poems. Instead they should be words they'd want said about them after they die.

3. God walks with us!

🔊 Scripture: Daniel 3:19-27 (the end of the story)

🔊 Recap the story, highlighting what it must have been like for those three guys to be thrown into the furnace, expecting to burn, watching the guards burn, and then realizing nothing was happening to them.

🔊 Say something like—Something strange happens when we refuse to bow down to the idols of our world. When we refuse to be as sexually active as other kids, when we choose God over grades, when we invite others to church. A very powerful God by the name of Jesus is standing right with us, delivering us from a meaningless life. He meets us in the furnace.

closing

The Grand Finale

📣 Every day every one of us is given an option. Will we bow down to the idols that surround us? Or will we have the conviction to stand and say, "No, I will not bow down?"

📣 Today God is calling all of us to find the courage and the conviction to stand up and not bow down.

discussion

Encore

Get It? — Middle School

📣 Describe your worst-case scenario. What situation would you least like to find yourself in?

📣 Describe some of the things in your life that might be considered idols.

📣 Do you think you would have the same courage and conviction as Shadrach, Meshach, and Abednego if you were in the same situation? Why or why not?

Get It? — High School

📣 Describe your worst-case scenario. What situation would you least like to find yourself in?

📣 What are some of the idols that you struggle with in your life?

📣 In the past, how have found the strength to stand up to these things and not bow down?

📣 How might the way we live today dictate how we will be remembered in the future?

What If? — The Big Picture

📣 These three boys could have bowed down to this idol and later on asked for forgiveness. What would they have missed out on if they had chosen this route?

📣 Describe a time when you have felt the presence of God helping you get through a really difficult time of temptation. Share this with the group.

So What?   It's Your Life

🔊 What are some things you can do to increase your courage and conviction when you are faced with the temptation to do wrong and not what God would want for your life?

🔊 Often it is when we have friends that share the same convictions as we do that we are more able to stand up and not bow down. Who are some of the people in your life that you can share your temptations and struggles with?

🔊 What are some of the things you can do to surround yourself with more people who share the same convictions as you?

Is Jesus the Only Way?

Primary theme evangelism	
Themes postmodernism, pluralism, theology	
Scripture 1 Timothy 2:3-4; Acts 10:34-35; John 3:18	
Approximate length through The Grand Finale 30-35 minutes	

You'll need

🔊 Nothing but Bibles

I n an increasingly pluralistic world, the traditional challenge of the exclusivity of the Christian message is coming under heavy fire. Many theologians and pastors are running far from the front lines in this discussion and rarely is such a topic addressed in the youth room. But today's high school students (more than junior highers) are confronting these issues all the time. As we move more and more into the reality of a postmodern world, it is becoming more difficult to defend the orthodox understanding of Jesus being the only way to heaven (at least with our traditional defenses). In this talk we examine three of the current theological understandings surrounding this discussion. As youth workers we all have a responsibility to educate our students and arm them with answers to this difficult and divisive debate. (Note: This talk is best suited for older students. And you should also know that it doesn't wrap things up neatly in the end and provide an answer. Instead it provides fodder for reflection, prayer, and discussion.)

Contributed by **James Prior**

This outline is saved as GT02_32 on the CD-ROM.

intro

The Opening Act

🔊 Illustration: The World Parliament of Religions (see sidebar)

🔊 The world is changing. We live in a melting pot of different beliefs and religious systems. Tolerance, the embrace of other cultures, political correctness, and openness are the values that thrive in our world.

🔊 Ask—How can the Christian faith, which holds such a strong position about the fate of people who do not agree with its belief system, thrive in a world like this? Is it possible or even worthwhile to cling to claims of "the only way" in light of our current culture?

🔊 Quote: Gandhi's Converts (see sidebar)

🔊 Discussion: Whatever Works for You (see sidebar)

🔊 Transition by saying—There are three basic responses to these questions. Now I know these are going to sound like really big, meaningless words but I am going to do my best to make them as easy to understand as possible. They are—pluralism, inclusivism, and exclusivism.

Illustration

The World Parliament of Religions

The year was 1893. The place was Chicago. Buddhists, Bahà'ís, and Bhakti Yogis had arrived from the East to attend the inaugural World's Parliament of Religions. While their contingent was sizable, they were vastly outnumbered by Bible believers from the West. Despite the disparity in numbers, however, the impact of the Eastern contingent was monumental. Swami Vivekananda, a disciple of the self-proclaimed "god-man" Sri Ramakrishna, used the Parliament to skillfully sow the seeds for a new global spirituality. Personifying tolerance and tact, he persuasively proclaimed the fundamental unity of all the world's religions.

One hundred years later—at the centennial celebration of the original Parliament (August 1993)—the impact of Vivekananda's message could be seen in living color. Buddhists outnumbered Baptists, and saffron robes were much more common than Christian clerical clothing. The swami's message of unification and universalism had undergone a metamorphosis as well. Almost imperceptibly, it had evolved into a new creed: The fundamental unity of all religions except one—historic Christianity. With alarming fanaticism orthodox Christianity was denounced as the obstacle to harmonizing the world's religions.

Gandhi's Converts

Someone once asked Gandhi why he sought converts in the political arena but precluded this among the religions. Gandhi replied, "In the realm of political and social and economic arena we can be sufficiently certain to convert, but in the realm of religion there is not sufficient certainty to convert anybody, and therefore there can be no conversions in religion."

Whatever Works for You

Ask your students to consider and discuss the following questions—
- Have you ever heard something like this statement—"You have every right to believe whatever you want. If that works for you—great. But what right do you have to insist it's the only way to believe?"
- Is the answer to just keep your faith to yourself? (This seems to be what more and more Christians are doing these days.)
- What are the weaknesses of that plan?
- What should you really believe? What are your options?
- How do we answer the question, "Is Jesus the only way to heaven?"
- In light of the religious state of the world do we even have a right to make such a claim anymore?

heart of the talk

The Main Event

1. Pluralism

🔊 Define pluralism: "All of the major world religions lead to a life in heaven with God."

🔊 The argument for pluralism, from a Christian perspective, is based on two foundations: biblical and moral.

🔊 Say something like—The first argument that Christians arguing the pluralist perspective make for their case is (believe it or not) from the Bible.

🔊 Explanation: The Exaggeration Gap (see sidebar)

🔊 The second argument that pluralists use to defend their position that anyone can go to heaven—even if they do not believe in Jesus—is called the Moral Argument. They ask the question, "How can we (Christians) claim to have the only way to God and true revelation when Christians do not live any better or any worse than followers of other faiths?" (Get some student responses to this question.)

🔊 They have a good point! Research shows that Christians lie, cheat, steal, and generally sin just as much as their non-Christian neighbors.

🔊 Wrap up this section by saying something like—Wouldn't it be great if pluralism were true? It would be great if everybody got to go to heaven. I think we can all agree with that. Just remember that in order to believe in pluralism, we have to give up a handful of important things—like belief that the Bible is God's inspired message to us and that Jesus is God's Son.

Explanation

The Exaggeration Gap

Pluralists argue that the Bible is simply a great collection of various documents complied by many authors. They say that since the earliest of the gospels in the New Testament was written at least 50 years after the death of Christ (a contention that is under heavy scholarly debate), by people who were not witnesses to the life and death of Jesus (also highly debatable), the time that passed between the occurrence of the real events and the compilation of the gospels was enough to let everyone's imaginations run wild. Therefore, in that time the people who were passionate followers of Jesus shifted from the reality of Jesus being a Spirit-filled prophet to the exaggerated claim that Jesus is God himself.

Continue by asking, What would this mean for us? What if the writers of the New Testament added in words that they wish Jesus had said?

2. Inclusivism

🔊 Define inclusivism: "Jesus IS the way of salvation. But he is saving everyone, including people who don't follow him here on earth."

🔊 Say something like—The difference between pluralists and inclusivists is this: While pluralists believe that salvation can be found in other religions, inclusivists teach that Jesus is in the process of saving the world, whether all know him or not.

🔊 There are three main points within this argument:
- Inclusivists do not glorify other religions like pluralism tends to do, but they believe that while light and beauty exist in other religions, darkness and bondage do as well.
- Inclusivists do not believe that other religions are vehicles of salvation. Salvation is found in the life, death, and resurrection of Jesus alone.
- Following God, even within other religions, will ultimately lead someone to faith in Jesus Christ (though that can happen after death, when confronted with the wonderful truth of Jesus).

◄») Quote: In This Life or the Next (see sidebar)

◄») Illustration: The Last Battle (see sidebar)

◄») Scripture: 1 Timothy 2:3-4 ("This is good, and pleases God our Savior, who wants all men to be saved and to come to a knowledge of the truth.")

◄») Scripture: Acts 10:34-35 ("'I now realize how true it is that God does not show favoritism but accepts [people] from every nation who fear him and do what is right.'")

◄») Wrap up this section by saying something like—Just as with pluralism, we should all hope for inclusivism to be God's truth! We shouldn't wish a life and eternity apart from God on anyone! But the inclusivist position has a hard time explaining many of the seemingly clear Scriptures in the Bible that talk of a verbal confession of Jesus and the life of love that follows that confession.

Quote

In This Life or the Next

Clark Pinnock, an evangelical theologian and inclusivist writes, "One receives the grace of God on the basis of an honest search for God and obedience to his revelation as heard in the heart and in the conscience…[this type of believer] is latently a member of Christ's body and destined to receive the grace of conversion and explicit knowledge of Jesus Christ at a later date, whether in this life or after death."

Illustration

The Last Battle

Some of you have probably read The Chronicles of Narnia. In the book *The Last Battle*, the pagan soldier Emeth learns to his surprise that even though he worshiped the pagan god "Tash" his whole life, at the end of the world Aslan (who represents Jesus in the stories) regarded the worship Emeth gave to Tash as worship unto himself.

Here's what the author C. S. Lewis says about this, "There are people in other religions who are being led by God's secret influence to concentrate on those parts of their religion which are in agreement with Christianity, and thus who belong to Christ without knowing it."

3. Exclusivism

◁») Define exclusivism: "Only those who hear the gospel of Jesus Christ and explicitly trust in him in this life can be saved."

◁») Say something like—In opposition to both pluralism and inclusivism, people who believe in exclusivism teach that the only chance people have for an eternity with God is if they accept him on earth.

◁») A couple things exclusivists believe:
  • Christianity is the only religion in the world with truth and is the only means of salvation. This salvation comes through a verbal, explicit, and personal faith in Jesus Christ.
  • The exclusivist teaches that a heart that seeks God will find him.

◁») Scripture: John 3:18 ("Whoever believes in him is not condemned, but whoever does not believe stands condemned already because he has not believed in the name of God's one and only Son.")

◁») Wrap this section by saying something like—The exclusivist view is the easiest to back up with the Bible. This doesn't necessarily mean that people who hold other views are not Christians; it just means that people who believe in the exclusivist view have a very strong foundation on which to rest their case.

closing

The Grand Finale

◁») So what are we to do?
  • Think, pray, seek God, and search Scripture.
  • Always act in love toward others.
  • Don't treat people with different perspectives as enemies or debate opponents.

◁») Conclude this difficult talk by saying something like—No one really knows who will and who won't go to heaven—that's not our job. Only God knows. Today you have been presented three views of this discussion. Even if we can't all agree on which is the right one, we should all be able to agree that following Jesus here on earth is a much better way to live our lives than not knowing him. Here's my advice: Share your faith as if the exclusivist view is true and pray that God's grace and goodness will extend to everyone alive.

◁») Quote: The Final Word (see sidebar)

The Final Word

Theologian Alistair McGrath writes, "We are assured that those who respond in faith to the explicit teaching of the gospel will be saved. We cannot draw the conclusion from this however that only those who respond will be saved. God's revelation is not limited to explicit human preaching of the good news, but extends beyond it. We must be willing to be surprised at those whom we will meet in the kingdom of God. In his preaching of the kingdom Jesus mentions some surprising characters—the Ninevites, the queen of Sheba, and those who lived in Sodom and Gomorrah."

discussion

Encore

Get It?	Middle School

(Note: If you use this talk with young teens, do some heavy modification first!)

🔊 Can you remember and explain the three views we talked about?

🔊 Have you ever been asked to defend the fact that Christians believe Jesus is the only way to heaven? Describe the conversation.

🔊 Do you think people in other religions have a hope of going to heaven? Talk about that.

Get It?	High School

🔊 Explain in your own words the pluralist view.

🔊 What about inclusivist?

🔊 What about exclusivist?

🔊 What do you find attractive about each position?

🔊 What do you see as being the problems of each?

What If?   The Big Picture

🔊 Is it harder today for people your age to accept that Jesus is the only way to heaven? Why?

🔊 Discuss the possibility that people could find salvation in other religions. What are some of the implications for us?

So What?   It's Your Life

🔊 How would you answer someone who came up to you and asked, "Do you believe Jesus is the only way to heaven?"

🔊 What if the exclusivist understanding really was the true and only view? How would that change the way you share your faith?

🔊 If the inclusivist position is the real deal, what does that say about how we share our faith with others?

🔊 What is the one new thing that you will take away from this message?

The Mystery, Beauty, and Hope of Easter

Contributed by **James Prior**

Primary theme Easter	
Themes evangelism, hope, salvation, Jesus	
Scripture Matthew 27:57-61; John 20:10-18; 1 Corinthians 15:50-55	
Approximate length through The Grand Finale 30 minutes	

You'll need

- *As Good As It Gets* (TriStar Pictures, 1997)
- TV and DVD player
- A personal story about a time when you felt like giving up
- A picture of a mean-looking dragonfly
- An video projector or overhead projector
- A screen (or a blank wall will do)

A few years ago on Easter Sunday some friends and I were sitting at a restaurant in San Diego. As we were talking about a new book that had just come out about proving the resurrection of Jesus, our waitress overheard our conversation. She told us she was a college student studying comparative religions and was on a journey of exploring spirituality. One of us asked her if she believed in Jesus. Her response is one that I will never forget.

She looked at us and said, "Of course I believe in Jesus, though probably not in the same way that you do." She went on to say, "You Christians are so consumed with proving that Jesus was who he said he was that you forget the mystery and beauty of what he said and did."

It seems to me that the goal of philosophy and theology for the last several hundred years has been to remove the mystery and replace it with solid irrefutable answers, to remove the beauty and replace it with rational understanding, and to remove the hope and replace it with the myth of progress and advancement. This message helps our students get back to the basics of the Easter message. It does not contain proofs of the resurrection, rather it dwells on the mystery, beauty, and hopefulness that the true Easter message inspires.

intro

The Opening Act

🔊 Quote: My Quest for Beauty (see sidebar)

🔊 Ask—What should it mean for this world that the Easter message is really true? What would it mean for those struggling with addictions and poverty, hurt and abuse, oppression and injustice, if it really is true that Christ is risen? (Field some student responses.)

🔊 Transition by saying something like—Surely this truth should mean that we are confronted with an amazing mystery, we are confronted with beauty beyond compare, and we are confronted with hope for the present and an amazing hope for the future.

Quote

My Quest for Beauty

A man by the name of Rollo May (who is not a believer in Jesus) wrote a book describing his lifelong quest for beauty. He recalls a scene from a visit to Mt. Athos, a peninsula filled with monasteries on the coast of Greece. He stumbled upon an all-night celebration of Easter. Incense hung in the air, and the only light came from candles.

At the end of the service the priest stood in front of all the people and declared, "Christos Anesti!" (Christ is risen!). Each person present replied according to custom: "He is risen indeed."

Rollo May writes, "I was seized then by a moment of spiritual reality: What would it mean for our world if he had truly risen?"

heart of the talk

The Main Event

1. Hope for the present

🔊 Movie clip: *As Good As It Gets* (see sidebar)

🔊 Point out Jack Nicholson's key line: "What if this is as good as it gets?"

🔊 Then say something like—So many people seem to be asking this question these days. Or to put it in a less hopeful way, people seem to be saying, "We are who we are, and there really is no hope for change."

🔊 Disillusionment with life is everywhere. Suicide is one of the leading causes of death for teenagers.

◄» In the Bible we read about a group of people who felt just as hopeless as many of us do in our darkest moments.

◄» Scripture: Matthew 27:57-61 (The disciples get Jesus' dead body ready for burial.)

◄» Have your students think through how hopeless the disciples must have felt as they got Jesus' dead body, cleaned and prepared it for burial, and then left it in a closed tomb.

◄» Ask—Have you ever felt hopeless?

◄» Personal illustration: My time of Giving Up (see sidebar)

◄» Quote: When Jesus Comes (see sidebar)

◄» It is when we are at our lowest point—feeling the most hopeless—that Jesus comes to us and offers us incredible hope for the present.

◄» Scripture: John 20:10-18 (Jesus reveals himself to Mary Magdalene after his resurrection.)

◄» Continue by saying something like—In this scene we see the opposite of the movie clip we saw earlier. When Jesus appeared to Mary after being in the tomb for three days, he presented to her the reality of a life filled with hope. Even when we are feeling our lowest, when we are feeling the most amount of pain, Jesus appears to offer us new life.

Movie clip

As Good As It Gets

Start 00:40:41 Melvin is cautiously walking down the sidewalk to his psychiatrist's office.
Stop 00:42:50 Melvin slams the outer office door.
Melvin Udall (Jack Nicholson) has been diagnosed with a severe case of Obsessive Compulsive Disorder. His life has become so entrapped that he can no longer step on cracks in the sidewalk or eat with regular utensils at a restaurant. In this pivotal scene, Melvin demands to see his psychiatrist, Dr. Green (Lawrence Kasdan), without an appointment. His doctor has no time for him and knows that if he gives in to Melvin's request, it will set Melvin back in his treatments. So the doctor leads Melvin back to the waiting room. Melvin grudgingly gives up the fight. But before he leaves the office, he looks around the waiting room and simply asks all the patients sitting there, "What if this is as good as it gets?"

Personal illustration

My Time of Giving Up

Share about a time in your life when you felt like giving up. The circumstances of your life had led you to a place where you truly felt hopeless—like there was no way out. Be as open and transparent with your students as you possibly can.

Quote

When Jesus Comes

The famous writer, Oswald Chambers, once wrote, "Our Lord begins where we would never begin, at the point of human [hopelessness]. The greatest blessing a person ever gets from God is the realization that, if they are going to enter into His Kingdom, it must be through the door of [hopelessness]."

2. Mystery, beauty, and hope for the future

🔊 Transition by saying something like—Not only do the death and resurrection of Jesus mean we don't have to go through life feeling trapped and hopeless. But they also mean we have a hope for the future—hope that when we die there is something more.

🔊 Illustration: The African Peppermint (see sidebar)

🔊 Ask—If you believed there was nothing beyond death, that life is just over, how would that affect your hope for the future?

🔊 The life, death, and resurrection of Jesus—what Christians call the Good News or the gospel—offers us the hope that after death we will live again.

🔊 Scripture: 1 Corinthians 15:55 ("Where, O death, is your victory? Where, O death, is your sting?")

🔊 Explanation: No Sting (see sidebar)

🔊 Illustration: The Dragonfly (see sidebar)

🔊 Illustration: No Day at the Beach (see sidebar)

Illustration

The African Peppermint

Philip Yancey describes a unique funeral custom conducted by African Muslims. Close family and friends circle the casket and quietly gaze at the body. No singing. No flowers. No tears. A peppermint candy is passed to everyone. At a signal, each one puts the candy in his or her mouth. When the candy is gone, each participant is reminded that life for this person is over. They believe life simply dissolves.

No Sting

In this kind of hard-to-understand passage, Paul is talking to a group of people who were denying that there is any hope for Christians after they die—a group of false teachers who were saying it is impossible that the resurrection happened. Paul restores hope to all of us by saying that because Jesus rose from the dead, we no longer have to fear death—there is no sting for us. In fact, it is something to look forward to!

The Dragonfly

By using either a video projector or an overhead projector (or just a big picture!) project a picture of a really mean-looking dragonfly onto a screen or empty wall. Get your students to take a good hard look at the insect and ask them to describe what about it makes the dragonfly look so mean. Dragonflies are some of meanest-looking insects in the world, yet they are completely harmless. They have no sting, and they have no bite.

The dragonfly is a lot like death for the person who has decided to follow Jesus. Death still looks kind of mean—there is something in it that makes us a little afraid—but Jesus offers us the hope that death is just like that dragonfly. It looks mean, but it has no sting, it has no bite, and it cannot hurt us anymore.

No Day at the Beach

Thomas Schmidt tells a tragic story at the end of his book on Easter, *A Scandalous Beauty*. On a fine day at a picnic, his nine-year-old daughter Susanna and her mother were on a hay wagon crossing a little creek. Suddenly the horses bolted and the wagon overturned. Everyone jumped off to safety except Susanna who was found several hours later drowned.

The last words in his book, which is all about hope for the present and the future, says this, "It matters to me that (death no longer has any power over us) is true, not merely interesting. The chaos of this life, the flood of waters have closed in over my head. Yet I choose against despair. I believe that death one day will die, that the love of God will prevail. In the meantime...I will follow Jesus in trust and hope until I see Susanna again...Not far from my apartment on a bluff overlooking the sea there is a marker on a new grave that bears the name of my only child and the following inscription: With joy still deeper than pain, gently flows the river where we shall meet again".

From *A Scandalous Beauty* by Thomas Schmidt (Brazos Press, 2002)

closing

The Grand Finale

🔊 Conclude this message by saying something like—This talk hasn't been about proofs for the resurrection—no evidences that demand a verdict. Rather, what I have hoped to present to you is an amazing gift. It is a gift given to us because of the reality that Jesus died and rose again. It is the gift of amazing hope for a life filled with joy and abundance here on earth. And it is a gift of amazing hope that even though our bodies might die, we will never feel the sting of death. May this mystery, this beauty, this hope transform your life this Easter.

discussion

Encore

Get It?	Middle School

🔊 In what ways do you see the world getting worse, not better?

🔊 Have you ever felt really disappointed? Describe that time to others in your group.

🔊 Do you fear death? Why or why not?

Get It?	High School

🔊 Describe some situations in the world right now that lead you to believe that things are getting worse, not better.

🔊 Describe a time in your life when you felt really hopeless, as if there did not seem much point in going on?

🔊 Have you ever experienced the pain of someone you love dying? If you feel comfortable talking about it, share with others in your group what that felt like.

What If?   The Big Picture

◁◁ If Jesus really did rise from the dead, how does that give you hope for the present? What about the future?

◁◁ Go around and have each person in your group answer this question using just a few sentences: What does Easter mean to me?

So What?   It's Your Life

◁◁ A philosopher by the name of Blaise Pascal wrote, "If I die and turn out to be right about Jesus, then Hallelujah! If I am wrong, well, it was a wonderful group of people to be wrong with and a satisfying life." Do you agree with this statement?

◁◁ If you fear death, what are some of the things you can do to understand that "death no longer has any sting"?

◁◁ How can you be a living example of the mystery, beauty, and hope of Easter to others?

Shaped by God

Contributed by **James Prior**

Primary theme God's will	
Themes grace, God's love, evangelism, forgiveness, trust, submission	
Scripture Jeremiah 18:1-4; Philippians 2:13	
Approximate length through The Grand Finale 25-30 minutes	

You'll need

 A couple pieces of beautiful, purely decorative pottery

 Some pieces of pottery that get used every day—an ugly coffee cup or a dish

 A big chunk of clay from an art store

O ne of the biggest struggles in my life is accepting the plans that God has for me. For many years I had a plan for my life; it was laid out clearly as far as I was concerned. Then God invaded my life, and one of the first things he made clear to me was this: "I know you have a plan for your life, but I want you to lay it down. I want you to understand that the plan I have for your life is better than the plan you have for your life." In a short passage from Jeremiah, God reveals to the prophet this exact same thing for the people of Israel. The message that he has for them is loud and clear. "I know you have plans, I know you have dreams—I am asking you to lay them down, not because I am a mean God, but because the plans I have for you are better than your plans." Many students struggle to understand this same thing. God is calling all of us to become moldable in the hands of a loving and caring potter.

This outline is saved as GT02_34 on the CD-ROM.

intro
The Opening Act

🔊 Scripture: Jeremiah 18:1-4 ("This is the word that came to Jeremiah from the Lord. 'Go down to the potter's house, and there I will give you my message.' So I went down to the potter's house, and I saw him working at the wheel. But the pot he was shaping from the clay was marred in his hands; so the potter formed it into another pot, shaping it as seemed best to him.")

🔊 Explanation: The Potter in the Ancient World (see sidebar)

🔊 So God is saying to Jeremiah, "Go down to the potter's house, Jeremiah; I want to show you some ordinary things"

🔊 Illustration: The Gift of the Artist (see sidebar)

🔊 Jeremiah was an artist just like many of the greats. God gave him a very simple task: Go to the potter's house. While in that place he saw a very ordinary thing—a pot being made. But God revealed to him an amazing lesson in this ordinary act that had the power to change a whole nation and has the power to change your life.

🔊 Say something like—What did Jeremiah see? Today we are going to look at just three things that God revealed to Jeremiah:

- The potter is committed to his work.

- The potter was creating something that was both useful and beautiful.

- The potter believes in do-overs.

Explanation

The Potter in the Ancient World

A potter's house in the time of Jeremiah (about 2,000 years before Jesus lived) was a fixture in every community. Almost every village or town had a potter. When God came to Jeremiah one day and asked him to go down to the potter's house, it would be as if God came to us today and said, "I want you to go down and hang out at the local gas station." Jeremiah would have been to the potter's house many times, and he would be very familiar with what happened there.

The Gift of the Artist

Ask your students this question—What makes someone a truly gifted artist, whether they are a painter, a comedian, or a photographer?

After a time of discussion respond to them by saying this—Some scholars believe that the true gift of an artist is their ability to see everyday normal things—things that might not seem special to another person—and make that ordinary thing extraordinary. Jerry Seinfeld excelled at this. As a comedian he could take something as simple as walking through a metal detector at an airport or buying soup and allow others to see these ordinary occurrences in hilarious ways. This is the gift of the artist.

heart of the talk

The Main Event

1. The potter is committed to his work.

🔊 Scripture review: Jeremiah 18:3 ("So I went down to the potter's house, and I saw him working at the wheel.") The first thing Jeremiah noticed when he went into that ordinary place was that the potter was working intimately at the wheel. Jeremiah didn't see a huge factory or rows of workers who didn't care about the quality of the work.

🔊 Illustration: Those Funny Scientists (see sidebar)

🔊 The God of these funny scientists is not like the God of Jeremiah at all. The Bible teaches us in many places that God longs to be in an intimate, personal relationship with all his creation. And this includes you!

🔊 Scripture: Philippians 2:13 ("For it is God who works in you to will and to act according to his good purpose.") Just as the potter was intimately involved with the creation of the pot, so God longs to be personally involved with you.

🔊 Transition by saying something like—The great news of the Bible is that God was willing to go to great lengths in order to be involved in your life, to know you, and to be known by you.

Illustration

Those Funny Scientists

There is a group of people in the science world known as theists. Theists believe that the universe and life could not possibly have come into existence without a creator. However, the creator that Theists believe in is not very much like the creator God that we read about in the Bible. Theists believe in a God that simply put all the ingredients for life to exist in a pan—so to speak—and watched the cake rise. This God is no longer associated with creation, nor is it possible to know him or be known by him.

2. The potter creates something useful and beautiful.

- Explanation: An Amazing Invention (see sidebar)

- Archeologists have found out something else about ancient pottery. It was always useful and was usually beautiful.

- Pottery that didn't get used was inconceivable to people back then.

- Object lesson: Beautiful but Not Useful (see sidebar)

- Object lesson: Useful but Not Beautiful (see sidebar)

- In our time we have separated usefulness and beauty. When you go to the grocery store, you are given two choices: paper or plastic. Very useful, but hardly beautiful.

- On the other hand we spend millions of dollars building museums to store priceless works of art. It is less common to find something that is both useful and beautiful.

- Continue by saying—What Jeremiah saw when he went down to the potter's house was the creation of something both useful and beautiful. God wants to do the same thing in you. He wants you to be useful to others but he also wants to give you a sense of how beautiful you truly are in his eyes. There is only one way we can become both useful and beautiful—we must allow him to mold us.

- Object lesson: Just a Lump of Clay (see sidebar)

- How do we stay moldable in God's hands? (Obedience. Saying to God, "I accept your plan for my life, and I am willing to become whatever it is that you want me to be.")

- Illustration: Alexander the Great (see sidebar)

- Transition by saying something like—Sometimes being shaped and molded is a painful process. Sometimes it might even feel like walking off a cliff! Being obedient to God is a very challenging thing. But the promise that he has for us is that if we remain moldable, he will make us both useful and beautiful.

An Amazing Invention

The invention of pottery is one of the most amazing, yet underrated, discoveries in the history of humanity. It might sound strange, but before pots existed, civilization could not begin. How? Good question.

Before the invention of pottery, the human race was filled with nomads. They could only gather food that they could eat that same day. If there is no way to store food, humans have to keep moving around and finding food.

So with the invention of pottery this all changed. Finally there was a way to store food and water so that it would not go bad. People did not have to keep moving and hunting—they could settle in an area and store supplies to get through winters or times of drought. Towns and villages sprung up, and as a result civilization could begin.

Beautiful but Not Useful

Show your students a piece of pottery that would never be used, only looked at. Explain to your students that the sole purpose of this pot (plate, vase, whatever) is decoration, nothing else.

Useful but Not Beautiful

Show your students a piece of unattractive pottery that would only be used for practical reasons, but never for decoration. Explain that the sole purpose of this item is usefulness, nothing else.

Just a Lump of Clay

Pull out a large lump of clay. If your group can handle it (without degenerating into a clay fight!), you could consider handing out small amounts of clay to each of them in order to give them a tactile experience while you continue talking. Explain to them that while this clay looks shapeless and ugly, in the hands of a professional it has the ability to become both useful and beautiful—as long as it remains soft and moldable.

Illustration

Alexander the Great

One of the greatest commanders in the history of war lived many centuries ago. He was a young man called Alexander the Great. A story is told that one day after a long and tedious march through very dry land, Alexander and his small, depleted force came upon a large fortress occupied by a provincial king.

Upon seeing the fortress Alexander simply marched to the front gate and demanded that the king immediately surrender. Hearing this proposal and seeing Alexander's worn-out army caused uproar in the fortress. They screamed down to him, "Why should we surrender to you? Your army is no match for us and this fortress."

Alexander simply turned around, ordered his troops to stand in a single-file line, and then ordered them to march over a sheer cliff. One by one Alexander's soldiers began to disappear over the edge to their death. After 10 or so soldiers had simply walked off the cliff, Alexander commanded them to stop. He turned back to the king in the fortress and repeated his command: "Surrender and I will let you live." The king immediately surrendered. It was clear that Alexander's soldiers would obey under any circumstance, which was more than the king could say for his own army.

3. The potter believes in do-overs.

- Scripture Review: Jeremiah 18:4 ("But the pot he was shaping from the clay was marred in his hands; so the potter formed it into another pot, shaping it as seemed best to him.") Something wasn't right with the first pot. But the potter didn't just throw it away—he squished it down and started to remold it.

- The best thing about our potter is his incredible love, patience, and forgiveness.

- Illustration: The Spanish Son (see sidebar)

- Quote: Marghanita Laski (see sidebar)

- Maybe you need to experience forgiveness—we all do from time to time! When we blow it, God does not throw us away; instead he is more than willing to simply forget our mistakes and start again. The potter believes in do-overs.

Illustration

The Spanish Son

One day a boy by the name of Pedro left his country home to find great riches in the city. His father was very displeased by his son's insistence to go despite it being against his wishes. After several years had passed, the father went into the city and placed an ad in the city newspaper. It read, "Dear Pedro, whatever you have done, wherever you have gone, all is forgiven, please come home. Meet me in front of this newspaper office at noon on Saturday. I love you, Your Father."

On that Saturday 800 Pedros showed up, looking for forgiveness and love from their fathers.

Marghanita Laski

Marghanita Laski was a famous secular humanist and novelist who died in 1988. It is said that her last words as she lay dying were, "What I envy most about you Christians is your forgiveness; I have nobody to forgive me."

closing

The Grand Finale

🔊 Conclude by saying something like—When Jeremiah went down to the potter's house, God gave him a clear and simple message, one that still has a lot of meaning and power for us today. The message was this: "I love you, I want to be intimately involved in every area of your life, I want to make you useful and beautiful. And if you mess up, I am here to forgive."

discussion

Encore

Get It?	Middle School

🔊 We talked about God longing to be involved in every area of our lives. What are some of the areas that you think God might be interested in becoming involved with in your life?

🔊 Talk about the word *obedience*. Is it as nasty as it sounds? What might it mean to obey God in everything?

🔊 What does it mean that we can be both useful and beautiful?

Get It?	High School

🔊 Describe a time when you have seen an artist take something normal and plain and turn it into art.

🔊 Do you believe God really wants to be involved in every area of your life? Why or why not?

🔊 What does it mean to you to be not only useful but also beautiful?

🔊 Describe a time when you and God needed to make a fresh start.

What If? | The Big Picture

🔊 What are some of your plans for your life? Share your hopes and dreams.

🔊 How hard would it be to give up those dreams if God had other plans for you? Do you honestly think you could obey?

🔊 What gets in the way of our believing that God is like a potter who can easily start again and forgive us when we mess up?

So What? | It's Your Life

🔊 Discuss what it means to moldable. What are some ways that you can remain soft in the hands of God?

🔊 If you need forgiveness today for something you may have messed up, what steps would you need to take to make it right?

The God Who Is There in Our Brokenness

The God Who Is There in Our Brokenness

Contributed by **James Prior**

This outline is saved as GT02_35 on the CD-ROM.

Primary theme grace	
Themes God's love, failure, hope	
Scripture John 8:1-11, 16:33; Luke 15:11-33	
Approximate length through The Grand Finale 30 minutes	

You'll need

- 🔊 A stack of magazines (preferably geared toward teens)

- 🔊 A personal story about a time in your life when you were really struggling and in pain

We don't have to be alive very long to realize and understand that the world in which we live is a broken place. The reality of war, poverty, disease, and economic breakdown is found in every one of our news bulletins. The Bible teaches that it is our individual brokenness that fuels the brokenness and the sorry state that the world is in. This talk aims to recognize the reality of this brokenness in both the world and in our lives, yet to offer hope to our students. Hope that is found in the realization that it is possible to worship and be intimate with a God who continues to remain in relationship with us in the midst of this broken world and our broken lives.

intro
The Opening Act

🔊 Activity: Real Life (see sidebar)

🔊 It would be nice to live in a fantasy world! But we don't.

🔊 Question: Good or Bad (see sidebar)

🔊 The Bible teaches that every single one of us is broken. We all have flaws and deep sinfulness in our lives that we try to hide.

🔊 Transition by saying something like this—Although many of us would dearly love for no one to know the brokenness that lives within us, the reality of life is that we live in a broken world—a broken world filled with broken, hurting people. The Bible teaches this, and we experience it every day. But the Good News of Jesus is this: God continues to work and move and make his presence felt in our lives and in our world even in the midst of our brokenness, our foolishness, and our weakness. It is when we are the most broken, when we are at our most foolish, when we are most weak that God's presence can really be experienced.

Activity

Real Life

Bring a stack of magazines (any kind will do, but teen magazines would be best). Have students flip through and look at the ads. Tell them to find ads that represent real life—the world they live in from day to day, not some fantasy world or idealized world. If your group is mid-sized or smaller, have students shout out when they find one, then hold it up for the group to see and explain why they chose it. If your group is larger, you may want to call on a few students to share what they found or do this activity in small groups where they can all share.

Question

Good or Bad

Ask this question—Are people basically good or basically bad? Sure, we're all capable of good and bad, but deep down, which is our true nature?

After fielding several responses with explanations, have the group vote. The results will greatly depend on your previous teaching along these lines—but it's fairly common today for people to want to believe that we humans are basically good. This is reflected in the Eastern religions that currently have found such popularity in media circles.

Some students will try to argue that God created people to be good and that's our true character. There's some truth to this—but it's ancient history. It hasn't been true since shortly after creation! The reality is: We are sinful people. Without God's strength we will choose evil.

heart of the talk

The Main Event

1. The God who is there in our broken world

🔊 Continue by saying—It seems kind of obvious to talk about the brokenness in the world around us today. Any one of us with a TV can see it with our own eyes.

🔊 Illustration: The African Epidemic (see sidebar)

🔊 Our broken world is not only evident in disease, war, poverty, and terrorism. If we pay attention, we notice this brokenness all around us, even in this room.

🔊 The question that many of us might be asking is, "Where is God in all this pain and suffering? Doesn't he care?"

🔊 Illustration: The Nazi Prisoner of War Camp (see sidebar)

🔊 Where is God in the midst of our broken world? God is right there in the midst of this pain, this suffering, and this hurting. He is right here with us, experiencing the reality of this broken world in a way we cannot even imagine.

🔊 Scripture: John 16:33 ("In this world you will have trouble. But take heart! I have overcome the world.")

🔊 Transition by saying something like—Jesus told us to expect trouble and pain in our world. The hope he offers us is that he has overcome this brokenness and that he is right beside us, guiding us through it all. But what about the hurt, the pain, and the brokenness that many of us feel in our own personal lives? What does Jesus say about that?

Illustration

The African Epidemic

There are more than 25 million people infected with the HIV virus in Africa. If you were between the ages of 18 and 30 and living on that continent, there would be a 50-percent chance that you have this disease. How do we even begin to comprehend this level of pain and brokenness?

Illustration

The Nazi Prisoner of War Camp

In the early 1940s, Auschwitz was full of Jews condemned to die. But on one side of the camp were kept the prisoners who worked and were not condemned to die. In many respects their lives were even worse than those who were murdered, though some of them lived. One of those who lived was a man who recorded in his memoirs this true story.

One day the Nazis discovered that three loaves of bread had been stolen. The order was given to have the entire camp line up in formation. Three gallows were erected, and those responsible were ordered to come forward and receive their punishment.

Two men and a small 13-year-old boy came forward to admit their guilt. As they made their way forward, this man who wrote about the story tells of a man behind him who began to mutter, "God where are you now? God where are you now?" As the noose was placed around the neck of the 13-year-old, this man began to repeat over and over again, "God where are you now? God where are you now?" As the officer pulled the lever that dropped the floor, which snapped the neck of the prisoners, this man began to become frantic. "God where are you now? God where are you now?" he kept repeating.

The person standing next to this man leaned over to him and whispered in his ear, "You want to know where God is? He is right there, hanging by his neck on that rope."

This man wasn't trying to say that God is dead—just the opposite; he was saying that God is here with us, right in the middle of our pain and suffering.

2. The God who is there in our broken lives

- 🔊 Transition by saying—Not only is our world a broken and hurting place, but the people who inhabit that world—you and me—are also broken and hurting. I know many of you have experienced great pain in your lives.

- 🔊 Illustration: The Cost of Pain (see sidebar)

- 🔊 Do you see or experience that hopelessness? It's everywhere. If you're not hurting, you can be sure some of your friends are.

- 🔊 Scripture: John 8:1-11 (the story of the woman caught in adultery)

- 🔊 Read this story aloud to your students and describe the life of a prostitute in Jesus' time. This woman was regarded as the lowest of the low. The pain she must have felt in her life would have been beyond most of our understanding. And the religious people despised and hated her. Yet Jesus refused to condemn her.

- 🔊 Paraphrase Jesus' words to the woman: "Woman, I don't condemn you, I don't judge you. You are free. Go and sin no more."

- 🔊 Personal illustration: When Jesus Met Me (see sidebar)

- 🔊 Transition by saying—Only Jesus has the power to invade our broken lives and make them whole. All we have to do is ask and believe.

The Cost of Pain

Ask—How much money do you think is spent on counseling and therapy sessions during one year? (Have students guess.) The answer, according to *The New York Times* is 96 billion dollars; and this does not include the 12 billion dollars spent on treatment for drug and alcohol addiction. It is estimated that one in four Americans—that's 25 percent—experience depression, anxiety disorders, or phobias. This article concluded by saying, "Across the land there is an unwarranted sense of hopelessness."

Personal illustration

When Jesus Met Me

Tell about a time in your life when you were really struggling and in pain. Be as open, honest, and transparent as you possibly can. Share how you felt during that time and how Jesus came up beside you and delivered you from that pain.

closing

The Grand Finale

🔊 Bible illustration: Coming Home (see sidebar)

🔊 Conclude by saying—We have a God who does not discard us because of our weaknesses, our pain, and our brokenness. We have a God who embraces us in spite of them. It is in the midst of a broken world and a broken life that we can begin to fathom the reality that though we might consider ourselves trash—useless and purposeless—with his presence in our lives we can dance and move and find beauty, meaning, freedom, and love.

Bible illustration

Coming Home

Remind students of the story Jesus told about the prodigal son (read it, if you have time, in Luke 15:11-33). Quickly retell the story, then point out to your students that the son was still messed up, still broken. All he did was come home; and the father—who represents God—ran to him, embraced him, and accepted him as he was.

discussion
Encore

Get It? | Middle School

🔊 Today we talked about living in a broken world. Where do you see the most pain and suffering in the world right now?

🔊 We also talked about living with broken lives. Do you know people who are experiencing the kind of pain we discussed?

🔊 As a middle schooler, what kind of signs do you see of brokenness in your friends and other people your age?

Get It? | High School

🔊 What are some of the things that contribute to the brokenness in the world?

🔊 Do you believe that Jesus has the capacity to bring healing to a broken world? How might this happen?

🔊 Discuss times that you have been hurting and have felt broken. How has Jesus carried you through these times?

What If? | The Big Picture

🔊 Describe what a world free of brokenness and pain might look like.

🔊 Describe what the life of an individual person free of brokenness and pain might look like.

🔊 Do you think it is possible for a human being to be truly free from brokenness and pain? Why or why not?

So What? | It's Your Life

🔊 What role can you play in bringing the power of God's healing to this world?

🔊 What are some ways that you can be active in allowing God to heal your personal brokenness?

🔊 What are some ways that you can be active in allowing God to heal the brokenness in the lives of those around you?

A Whole New You

Contributed by **Alex Roller**

Primary theme sanctification
Themes sin, forgiveness, change, transformation, choices, the gospel
Scripture Romans 3:23; 2 Corinthians 5:16-17; Ephesians 4:20-24; Colossians 3:5-10
Approximate length through The Grand Finale 30-35 minutes

You'll need

- White T-shirts (one shirt for every group of six to eight students)
- Washable markers (washable is key)
- Large plastic tub or bucket full of bleach water
- A trash can (if you can find a smelly one, even better!)
- Can of air freshener
- Stick of deodorant
- Bottle of cologne/perfume

 et's face it—our lives are covered in yuck. We are sinners. But for whatever reason we try and make our sin look pretty. We cover it up with smiles and things—whatever we can do to make it look like we've got it all together. In reality, the more we try to cover up our sin, the more it will begin to stink. We need God to come in and clean us up, give us a makeover, make us a new creation. We have to be willing to let go of our old selves to accept and put on the new us. (Note: This talk is better suited to younger students.)

intro

The Opening Act

🔊 Activity: Dirty Shirts, Part 1 (see sidebar)

🔊 Illustration: Mom Knows Dirt (see sidebar)

🔊 Transition by saying something like—We all get dirty. It's a part of life. We dribble spaghetti sauce, someone splashes mud on us, we pee our pants, whatever. The fact is, we get dirty. But it's not just our clothes that get dirty.

Activity

Dirty Shirts, Part 1

Have students break into groups of six to eight. Give each group a few washable markers and a white T-shirt. Have students write on the T-shirts anything that keeps them from their relationship with God—sins, bad priorities, idols (anything they make more important than God), relationships, habits, and so on. Encourage students to be honest as they write. Give them five to eight minutes to cover their shirts. When they are done, have them bring the markers and T-shirts up to you.

Illustration

Mom Knows Dirt

Say something like this—Do you remember when you were little, and you'd be out playing in the dirt? You'd come home and set one foot in the door—your mom might not have even seen you yet—and she'd say, "Outside! Take that dirty stuff off!" Has that ever happened to any of you?

heart of the talk

The Main Event

1. We're all dirty.

🔊 Our lives are dirty, and the Bible calls this sin. It makes us impure and unclean.

🔊 Scripture: Romans 3:23 ("For all have sinned and fall short of the glory of God.") We have all done things that God is not thrilled about. We have made unclean that which God created clean and pure.

◀◗ Illustration: Dirty Shirts, Part 2 (see sidebar)

◀◗ Transition by saying something like—As you can see, we all deal with lots of sin. Some of the sins are common; others aren't. Many of us wouldn't be able to tell that someone is dealing with a particular sin just by looking at them. Sometimes we hide.

Illustration

Dirty Shirts, Part 2

Hold up the shirts covered with writing. Take time to look at and read each T-shirt aloud, highlighting the different sins, idols, and so on. Pay special attention to the recurring ones and especially those that people may not have thought about in other groups.

    After you hold up each shirt, put it in the bucket or tub of bleach water. Push it down under the water and swirl it around a bit. (Tip: Plant a white shirt in the bucket before you start, just in case the bleach water isn't strong enough.) Once you have put each shirt in the water, leave them. You'll come back and use them at the end of the talk.

2. The great cover-up

◀◗ Object lesson: Smells Good! (see sidebar)

◀◗ When we say yes to Jesus, he makes us clean; he erases our sins and purifies us.

◀◗ But then we go back and put on the same old person that we were— stinky, smelly, and dirty. It's like taking a shower and putting stinky, dirty clothes back on your clean body. How much sense does that make?! Then we try to hide or cover up our stinky old selves, rather than allowing Jesus to really change us as he wants to do.

Object lesson

Smells Good!

Bring out the trash can. If it's a smelly one, even better! Have a student smell the trash can and describe what they smell. If your janitors do a really good job and all your trash cans are clean, just have students describe what a really smelly trashcan is like. Or, if you're willing to put in some extra effort, go to the nursery in your church, borrow a poopy diaper, and leave it in the bottom of the trash can.

Next, take out a can of air freshener. Spray a little in the air as you ask—What do we use this stuff for? We want to cover up the bad smell with something good, right?

Now take out the deodorant. If you have a bunch of junior highers, you might have to explain what it is. Ask—Why do we wear this stuff? To cover up our body odor, right? Sometimes deodorant is not enough.

Take out the cologne or perfume. Spray a little on yourself and have a student get a good whiff. As you do this, ask—Why do we wear this?

All of these things are designed to cover up bad smells, but they don't get rid of the real problem—the smell themselves.

3. The old is gone.

◀》 Continue by saying something like—When we give our lives to Jesus, he wants to take the old stuff—our old sinful selves—and replace them with new pure stuff.

◀》 Scripture: 2 Corinthians 5:17 ("If anyone is in Christ, he is a new creation; the old has gone, the new has come!") If we are new creations, we should want to have nothing to do with the old us—our former lives.

◀》 Scripture: Colossians 3:9-10 ("Since you have taken off your old self with its practices and have put on the new self, which is being renewed in knowledge in the image of its Creator.") We have to get rid of the old stuff—our old sins, our old attitudes, our old way of thinking—we have to get rid of ourselves!

◀》 The cool thing about God is that he wants to take charge of that change process in our lives, which is a good thing, since we couldn't do it ourselves.

◀》 The Bible has a big word for this: sanctification.

closing

The Grand Finale

◀》 Transition by saying something like—Some of the stuff, some of the sin in our lives, can be pretty gross. It seems like it might stain us pretty deeply. But Jesus' cleansing power is pretty strong detergent.

◀》 Object lesson: Dirty Shirts, Part 3

◀ᴺ Remember—Jesus wants to change us, but we have to choose to let him. We have to choose to "put on our new selves."

◀ᴺ Scripture Ephesians 4:22-24 ("You were taught, with regard to your former way of life, to put off your old self…and to put on the new self, created to be like God in true righteousness and holiness.") He wants to give us a full makeover. Guys, don't worry—there's no makeup involved (that would only be a cover-up, anyhow!).

◀ᴺ People might not recognize you in your new self. The disciples were scared of Paul because of his former reputation.

◀ᴺ People will get used to the new you. And you can prove you've changed by the way you live.

◀ᴺ Close in prayer, asking God to give your students the courage to quit the big cover-up and wear their new selves proudly!

Object lesson

Dirty Shirts, Part 3

Go over to the bucket or tub and pull out one of the T-shirts. (Note: Look at them before you pull them out. If you're not sure the marker washed out, grab the one you planted at the bottom.) As you pull the T-shirt out, say something like—When Jesus washes our sins, he makes us more than clean, he makes us brand-new. He doesn't leave any stains behind. If you want to add to the effect, pull out all the shirts and lay them over the side of the tub. If you don't have a lot of time (or if you can still see the writing on some shirts!), one clean shirt will illustrate the point just fine.

discussion
Encore

Get It?	Middle School

◀ᴺ Was it easy or hard to come up with things that get in the way of your relationship with God? Why?

◀ᴺ What things seem to get in the way the most?

◀ᴺ How do we try to cover up the bad stuff in our lives? How do we act like everything is okay? Is this good or bad? Why?

◀ᴺ Is it easy or hard to quit doing the bad things you did before, to leave behind your old self? Why?

Get It? | High School

- How do we cover up the bad stuff in our lives? How do we act like everything is okay? Is this good or bad? Why?

- If you left your old self behind, did you (or would you have to) lose certain friends in the process? Why or why not?

- If so, is the change in you worth the loss of those friends?

- Many times we ask God to forgive us of a certain sin, then we turn right around and do it again. Why is it harder for us to let go of it? Does this mean God hasn't forgiven us?

- What is the difference between asking for forgiveness and repenting?

What If? | The Big Picture

- Imagine that everyone's sins were tattooed on their foreheads so everything was out in the open. How would that affect the way people interact? Would it be a good or bad thing? Why?

- Is it easier to be around people and change the way you act or go into a new group of people and start fresh? Why?

- What is the hardest part about leaving your old self?

- How do Christians rationalize continuing to do things from their old selves, while they are new creations in Christ?

So What? | It's Your Life

- Have you asked Jesus to make you clean, to make you a new creation? If so, how has life been different since then? If not, what's keeping you from asking him to clean you up?

- What is one thing from your old self that you are still hanging on to?

- What would it take for you to let go of that thing?

- Who is someone who can help you avoid the big cover-up and can help you keep clean (hold you accountable)?

Be a History Maker

Contributed by **Alex Roller**

Primary theme making a difference	
Themes purpose, God's power, gifts and abilities	
Scripture Ephesians 4:1-3; Hebrews 12:1-3; Jeremiah 29:11-13; Isaiah 26:8; Matthew 19:26; John 14:9-14; 1 Timothy 4:12	
Approximate length through The Grand Finale 20-25 minutes	

You'll need

- *Dead Poets Society* (Touchstone Pictures, 1989)
- *Chariots of Fire* (Warner Brothers, 1981)
- TV and DVD player
- Flashlight
- Batteries
- Lamp
- *Pinocchio* (Walt Disney Pictures, 1940)
- Printer sheets containing perforated business cards (you need one business card per student)
- Pens or pencils

**A**re your students the church of the future or the church of today? This is a significant question. Many adults, and many churches, give kids the impression that any gifts they possess are merely in the development stage to be used only when they're adults. Of course, advertising executives don't see it that way. They know that teenagers represent one of the most significant buying segments of the world's population; therefore, they really care about teens' opinions and input. Our students can make a difference today—in our churches and in their worlds. They are gifted, they are empowered, and God wants to use them. In this message, they'll be encouraged to be open to how God wants to use them now.

intro
The Opening Act

🔊 Movie clip: *Dead Poets Society* (see sidebar)

🔊 Illustration: What Legacy? (see sidebar)

🔊 Transition by saying something like—God created us to be impact players, to leave a legacy. Let's look at what that means in our lives.

Movie clip

Dead Poets Society

Start 00:11:16 The students enter Mr. Keating's classroom.
Stop 00:16:37 Ends with a close-up of an old photograph of a football team.
John Keating (Robin Williams) is a new English literature professor at Welton Academy, an all-boys prep school in New England. In this scene, it's the first class of the fall semester. Without a word, the teacher leads his students out into the hallway and over to a trophy case full of alumni pictures and awards. Once they've gathered around the great alumni wall of fame, Mr. Keating asks his students to consider what kind of a legacy they will leave behind. He tells them that the young men they see in those old photographs aren't that different from them. Then he encourages the class to listen to what the "old boys" are saying to them—"*Carpe diem*"—that wonderful Latin adage meaning "seize the day."

Illustration

What Legacy?

Ask students if they've heard of the following people and what they know about them:
• Abraham Lincoln
• Adolph Hitler
• Martin Luther (Note: Unless you're in a Lutheran church, many of your kids won't have heard of Luther, the primary figure who started Protestantism—many will think you're referring to Martin Luther King, Jr. instead.)
• For the last person, name a personal friend or relative of yours who they don't know.
Everyone leaves a legacy (the results of your life)—some good, some bad. Some aren't world-famous, but they leave an impact nonetheless.

heart of the talk

The Main Event

1. You can write your history now!

🔊 What is your legacy at this moment? If you were to die right now, how would you be remembered?

🔊 Regardless of what specific plan God has for us, we are called to be seekers of God.

🔊 Scripture: Ephesians 4:1 ("I urge you to live a life worthy of the calling you have received.") We remember many biblical figures. Why? Because they each lived a life that was worthy of their calling.

🔊 Scripture: Hebrews 12:2 ("Let us fix our eyes on Jesus, the author and perfecter of our faith.") In Jesus we have a great example of how to leave a legacy and what kind of legacy to leave.

🔊 Like those old pictures at Welton Academy, we are surrounded by those who have gone before us, saying, *"Carpe diem"*—seize the day for the Lord.

2. How to be a history maker

🔊 When we seek God with our whole heart, we don't have to worry about whether or not we're doing the right thing or what kind of legacy we're leaving—it just comes naturally.

🔊 Scripture: Jeremiah 29:11 ("'For I know the plans I have for you,' declares the Lord, 'plans to prosper you and not to harm you, plans to give you hope and a future.'") God has a great plan for each of you, something he uniquely designed specifically for you. When we seek him with our whole heart, we begin to get glimpses of how we can live in that plan.

🔊 Movie clip: *Chariots of Fire* (see sidebar)

🔊 God has chosen to use us to spread his message of love and to accomplish his plan on the earth.

🔊 The key is that our legacy isn't about us—it's about God.

🔊 Scripture: Isaiah 26:8 ("Yes, Lord, walking in the way of your laws, we wait for you; your name and renown are the desire of our hearts.") "Renown" is like your reputation. We want God's reputation, name, and message to be the most important things in our lives so that other people see him in us instead of seeing our own agendas.

🔊 Transition by saying something like—We want to make history for him. That can seem like a pretty scary task—and more than we can handle. The cool thing is that God wants to help us accomplish his plan in our lives. The reality is that we can't do it without him.

Movie clip

Chariots of Fire

Start 00:56:11 Eric runs into the church.
Stop 01:00:18 Jennie hugs Eric and walks away.

Before showing this clip, tell your students that *Chariots of Fire* is based on a true story, then share a little background information about Eric Liddell. He grew up in China in the early 1900s, the son of Scottish missionaries. He was one of the fastest runners in history. However, besides his tremendous speed and unusual running style, Eric is most remembered for choosing to honor God by not running in the heats for the 100-meter dash at the 1924 Olympic Games in Paris. The 100-meter dash was one of Eric's best races, and he was sure to do well, maybe even win a gold medal. But the preliminary trials were being held on a Sunday—Eric said he would not run on the Sabbath. Instead he chose to focus on the 200- and 400-meter races, and he ultimately won a bronze and gold medal, respectively.

In this scene, Eric (Ian Charleson) hasn't qualified for the Olympics yet, but he's training hard to do so. Meanwhile, his sister Jennie (Cheryl Campbell) is very concerned about the amount of time Eric devotes to running and training for the races. She's afraid his pursuit of an Olympic medal is distracting him from his pursuit of the Lord and from his "true calling"—being a missionary to China. So she wants him to give up running altogether and go back to China to head up his parents' mission organization.

So Eric tells Jennie that God made him fast. He says, "When I run, I feel his pleasure. To give that up would be to hold him in contempt. You were right—it's not just 'fun.' To win is to honor him." Then Eric goes on to reassure her that he still plans to resume his mission work, but he has a lot to do first—like get his degree from the university and qualify for the Olympics in Paris. In the end, he did all three—and did them well.

3. Connect with the inventor of history!

📢 Here's a brain-bending thought: Before God created the universe, there was no such thing as time. So God invented the idea of history!

📢 Scripture: Matthew 19:26 ("Jesus looked at them and said, 'With man this is impossible, but with God all things are possible.'") We are pretty stubborn and independent people. We think that we can do things on our own. The reality is we can't—we'll fall flat on our faces.

📢 Object lesson: Who's Got the Power? (see sidebar)

📢 Scripture: John 14:12 ("[Jesus said,] 'I tell you the truth, anyone who has faith in me will do what I have been doing. He will do even greater things than these.'") That's a pretty amazing thing—we can do greater things than Jesus did!

📢 The main thing for us to remember is that we can do the things that God wants and has in store for us to do.

📢 With us, things are impossible. With God, tapping into his power source, all things are possible. The advantage of God's power source is that it never runs out.

Who's Got the Power?

Bring out a flashlight that has no batteries in it. How good is it? What does it need? Put the batteries in and "*voila!*" It works! But what will happen after the batteries have been in the flashlight awhile? They run out of power. We are often like this in our relationship with God. We charge up, and then we run on our own for a while—until our batteries run out of juice.

Now bring out the lamp and plug it in. How long can the lamp stay on (assuming it's using the world's best light bulb)? We need God's constant power in our lives if we are truly going to make history for him. We need to tap in to that power source.

closing

The Grand Finale

- Recap by saying something like—When we run hard after God, he shows us the plan for our lives. In order to accomplish this, we need to tap in to his ultimate power source. We can become history makers for him.

- Movie clip: *Pinocchio* (see sidebar)

- Quote: Become Yourself (see sidebar)

- When we live our lives this way—plugged in to God's power source—people will begin to see the legacy we're leaving behind even before we're dead.

- Scripture: 1 Timothy 4:12 ("Don't let anyone look down on you because you are young.") You can make a difference. Be a history maker for God.

- Take-home item: History Maker Cards (see sidebar)

Pinocchio

Start 01:24:25 Pinocchio is lying on the bed, and Geppetto is kneeling next to him.
Stop 01:27:30 The scene fades to black as the movie ends.
Pinocchio (voice of Dickie Jones) becomes what he wanted to be all along and what Geppetto (voice of Christian Rub) planned and hoped for—a real boy. (Note: You can use any Pinocchio film, really—just find the similar scene.) This works great with the quote from Kierkegaard.

Quote

Becoming Yourself

"Now with God's help, I shall become myself."
— Soren Kierkegaard

Take home item

History Maker Cards

Ahead of time go to an office supply store and buy a pack of printer sheets that contain pre-perforated business cards. Design a simple card that says, I'M A HISTORY MAKER, and a place for students to sign their name.

Now pass out these cards and challenge your students to sign their cards and put them in their wallets or purses to remind them of who they were designed to be.

discussion

Encore

Get It?	Middle School

◁» What's a legacy?

◁» What talents and abilities do you have? (Note: Middle school students often come up with just the expressive or performance skills, like athletics, art, or music. Make sure they understand that our talents and abilities can also be quieter—things like listening, problem solving, or compassion.)

◁» How can you use those gifts to point to God?

◁» What do you think God has in store for your life?

◁» Where does our power and strength come from? What does that look like in real life?

Get It?   High School

🔊 What talents and abilities do you have?

🔊 How can you use those gifts to glorify God?

🔊 How might your gifts be creating a legacy in your life?

🔊 Where does our power and strength come from? What things do you do to tap in to God's power?

🔊 How can you tell if you're using your gifts to promote only yourself or to point people to God?

What If?   The Big Picture

🔊 If you died today, what would people say about you at your funeral? What would you like them to say if it were up to you?

🔊 What can you do to get your life in alignment with what you wish people would say about you?

🔊 Who has left a legacy or made a great impact on your life? What was it? Why did it make such a difference?

🔊 Where and when have you seen someone be a history maker for Jesus in your school or community?

So What?   It's Your Life

🔊 What do you want your legacy to be?

🔊 How do you think God can use your gifts to help accomplish his plan?

🔊 What is one way you can make a difference on your campus for Jesus? In your home? With your friends?

🔊 What do you need to do to rely more on God's power? How can you make him more of a priority?

🔊 How can you move from the "rechargeable batteries" kind of reliance on God to the "plugging in to the constant source of power" kind of reliance on God?

Check the Mirror

Contributed by Alex Roller

Primary theme witnessing

Themes Christian life, accountability, evangelism

Scripture Galatians 2:20; 2 Corinthians 5:17; Acts 1:8; Matthew 28:19-20; Colossians 3:1-5, 12-14; Galatians 5:22-23; Romans 12:1-2

Approximate length through The Grand Finale 20-25 minutes

You'll need

- *Shrek* (DreamWorks SKG, 2001)
- TV and DVD player
- Your personal testimony of salvation
- A large mirror (a cheap floor mirror works great)
- A six-inch square of aluminum foil for each student
- Markers (red and black)

Missionary E. Stanley Jones met with Gandhi and asked him, "Mr. Gandhi, though you quote the words of Christ often, why is it that you appear to so adamantly reject becoming his follower?" Gandhi replied, "Oh, I don't reject your Christ. I love your Christ. It's just that so many of you Christians are so unlike your Christ."

What a biting commentary on the face of our Christian witness in the world! We may believe in our hearts and minds that our faith affects how we live, but does it really? This talk will help students examine what other people really see in their lives. How we live, act, speak, and treat other people often makes more of an impact on people's perception of Christ—positive or negative—than our words do. When others look at your life, who do they see—you or Christ?

intro
The Opening Act

🔊 Ask—You've all heard of Snow White and the Seven Dwarfs? Which is your favorite dwarf? (For your information, they are: Grumpy, Happy, Sleepy, Sneezy, Dopey, Doc, and Bashful.)

🔊 Talk briefly about the coolest part of the story—the magic mirror.

🔊 Ask—What was so special about the mirror? (It always told the truth.)

🔊 Movie clip: *Shrek* (see sidebar)

🔊 Transition by saying something like—The magic mirror doesn't always tell us what we want to hear. It tells it like it is. Many times we wouldn't like what we'd hear or see, but today we're going to take a good hard look in the mirror and examine what other people REALLY see when they look at our lives.

Movie clip

Shrek

Start 0:15:58 Lord Farquaad is walking down the hall.
Stop 0:20:08 "We're going to have a tournament!"
Lord Farquaad (voice of John Lithgow) wishes to rid the kingdom of all fairy tale creatures, and he'll do anything to accomplish this task and become the king—even torture the innocent Gingerbread Man (voice of Conrad Vernon) to find out where the other creatures are hiding. When Lord Farquaad's henchmen bring in Magic Mirror (voice of Chris Miller), it tells the wannabe evil king that if he wants to become the real king, then he must marry a princess. The mirror gives Lord Farquaad three choices: Cinderella, Snow White, or Princess Fiona.

Farquaad chooses Princess Fiona before the mirror can reveal that in order to marry her the diminutive lord will first have to free her from her prison cell at the top of a tall tower surrounded by lava and guarded by a large dragon. So Farquaad takes the coward's way out and decides to have a tournament to decide who will get the honor of freeing his future bride.

heart of the talk
The Main Event

1. The problem with Christians

🔊 Continue by saying—As we check the mirror today, I might be stepping on some toes, pushing you a little bit. Sometimes we have to ask the tough questions.

- ◀)) Ask—What do people think about Christians?

- ◀)) Many people don't care about knowing anything about Jesus because of how they see so many Christians acting—like the hypocritical, crazy tele- vangelists asking for money; the numerous scandals occurring in the church today; and stuff like that.

- ◀)) Ask—Can anyone tell me who Gandhi was? (The following story about Ghandi won't have much punch if kids don't know he was a Hindu man from India who brought about major change in his home country—and the world—through his peaceful, nonviolent protests. Many consider him a counterpart to Martin Luther King, Jr.)

- ◀)) Quote: Gandhi and Jesus (see sidebar)

- ◀)) They don't see us acting any differently than the world around us; often- times, they see us acting worse.

- ◀)) If we can act the same way with Jesus as we can without him, why would people want to be a part of Jesus' family?

- ◀)) Actions really do speak louder than words. Sometimes our actions speak so loudly that those around us can't hear what we are saying.

Quote

Gandhi and Jesus

Dozens of years ago, missionary E. Stanley Jones met with Gandhi and asked him, "Mr. Gandhi, though you quote the words of Christ often, why is it that you appear to so adamantly reject becoming his follower?"

Gandhi replied, "Oh, I don't reject your Christ. I love your Christ. It's just that so many of you Christians are so unlike your Christ."

2. It's not your life.

- ◀)) Scripture: Galatians 2:20 ("I no longer live, but Christ lives in me.") When Christ comes into our lives, he takes over. We're no longer in charge.

- ◀)) Scripture: 2 Corinthians 5:17 ("If anyone is in Christ, he is a new creation; the old is gone, the new has come!") We are creations of God, made in his image.

- ◀)) Personal illustration: The Change in Me (see sidebar)

The Change in Me

Take a moment to share a brief version of your personal testimony. Specifically, think about aspects of your life—attitudes, actions, thoughts, desires—that changed when you gave your life to Christ or over the years since then. What was something old that went away? What was something new that came?

3. We are God's witnesses.

◀» Continue by saying something like—God is excited about the new things he puts into our lives. Plus, he completely forgets about the old things he took away. He doesn't want us to take what he's given us and hide it in a closet. He wants us to tell our story!

◀» Scripture: Acts 1:8 ("[Jesus said,] 'And you will be my witnesses in Jerusalem, and in all Judea and Samaria, and to the ends of the earth.'")

- Judea—your immediate surroundings: school, neighborhood, and city

- Samaria—your region: county, state, and country

- To the ends of the earth—duh!

◀» It is God's desire that everyone would come to know him and be saved by him through Jesus.

◀» Scripture: Matthew 28:20 ("[Jesus said,] 'Therefore go and make disciples of all nations.'") Spreading the news about Jesus is our role—our responsibility.

◀» Illustration and drama activity: Human Bible (see sidebar) (optional)

Human Bible

A familiar churchy quote is, "You may be the only Bible someone ever reads." Invite your students to share what this means to them. How can we be the Bible to other people?

Optional Drama Activity

Have students get in groups of four to five and come up with a one-minute sketch to illustrate this quote. Then have students perform their skits for the entire group.

4. Living it out

🔊 Continue by saying something like—If we are to live our lives as witnesses for Jesus—as a Bible for those around us—we have to figure out what that looks like.

🔊 Scripture: Colossians 3:2 ("Set your minds on things above, not on earthly things.")

🔊 Scripture: Galatians 5:22-23 ("But the fruit of the Spirit is love, joy, peace, patience, kindness, goodness, faithfulness, gentleness and self-control. Against such things there is no law.")

🔊 Scripture: Romans 12:1-2, *The Message* (see sidebar)

🔊 We don't run away and hide from the culture we live in, but we are supposed to look different within the culture. When others see us, they should see Jesus.

Scripture

Romans 12:1-2

So here's what I want you to do, God helping you: Take your everyday, ordinary life—your sleeping, eating, going-to-work [school], and walking-around life—and place it before God as an offering. Embracing what God does for you is the best thing you can do for him. Don't become so well-adjusted to your culture that you fit into it without even thinking. Instead, fix your attention on God. You'll be changed from the inside out. Readily recognize what he wants from you, and quickly respond to it. Unlike the culture around you, always dragging you down to its level of immaturity, God brings the best out of you, develops well-formed maturity in you.

From *The Message* by Eugene Peterson (NavPress, 2002)

closing

The Grand Finale

🔊 Say something like—Some of you are thinking, "Wow. I need to think about what my life looks like. Do others really see Jesus in me?"

🔊 Object lesson: Look in the Mirror

🔊 We have different mirrors we can look in—different ways we can examine our lives to see how well we're showing Jesus to other people:
- the mirror of self-examination,
- the mirror of Scripture, and
- the mirror of friends and accountability.

🔊 Activity: My Mirror (see sidebar)

🔊 Close in prayer, asking God to help each of us show Jesus to others.

Object lesson

Look in the Mirror

Ask—Why do we look in mirrors? (To check our makeup, hair, zits, clothes, and so on.) Just like we regularly check to see how we look on the outside, we also need to examine our lives and discover what people really see in us.

Take a large floor mirror and pan it across the audience (with the mirror facing them, of course). While doing this, ask, "What do others see when they look at you—you or Jesus?"

Activity

My Mirror

Invite students to look in the mirror of their own lives and ask the question, "What do other people see in me?" This activity will give them the opportunity to see what they're doing well (when it comes to showing Christ in their lives) and what they still need to work on. It will also give them a chance to pick someone who can be a mirror for them, someone to hold them accountable.

Stack six-inch-square pieces of aluminum foil in the middle of the room. Invite students to come forward and take a piece of foil. Ask them to use the black Sharpie markers to write on their "mirror" the things they are doing well to allow people to see Jesus in their lives. Then have them use the red Sharpies to write down the things they need to work on.

At the bottom, have them write MY MIRROR and add the name of the person they will allow to hold them accountable.

For a more subtle approach pass the squares down the rows and have students share the markers. Invite students to put their "mirror" in their backpack, purse, wallet, or on their bathroom mirror at home to serve as a reminder that they need to check the mirror and ask, "Do others see Christ in me?"

discussion

Encore

Get It? — Middle School

- If you asked your friends to describe you, what would they say? Would *Christian* be one of the words they used?

- If you are a Christian, what is something different about you now than before you said yes to Jesus? Or if you've been a Christ follower all your life, what is an area of your life that you've allowed Jesus to change recently?

- What are some reasons that your non-Christian friends don't believe or aren't interested in Jesus?

- How have you seen Jesus in other people's lives?

Get It? — High School

- Think back to the quote from Gandhi about not seeing Christians act like Christ. Where have you seen this recently?

- Is it hard to be a new creation at your school? Is it hard to leave the old life? Why?

- What keeps you from sharing Jesus on your campus?

- What is difficult about living a life that shows Jesus, especially around your non-Christian friends?

What If? — The Big Picture

- What if you really were a Bible? What verses would you be?

- What if you could sit down and talk with Gandhi—what would you say to him?

- What are some areas where Christians tend to blend in with the culture around them? Why do you think that is?

So What? — It's Your Life

- What areas of your life aren't reflecting Jesus? What can you do about that?

- In Acts 1:8 Jesus said we would be his witnesses in different areas. What are the areas where you can be his witnesses? How?

- Who is someone that can be a mirror for you and hold you accountable to showing Jesus in your life?

I'm NOT All That

Contributed by **Alex Roller**

Primary theme humility	
Themes pride, servanthood, honoring God	
Scripture John 15:5; Philippians 4:13; Philippians 2:1-11; James 4:6-10; Revelation 4:10; Matthew 23:11-12; John 13:12-17	
Approximate length through The Grand Finale 30-35 minutes	

I n our culture today, it's all about each person doing everything she can to get ahead and make a name for herself. But Jesus had a very different attitude about how he viewed himself. Jesus was God, but he didn't claim any special privileges while he was on earth. It's hard for our students to understand the concept of thinking that other people are more important than them. No one else in our culture models that today. If we are to live our lives like Christ, we need to adjust our attitudes and our perspective on what matters and who is really important.

You'll need

- A saw (or hammer and nails)
- A piece of wood
- Needle and thread
- A piece of fabric
- A button
- A candy prize
- *The Princess Bride* (MGM Home Entertainment, 1987)
- TV and DVD player
- A trophy
- A personal story about a time when you were "first" at something—when you won a competition or event
- A toy crown
- A pair of jeans with the knees worn out
- A bowl
- A pitcher of water
- A towel

intro

The Opening Act

🔊 Activity: Role Reversal Challenge (see sidebar)

🔊 Movie clip: *The Princess Bride* (see sidebar)

🔊 Transition by saying something like—When we're good at something, it's easy for us to get caught up in how good we are. We like to tell everyone around us how good we are.

Activity

Role Reversal Challenge

Get two student volunteers—one guy and one girl. Play to the students' sense of pride by asking for the best male and female athletes. When they get up front, reveal the game. It is a race between the two students—the guy must sew a button onto a piece of fabric, while the girl must saw a board in half (another option is to have her hammer several nails into a board). (Note: You really have to be aware of the girl's safety while she's sawing. It will be a major distraction to your point if she saws her finger off!) The first person to finish their task wins a small prize. Or, if you're feeling generous, they can win candy for everyone of their same gender!

Movie clip

The Princess Bride

Start 00:29:27 Westley runs up the hill to meet Vizzini.
Stop 00:34:12 Vizzini laughs and falls over dead.
In this clip, Vizzini (Wallace Shawn) thinks he is the smartest man in the world. So in order to win the release of Princess Buttercup (Robin Wright Penn), Westley (Cary Elwes) challenges Vizzini to a battle of wits—to the death. After much bravado and endless explanations of why he is so very clever, Vizzini falsely believes he has tricked and defeated Westley. Instead he dies. Needless to say, Vizzini wasn't as great or smart as he thought he was. He was all talk and no action. Getting a big head about ourselves can lead us to disastrous ends!

heart of the talk
The Main Event

1. We all like to be first (or at least close to it!).

◀)) When we do well at something, we like recognition. We like to be told we did a good job.

◀)) Personal illustration: Trophy Room (see sidebar)

◀)) Ask—What is pride? What is humility? Are they good or bad? Why?

◀)) It's good to be excited about the things we do well, especially when they are things God has given us the abilities to do.

◀)) Illustration: King Me! (see sidebar)

◀)) One big problem with letting other people know how important you think you are, or how good you are at something, is that it can get in the way of your relationships with other people.

Personal illustration

Trophy Room

If you have an old trophy or award that you won at some point in the past, bring it and talk about what took place when you won it. Talk about how you felt when you received it. If you don't have a trophy, just share a personal illustration about a time from your childhood or teenage years when you were "first" at something—when you won a competition or event. Don't use this to make yourself sound great. Instead tell it a bit tongue-in-cheek, making it seem a bit silly that you thought that at that moment you were the best you were ever going to be.

Illustration

King Me!

Bring out a toy crown. Ask students to identify it, then ask—Why do people wear crowns? Explain that the gold and jeweled crown was a symbol of importance and authority. A king's crown was bigger and more ornate than the queen's or a prince's. The size and decoration indicated importance. Royalty would wear the crown to show how important they were.

2. Jesus turned things upside-down.

🔊 We may be good at certain things, but we must remember where those talents and abilities came from.

🔊 Scripture: John 15:5 ("[Jesus said,] 'I am the vine; you are the branches. If a man remains in me and I in him, he will bear much fruit; apart from me you can do nothing.'") Apart from Christ we can't do anything—we are nothing.

🔊 Scripture: Philippians 4:13 ("I can do everything through him who gives me strength.") With Christ all things are possible. We won't receive all that God has in store for us unless we humble ourselves and admit our own personal weakness.

🔊 Scripture: Philippians 2:1-11, *The Message* (see sidebar)

🔊 We are called to be like-minded with Christ. In humility we need to consider others better than ourselves, think about them first.

🔊 God doesn't like it when think we're the greatest. Even Jesus didn't think he was the greatest—and he was!

🔊 Scripture: James 4:6 ("Scripture says: 'God opposes the proud, but gives grace to the humble.'")

🔊 People expected Jesus (the Messiah) to show up and be an earthly king, to assume a throne, and wear a crown. Instead, he was born in a stable and lived a lowly, humble life!

🔊 Transition by saying something like—It's a hard thing to do—admit that someone is better than we are and acknowledge where the true source of our gifts and talents lies.

Scripture

Philippians 2:1-11, *The Message*

If you've gotten anything at all out of following Christ, if his love has made any difference in your life, if being in a community of the Spirit means anything to you, if you have a heart, if you care—then do me a favor: Agree with each other, love each other, be deep-spirited friends. Don't push your way to the front; don't sweet-talk your way to the top. Put yourself aside, and help others get ahead. Don't be obsessed with getting your own advantage. Forget yourselves long enough to lend a helping hand.

Think of yourselves the way Christ Jesus thought of himself. He had equal status with God but didn't think so much of himself that he had to cling to the advantage of that status no matter what. Not at all. When the time came, he set aside the privileges of deity and took on the status of a slave, became human! Having become human, he stayed human. It was an incredibly humbling process. He didn't claim special privileges. Instead, he lived a selfless, obedient life and then died a selfless, obedient death—and the worst kind of death at that: a crucifixion.

Because of that obedience, God lifted him high and honored him far beyond anyone or anything, ever, so that all created beings in heaven and on earth—even those long ago dead and buried—will bow in worship before this Jesus Christ, and call out in praise that he is the Master of all, to the glorious honor of God the Father.

From *The Message* by Eugene Peterson (NavPress, 2002)

3. It's all about God!

🔊 Continue by saying something like—So what does it look like to live a humble life? As we read in Philippians, we must consider others better than ourselves, which can only come from focusing on God being number one.

🔊 Scripture: Revelation 4:10 ("The twenty-four elders fall down before him who sits on the throne, and worship him who lives for ever and ever.")

🔊 Illustration: Crowns Down (see sidebar)

🔊 Scripture: Matthew 23:11-12 ("The greatest among you will be your servant. For whoever exalts himself will be humbled, and whoever humbles himself will be exalted.") We need to kneel down before the almighty God and remind ourselves that he is the one who is in control. (Note: If you're speaking to young teens, they may think you mean this literally if you don't unpack it a bit.)

🔊 Illustration: Worn-Out Knees (see sidebar)

🔊 Getting on our knees should be a daily task. Sometimes we need to do it more often, to remind ourselves—and others—that God is in control and we are not.

🔊 Quote: Our Names (see sidebar)

Illustration

Crowns Down

Bring back the crown from earlier and demonstrate what this verse might look like. Back in medieval times and even today people kneel in the presence of a king or queen. It was a sign of submission and realization of authority.

Object lesson

Worn-Out Knees

Bring out a pair of jeans with worn-out knees. For added effect, you could put them on. Show how being on your knees, an act of submission, wears out the knees of the pants. We need to kneel down and acknowledge God so much that we wear the knees out of our pants. (Note: While this object lesson will have more impact if you actually show a pair of worn-out jeans, it will still work as an illustration by describing a pair of worn-out jeans without having a pair to show.)

Quote

Our Names

Louie Giglio says that since God says that his name is, "I Am," our names are, "I am not."

closing

The Grand Finale

- Transition by saying something like—One really good way to keep Jesus' humble attitude active in our lives is to serve other people. After all, that's what Jesus did!

- Scripture: John 13:12-17 (Jesus washes the disciples' feet.)

- Object lesson: Foot Bath (see sidebar)

- For many of us our pride is standing in the way of us serving others. It can even stand in the way of our relying on God.

- What are some areas in your life where you need to get down on your knees and acknowledge God? Which of your crowns do you need to lay at the fee of Jesus?

- How can you serve others this week?

Object lesson

Foot Bath

One of the most obvious illustrations Jesus gave of this servant attitude came on the last night that he was hanging out with his disciples. Talk a bit about how dirty and smelly their feet would have been—no sidewalks, open shoes, hot weather, and so on. As you're talking about this, bring a student on stage and sit him in a chair. Begin to take off his shoes as you tell the story of Jesus washing the disciples' feet—how he took off his outer garment, wrapped a towel around his waist, and so on. Explain that this was normally a role that a household servant would play. A guest of honor or someone who was trying to be first in life would never have done this for others. Using a bowl, a pitcher of water, and a towel, wash the students' feet. Be prepared for some interesting reactions from the crowd (and also from the student volunteer!).

discussion
Encore

Get It?	Middle School

- What are some things that you are good at doing?

- What happens when we make sure that people around us know how good we are?

- When is pride a good thing? When can it turn into something harmful?

- What was Jesus' attitude about who he was and how good he was at so many things?

- How should we think about others when compared to ourselves? Are they better or worse, more important or less important?

- What is the source of our talents and abilities?

Get It?	High School

- What happens when you let people know how good you are in different areas? How does your ego affect your relationships?

- What is an area in your life where you find it difficult to acknowledge someone else's authority?

- What's the difference between having a lousy self-image and having God-focused humility?

- What's so amazing about Jesus' attitude? Why is that foreign to us humans today?

- How often and in what ways do you compare yourselves with others around you? How does it affect the way you treat them?

What If?	The Big Picture

- What would happen if every professional athlete had a change of attitude to become like Jesus? What would things be like?

- Imagine you lived back in medieval times. What would your crown look like? How important would you have been? How is that different today?

- Is it difficult to think about others as being more important than yourself? Why or why not?

- Who do you know who really lives this way, who is a model of this kind of humility and servanthood?

So What? | It's Your Life

🔊 How can you serve someone this week? Who can you serve?

🔊 What is one area in your life where you are focused more on yourself than on other people? What can you do to change that?

🔊 What can you do this week to remind yourself that God is the one in control and he deserves all the credit?

🔊 Who is someone that can remind you to work on those things this week?

Wearing Other People's Stuff

Primary theme compassion
Themes Christian service, making a difference, serving others, sacrifice
Scripture Acts 2:42-47; Acts 4:32-35; Galations 6:2-3; Colossians 3:12; 2 Corinthians 1:3; Matthew 14:13-14; John 4:4-26; Luke 5:17-26; Mark 10:46-52; Matthew 9:18-26; John 11:1-44; 1 Peter 5:7
Approximate length through The Grand Finale 25-30 minutes

The Christian life is a tough road. In fact, life in general can be very difficult. But the nice thing is that God didn't design us to go through life alone. We do life together, and compassion is a key component of this. It means we carry each other's burdens. In Colossians 3:12, Paul writes, "Therefore, as God's chosen people, holy and dearly loved, clothe yourselves with compassion, kindness, humility, gentleness and patience." The Greek words for compassion (*splagna oiktrimou*) spell it out for us. *Splagna* means innards or guts, and *"oiktrimou (mas)"* means compassion, pity, mercy. So basically Paul is saying that having compassion toward someone means having guts of mercy and pity. Compassion, especially within a community, should be a gut reaction.

You'll need

- Two sets of extra-large clothes (pants, shoes, shirt, hat, and a sweatshirt or sweater)
- Two inflated balloons
- Candy prize
- A personal story about a time when you had to borrow someone else's clothes
- *Patch Adams* (1998)
- TV and DVD player
- Bibles
- A backpack
- A textbook
- A box of tissues
- A box of bandages
- A thermometer
- A big question mark (cut out of foam board or printed on paper)
- A photograph
- A can of food

intro
The Opening Act

🔊 Game: Balloon Clothing Challenge (see sidebar)

🔊 Ask—Have you ever had to borrow someone else's clothes?

🔊 Personal illustration: Clothing Nightmare (see sidebar)

🔊 Transition by saying something like—We have all had to wear someone else's clothing at some point in our lives. Many times it is an outfit we would never be caught dead in otherwise. The crazy thing is, Jesus calls us to wear each other's stuff all the time!

Game

Balloon Clothing Challenge

Get four student volunteers. This is a great game for guys versus girls (so you would need two guys and two girls—duh!). Each pair will need an identical pile of clothes. (Note: The game is SO much easier if the clothes are really big.) One person from each pair will be the contestant; the other will be the assistant.

The goal of the game is for each contestant to get all of the clothes on (over their own clothes) while keeping the balloon in the air. The only person allowed to touch the balloon is the contestant. The assistant's job is to get the clothes ready and hand them to the contestant.

If the balloon touches the ground, the contestant must take off one of the too-big articles of clothing and start again. The first team to get all the clothes on their contestant wins!

Personal illustration

Clothing Nightmare

Think of a time when you had to borrow clothes from someone else—maybe a swimsuit, clothes from someone's parents, and so on. What did you have to wear? Any funny things happen as a result? Were you able to find something that matched your personality, or was it "sooo not you" or "so five minutes ago"?

heart of the talk
The Main Event

1. Wearing each other's stuff

🔊 Ask—Do you, especially you girls, ever share clothes with each another? When and why?

◀)) Believe it or not, we are called to wear each other's stuff. Not just clothes—but all our stuff!

◀)) Scripture: Acts 2:42-47 and Acts 4:32-35 (A description of the early church.) All the believers were together and shared with one another. They helped meet each other's needs.

◀)) Scripture: Galatians 6:3 ("Carry each other's burdens, and in this way you will fulfill the law of Christ.") We are supposed to carry each other's burdens or wear each other's stuff. This is called compassion.

2. Carrying each other's burdens

◀)) Definition: Compassion (see sidebar)

◀)) This deep urge to help should be a gut reaction.

◀)) Illustration: It's Greek to Me (see sidebar)

◀)) Movie clip: *Patch Adams* (see sidebar)

◀)) That's compassion—it's a gut reaction. It's not just an outside or passerby thing. It comes from deep inside.

Definition

Compassion

According to Webster's the definition of *compassion* is, "Sorrow for the sufferings or trouble of another or others accompanied by a deep urge to help."

Illustration

It's All Greek to Me

The Greek language, which was used to write the New Testament, spells it out. In Colossians 3:12 the original words for compassion are *splagna oiktrimou*. *Splagna* means innards or guts, and *oiktrimou (mas)* means compassion, pity, mercy.

It's the same word that's used when God is called the Father of mercies (2 Corinthians 1:3, NASB or KJV). So basically Paul (the writer of Colossians) is saying that compassion is guts of mercy and pity. When we see a need or someone hurting, we should want to make things better, to help in some way. It should be a gut reaction.

Movie clip

Patch Adams

Start 0:38:07 Carin says, "An enema bulb?
Stop 0:41:58 Patch says, "How about a poodle?"
Patch Adams (Robin Williams) is a medical resident who desires to do things differently, like treating his patients with compassion. As he says at one point in the movie, "You treat a disease, you win, you lose. You treat a person, I'll guarantee you'll win." So Patch works hard to help the patients feel better emotionally as well as physically.

In this clip Patch enlists the help of two fellow residents as he sneaks into a hospital ward late one night and fulfills the fantasy of one of his terminal patients who's always wanted to go big-game hunting. Granted, he does so with balloon animals and a rubber dart gun, but the patient feels better just knowing Patch really listened to him and remembered his desire to go on a safari. Patch is a great example of compassion, as he feels right along with his patients—in fact, it seems he just can't help himself.

3. How did Jesus do it?

- Continue by saying something like—Jesus had the same kind of reaction many times. Scripture records countless stories of Jesus being moved to help other people.

- Scripture: Matthew 14:14 ("When Jesus landed and saw a large crowd, he had compassion on them and healed their sick.") Jesus was moved by what he saw. Something stirred inside him that made him want to help.

- Storytelling: Raising Laz (see sidebar)

- Jesus saw how hurt Mary and Martha were, and he raised Lazarus from the dead. He did it to ease their suffering, but ultimately, it was to show God's love and power.

- Scripture: (optional)
  - John 4:4-26—Samaritan woman at the well
  - Luke 5:17-26—Jesus heals a paralytic
  - Mark 10:46-52—Jesus heals blind Bartimaeus
  - Matthew 9:18-26—a dead girl and a sick woman

Raising Laz

Use these notes to tell the story of Jesus raising Lazarus from the dead. Familiarize yourself with the story beforehand so you can comfortably tell it without notes.

John 11:1-10: Jesus was hanging out with the disciples after he'd just escaped from some Jews who wanted to stone him. Mary and Martha sent for Jesus, saying their brother, and Jesus' friend, Lazarus, was sick. Jesus said it would be okay and that God would be glorified, so he and the disciples stayed put for two days. Then Jesus said they were going back to Judea. The disciples couldn't believe it, since that's where the Jews had tried to stone Jesus.

John 11:11-16: Jesus told the disciples that Laz had fallen asleep, but that he was going to go wake him up. The disciples told Jesus that sleeping would help Lazarus get better. They didn't get it, so Jesus spelled it out for them—Laz was dead.

John 11:17-37: When Jesus got to Bethany, Laz had already been in the tomb for four days. Laz's sister Martha met Jesus on the road and told him, "Lord, if you had been here, my brother would not have died" (verse 21). Martha went back and told Mary that Jesus was there, so Mary ran out of the house to meet Jesus. Everyone who was at the house ran after her, thinking she was going to the tomb. When she got to Jesus, she said the same thing as Martha, "Lord, if you had been here, my brother would not have died" (verse 32). When Jesus saw her crying, he was moved to tears. He asked where they had buried Lazarus and went there.

John 11:38-44: When Jesus got to the tomb, he told them to roll away the stone. Remember—Laz had been dead in there for four days, so he was pretty smelly already. Jesus yelled, "Laz, come out!" The dead man came out of the tomb with his hands and feet still wrapped in the grave clothes—they even covered his face. Jesus told the people standing there to take off Laz's grave clothes and let him go.

closing
The Grand Finale

- 🔊 Transition by saying something like—You may be thinking, "Well, sure, Jesus can do really cool things to carry other people's burdens. He was God. I can't do cool stuff like that!" But the truth is, we can carry each other's burdens, just in a different way. We can have a great deal of compassion for others.

- 🔊 Object lesson: Carry This

- 🔊 Scripture: 1 Peter 5:7 ("Cast all your anxiety on him because he cares for you.") Regardless of what we think we can do for others, the reality is that Christ carries all of our burdens.

- 🔊 Jesus has a gut reaction (a *"splagna oiktrimou"*) when he sees our suffering. We need to have the same reaction toward other people.

◀ Scripture: Galatians 6:2-3, *The Message* (see sidebar)

◀ Challenge students to think of one person in their lives whose stuff they could wear.

◀ Close in prayer, asking God to give you and your students gut reactions of compassion toward others.

Object lesson

Carry This

Using the backpack and objects listed below, show students how they can practically carry each other's burdens on a daily basis. As you talk about each item, place it in the backpack.

Textbook—schoolwork, studies, homework

Tissue—emotional issues and hard times

Box of bandages and a thermometer—sickness and injury

Giant question mark—decisions, advice

Photo—family problems

Can of food—hunger and other physical needs

Encourage students to share some more ideas. Remind them that they can carry each other's burdens no matter what kind of burden it is and no matter who the person is—a friend, a family member, or a total stranger.

Scripture

Galatians 6:2-3

Stoop down and reach out to those who are oppressed. Share their burdens, and so complete Christ's law. If you think you are too good for that, you are badly deceived.

From *The Message* by Eugene Peterson (NavPress, 2002)

discussion

Encore

Get It?	Middle School

◀ What is compassion?

◀ What are some tough times and burdens in your life that you've had to deal with? How did you handle them?

◀ When has someone really helped you out with a tough time in your life? How did that make you feel?

◀ Have you ever helped someone out with a tough time in her life? Share that story. How did it make you feel to help her?

◀ What are some burdens that you can carry for your friends?